DYNAMIS OF HEALING

ORTHODOX CHRISTIANITY AND CONTEMPORARY THOUGHT

SERIES EDITORS
Aristotle Papanikolaou and Ashley M. Purpura

This series consists of books that seek to bring Orthodox Christianity into an engagement with contemporary forms of thought. Its goal is to promote (1) historical studies in Orthodox Christianity that are interdisciplinary, employ a variety of methods, and speak to contemporary issues; and (2) constructive theological arguments in conversation with patristic sources and that focus on contemporary questions ranging from the traditional theological and philosophical themes of God and human identity to cultural, political, economic, and ethical concerns. The books in the series explore both the relevancy of Orthodox Christianity to contemporary challenges and the impact of contemporary modes of thought on Orthodox self-understandings.

DYNAMIS OF HEALING

Patristic Theology and the Psyche

PIA SOPHIA CHAUDHARI

FORDHAM UNIVERSITY PRESS
New York • 2019

For those who have taught me about healing from their own hard-won knowledge.

For those who seek hope of healing.

And to St. Maximus the Confessor, for bringing fire.

CONTENTS

Dynamis of Healing

INTRODUCTION

I am the Way, and the Truth, and the Life.

—John 14:6

While conscious hypocrisy, being the voluntary falsification of human authenticity, is easily perceptible by one's own self and by others, involuntary and unrecognizable existential falsehood presents the greatest problems. It is difficult to diagnose, even more difficult to confess, and most difficult to cure. Besides, it is existential falsehood that raises the question of personal truth, since the absence of truth has been perceived throughout the centuries as alienation.

—Vasileios Thermos, *In Search of the Person*

The feminine symbolizes that route that seeks the center by being firmly in the midst of things, touching, immersing oneself. When this mode of approach is lost, repressed, or split off, we lose our ability to feel connected, to feel in a living way that what we inherit from the storehouse of our religious tradition matters, that we really can live from the source. For many, the distance from religious tradition is so great that they doubt its truth. Religion then goes up into our heads and we live at a great distance from what matters.

—Ann Belford Ulanov, *The Wisdom of the Psyche*

Preface

I have long been drawn to reflect on the relationship between Christian understandings of salvation rooted in the patristic tradition, and the healing of psychological suffering at the deepest levels. As an Orthodox Christian scholar of theology and depth psychology[1] with experience in psychiatric and medical chaplaincy, and as a Jungian analyst in training, I find myself drawn to reflection on this relationship with the following questions in mind: How may an encounter with some of what is revealed of God in the vast breadth of Orthodox Christian theology bring healing to the psyche at its deepest levels? And how might the insights of depth psychology further enflesh Orthodox Christian understandings of how healing arrives and manifests? These questions set the basis of exploration that became this book. It is a work that, while engaging with the disciplines of theology and depth psychology, is not a systematic comparison so much as a genuinely exploratory initiative and a seeking to elucidate possible connections, doing so with a constant emphasis on healing tropes in the hope of bringing them to bear as resources in both fields.

In my own work, I found a meaningful route into these questions through the work of Ann Belford Ulanov, Jungian analyst and Christian theologian. Her work not only brings these two fields into conversation, but does so uniquely through her many years of engagement with what she has described as "the feminine mode of being."[2] She describes it succinctly:

> For [Carl] Jung, the feminine and its psychology describe not only factors which form a specific female sexual identity but also certain modalities of being which belong to all human beings. These modalities are *styles of being and of awareness, ways of relating to reality, digesting reality, and making judgments about it.* . . . To understand the feminine in this way is to see it as a symbolic form that shapes as well as articulates our meeting with the reality it seeks to express.[3]

This mode of being, while belonging to both men and women, has typically been more associated with women and, therefore, left out of the dominant discourses in both theology and psychoanalytic theory. Yet this mode holds true riches, as it asks of us the willingness to suspend the modes of perception—in particular perhaps some of the academic modes of perception—that we have been taught, and to open to new ways of perceiving. As Ulanov has written of (depth) psychology:

> This whole movement of psychology is, in a sense, an expression of the feminine, because its pursuit of ceaselessly emerging images, of

nonrational wisdom, of the gestating, healing capacities of the psyche, its wish to make tangible to us our diffuse and intuitive feeling tones, and its charting of the non-spatio-temporal and non-causal matrix are all fervent attempts to capture the feminine modality of being in relation to the more masculine consciousness of persons.[4]

I bring this up here, early on, because while this work is not an exploration of the feminine mode of being per say, it is rather an exploration *from* the feminine mode of being. It is not specifically about the feminine, or even less so, women, in the fields of depth psychology or patristic/Orthodox theology, but is rather an attempt to look at those fields using the tools of the feminine mode of being, with an emphasis on imagery, on attunement to energies and intuition, on a letting phenomenon be what they are and—while of course reflecting on them—not overly determining them. Of utmost import, it is a dwelling with experience, in its vagaries and even its unknowns. As Ulanov writes:

> Associated with feminine consciousness and spirit is the downward going road, down into the midst of things . . . the feminine mode goes right into . . . controversies; we get nowhere by rising above them to some general agreement. We go down, further down, for at the heart of our love for God, connections to each other grow among us. The feminine mode directs us into connection, linking, communion with each other, being for and with each other, accepting our body, the animal root-impulse, the ambiguities and mess of living, going into the wound, including all the parts, the bad ones we fear, the ones we suffer, the broken parts, not fixing but listening, knowing the new accumulates slowly out of slime, suddenly then to be born and address us with what could not consciously have been created by ourselves.[5]

Such a framework undergirding my approach may prove frustrating to some, particularly as our Western academic culture is highly "logos" oriented in its thinking patterns, and throughout this book I am attuning more to "eros."[6] However, I stand by it for several reasons.

The first is in the epigraph by Ulanov at the start of this chapter, that without this connective capacity, religion—or indeed psychoanalytic theory—can become a meditation on abstract dogma or theory that, while remaining elegant and even profound, can leave the depths of the person

and his or her sufferings entirely untouched. This does no justice to the
mandate of healing found in either discipline. Yet to access the depths we
often have to let go of our primary, conscious, and "regular" mode of perceiving or understanding.

Secondly, while I agree with Ulanov's emphasis that the feminine mode,
as an *archetypal* mode, belongs to both male and female individuals, it is
also the case that this mode has been undervalued (or else overdetermined
and undifferentiated) in its association with actual females. I believe this
has contributed to women seeking, and being forced, to adapt to arche-
typally masculine modes of consciousness in order to survive at the expense
of their own feminine modes, rather than valuing them for the rich gifts
they contain.

Thirdly, and related, while it may not be a moment in our culture in
which it is popular to talk about "masculine" or "feminine" in any form
of descriptive manner, and for many very good reasons, I remain keenly
aware of a prescient observation made by Ulanov already in the early 1980s,
which is that to overlook the "feminine" mode in favor of androgyny or
sexual nondifferentiation is to once again silence the feminine in its many
forms of being and, upon closer inspection, "[reveals hatred of] the female
elements of being" born out of a refusal to engage with all aspects of ourselves, and it is correlated—from a psychoanalytic perspective—to the
avoidance of the inevitable stresses of a move from a pre-Oedipal stage of
development to post-Oedipal stages that fully engage with sexuality.[7] Again,
while this book is not an apology for this viewpoint, nor an in-depth exploration of this discussion, I believe it does show the power of such perceiving as correlated to the "feminine" and, as such, is a refusal to let it be
silenced.

Lastly, and correlated to the above, I know of no other discourse about
Orthodox Christian theology and depth psychology that approaches the
two from the emphases contained in this mode, and I have come to believe that this is an important and fruitful vein from which to contemplate
both traditions. In an essay on the Virgin Mary, whom in the East we
reverence as the Theotokos, the God-bearer, Ulanov imaginatively postulated that much of the vigorous feminine energy that used to belong to
the veneration of Mary, who was not sentimentally pious but powerful in
her own female self, had now gone underground into depth psychology.[8]
While this may or may not resonate, as an image it opens the door for us
to be genuinely appreciative of not only the "feminine mode of being," but

of Mary's presence herself in our engagement with healing. As we shall see in the last chapter, she may bring rather more to bear than we generally realize.

Having said that, let us now return to the exploration itself.

Meeting Places

Patristic writings often speak of the categories of being and nonbeing. God alone exists and bestows being; evil is nonbeing.[9] Humans were created to participate fully in being, and yet through sin are corrupted and participate in death.[10] Sin brings death, and God brings life.[11] Depth psychologists also speak—though from a different location—of feeling alive, deeply rooted in one's proper "destiny," a joyous and full living that can come from the work of healing in analysis.[12] They also know the sufferings of deadness, the stifling cocoon of being trapped in one's complexes (Jung), the futility and despair of the "false self" (Winnicott), the repetitive traps that feel like "fate" (Bollas), or the compulsive "search for glory" of the neurotic self, martially enforced by the twin guards of pride and self-condemnation (Horney).[13]

The question, then, is whether there are "meeting places" between the patristic ontological articulations around being and nonbeing, life and death, and those of depth psychology around livingness and deadness?[14] Does the potential for healing live in such places? I believe that this exploration shows that the answer is yes. There *are* meeting places, and these places are some of the core places where healing can occur, where grace can become incarnate in a person's life.

Thus, in this book I broadly reflect on salvation as that ontological movement from death to life, nonbeing to being, proclaimed by the ancient Christians, and the recovery of the experience of livingness experienced in the analytic setting.[15] *I do not directly equate them or conflate them*, but I hold them together to see if sparks jump across from one to the other and back again. More specifically, I consider possible *traces* of the ontological and soteriological claims that inform the Orthodox tradition as *experienced* in the depths of the psyche, particularly in light of the processes of healing known to different schools of depth psychology.

I think of these traces as the above-mentioned "meeting places," where the person engages with the divine, that which is ultimately real, and comes through this meeting having encountered something powerful, something that brings healing and the possibilities of new life. Orthodoxy Christianity is filled with such places, with seven "official" sacraments, more commonly called *mysteria*,[16] and others that are not as easily named. I will briefly discuss the some of the *mysteria* toward the end of the book, but in Orthodoxy all of creation can also be understood as a place of sacramental encounter, a locus of divine presence.[17] I wish therefore mainly to consider the *mysteria* of God's presence and energies in creation and in each person, as naturally encountered within the psyche, and as restored through communion with God.[18]

As I will discuss, my hypothesis is that such traces do exist in the psyche, and may even form the core of what many depth psychologists rely on and engage with in the course of an analysis, even if not articulated as such. If this is so, then depth-psychological work in these areas can also become a work of the *askesis* (exercise) of faith, as it seeks to bring to fuller fruition the potentialities encountered in these traces.

What will the framework be for this discussion? In this work, I will explore two central areas of depth psychology: that of reliance on the psyche qua psyche to contain within itself a healing impetus, and that of the importance of eros. Undergirding these two realms, I will attempt to track the movement of the ontological energies gifted to creation by God, and assumed and restored in Christ, that seem in some way to be correlated, and to discuss how they might possibly be extrapolated to the insights of depth psychology and even, ultimately, contribute further to the healing of the person.

I have structured this book in four simple but substantial chapters. In Chapter 1 I will spend some time discussing the basis for interaction between Orthodox/patristic ontology and depth psychology, through the lens of the Orthodox understanding of creation as sacramental and hence including the psyche. I will also look briefly at areas of divergences and possible conflicts. In Chapter 2, I will offer a central image of salvation found, and emphasized, in the Orthodox tradition, which undergirds the discourse of this exploration, as well as opens up to the vast and lively streams of theology that informed this image and in turn arose out of it. I do this in the hopes that the reader may continue on with a better sense of the experiences and energies of transformation that Orthodox Christianity deems salvific, and carry that sense into the next chapters. In Chapter 3, I will turn to the first main area of exploration of "traces" of Orthodox ontology: that of being qua being and that of the healing impetus embedded in the psyche. In Chapter 4 I will explore traces of the ontological energies of eros and desire in conversation with the importance of eros and desire from a depth-psychological perspective. My hope is that by setting the discussion up in this way, the reader may encounter what I have encountered in my own research by way of converging images, energies, and experiences between Orthodox Christian theology and spirituality, and depth-psychological healing.

I would emphasize, once again, that this discussion is not intended to be a definitive argument, but rather to hold various images and energies and experiences in close proximity to each other, in order to notice how they relate and where they seem to lead organically. The area covered is vast, deep, and untamable—it cannot be corralled into a neat argument, but it can be engaged with and reflected upon. This approach may be more familiar to readers immersed in depth-psychological methods, and less to an academic audience but, when dealing with the depths, I prefer to honor Carl Jung's observation (one that was perhaps influenced as well by his reading of early Church Fathers) that "everything of which we are conscious is an image, and that image *is* psyche."[19] The human psyche represents what it perceives through what we may broadly call images (not just pictures but all forms of representation), and that this is the language it speaks before we sweep it up into conceptual discourse and logic (as commonly understood). If we are going to discuss the depths, we also need to be open to engaging with them, and in this work I attempt to do both. I will touch on this again shortly.

Brief Excursus on Death

As life and death are themes that will weave in and out of this work in its entirety, especially as arising from patristic and Orthodox theological reflection, I wish to address up front the nuanced understanding of death that will be encountered throughout.

As twentieth-century Orthodox theologian Alexander Schmemann observed, modern thinking on death, even from a Christian perspective, tends to fall into what is actually a Platonic bifurcation between biological life (and its inevitable termination) and the hope of spiritual immortality entered into upon the arrival of physical death.[20] However, as he points out, this has resulted in a loss of existential understanding of the axiomatic import to patristic and Orthodox faith that Christ *destroyed death*, "trampling down death by death and upon those in the tombs bestowing life."[21] (I will consider this in much greater detail in Chapter 2, in reflecting on images of salvation as offered by several key patristic theologians.)

As Schmemann observes, the reason for this diminished understanding of death having been decisively defeated lies in the fact that, biologically speaking, "nothing indeed has happened to death after Christ's death."[22] But as he explains, what the modern sensibilities have lost sight off—though perhaps *not* from a depth-psychological perspective as I will attempt to show—is that biological death is not the "whole death."[23] He writes:

> [In the] Christian vision, death is above all a *spiritual reality*, of which one can partake while being alive, from which one can be free while lying in the grave. Death here is man's *separation from life*, and this means from God Who is the only Giver of life, Who Himself *is* Life. Death is the opposite term, not of immortality . . . but of the true life. . . . This true life man has the power to reject and thus *to die* so that his very "immortality" becomes eternal death.[24]

In willing, indeed desiring, separation from God, from Life itself, we have succumbed to the "spiritual death, the one that . . . makes man's life solitude and suffering, fear and illusion, enslavement to sin and enmity, meaninglessness, lust and emptiness."[25] This comes about—as we will also see from the various theologians lifted up in this discussion—from the love of one's own self *more* than God, from seeking life in oneself rather than in God, and succumbing to an illusory world of our own creation that must always exist in ontological anxiety. This turning away from God's life to a life of our own creation constitutes the Original Sin[26] and is the archetypal instance of the misuse of our free will and *desire*. This is why the voluntary death of Christ, and the willing symbolic[27] death of the person in the sacrament of baptism, both speak of a healing of desire—dying to the desire for a self-created, solely self-referential life, or life ensnared entirely by the limits of biology, and reborn in desire for God, for true life.

Hence, it is not biological death, which is even a part of the principle of life and growth,[28] that is the "enemy," so to speak. The terms used here, of life and death, encompass a far greater spectrum than biology, while also including it. I will return to these themes throughout.[29]

The Unassumed Is the Unhealed

In Chapter 2, I will discuss a core maxim of patristic soteriology that—arising out of a rich understanding of salvation redolent with images of healing, empathy, and exchange of natures—proclaims that the essence of human nature has been assumed by God in Christ, such that it may be healed. First stated by Origen in his *Dialogue with Heraclides*, this maxim was made famous by St. Gregory of Nazianzus in his *Letter to Cledonius*, where he wrote "that which is not assumed is not healed."[30]

Given this image, I came to wonder how the radiant *mysteria*[31] described in two thousand years of Orthodox spirituality and praxis might meet the deepest spiritual needs and darkest sufferings of a depressed, or even a psychotic, patient? Could a conversation between the two disciplines fill out, flesh out, the image offered by St. Gregory, which arose from the theological reflections on healing and salvation that preceded him, elucidating its existential truth even when we feel furthest from God?

In Orthodox liturgy, God is worshipped as "the Existing One."[32] Orthodox theological reflection also generally considers itself largely empirical, i.e., based in confessed experience not abstract theory or speculation.[33] It is my belief and central hypothesis, as discussed earlier, that if Orthodox ontological claims concerning God and the person are, in fact, ontologically true, then those truths should leave observable traces in our experiences and dynamics of psychological healing and transformation.[34] I am writing, therefore, in part to explore how this truth of salvation shows up in the psyche.

At the same time, depth psychology has long had a ministry, even if not framed as such, to the parts of our psyches and lives often overlooked or disavowed—especially from "moral" perspectives—as unworthy, ugly, illegitimate, embarrassing, and "sinful," and yet that can be the unexpected doorway through which great healing arrives when engaged with acceptance and compassion (which is not the same as to condone all behaviors). Could the existential reach and healing possibilities of Orthodox ontology and experiences of transformation be more fully illuminated if we turn to depth-psychological exploration as to how our dark moods, our sludge, our irrational terrors, our obsessions, still share, in some sense, in the good and the purposive and, when engaged with courageously and compassionately, can yield hidden gold?

Reflections on Method of Interdisciplinary Conversation

It is challenging to bring together two disciplines, theology and psychology, that—given that each contains a vast spectrum of approaches—have often been set up as at odds with each other. This has to do, in part, with how one frames the conversation. In the preface I wrote about the "feminine mode of being" as a helpful way of understanding the approach I was taking to the material. Here it may also be helpful to further discuss aspects of the method I employ.

If seen as a conversation between two schools of thought, with their respective philosophical underpinnings, then one can fall into a comparison of divergences and convergences without any real synergistic meeting. However, there exists an important assumption in a conversation of that nature: namely, that one is primarily dealing with descriptive, and even speculative, systems, rather than with reality. But the apprehension of truth solely through the intellectual appropriation of "correct concepts" is not an inherently Eastern Orthodox, or patristic, epistemology. Rather, here, truth is also experienced directly.[35]

In a postmodern context, where Truth with a capital "T" is suspect, any claim to reality becomes suspect as well. However, Orthodoxy, though in some ways extremely compatible with postmodern thought, in other ways refutes any notion of the relativization of Truth.[36] As will be shown, although Orthodox theological reflection is wide and varied, there is no reality "outside" of God, as though faith could be partitioned off and lived separately from the rest of life. This is held together with the understanding that God also accommodates us, meeting us where we are.[37] Truth is both absolute and particular, unknowable in essence and knowable in energies.[38] Hence, ontology—understood as discourse about that which is ultimately Real, about structures of being itself[39]—is central to an understanding of Orthodox theology, in particular if attempting to reflect on the meaning of certain experiences of healing.

For some years now, I have sensed in patristic theology a worldview that seemed unexpectedly compatible with the experiences articulated in depth-psychological literature, perhaps especially that of analytical psychology (Jungian). Depth psychology also has its own languages for dealing with reality with a capital "R," as is seen, for example, in Wilfred Bion's discussion of "O," Donald Winnicott's gesturing to the "true self," and in the depth work of Carl Jung who famously stated "Only what is really oneself has the power to heal."[40] Jung was, of course, no stranger to the writings of various Church Fathers, so the intuition to correlate theology and psychology from these times and places, across the centuries, was perhaps not entirely misplaced. There seemed to be an explicit metaphysic in patristic theological reflections, and perhaps an implicit one in much of depth-psychological experience. It is important to state here that I am not seeking to conflate the two disciplines: i.e., I will let theology speak about revelation, the metaphysical, and the ontological, and let psychology speak about the psyche, the unconscious, and personal experience. *Each is to be taken on their own terms of experience and self-identification.* Of course in an actual life, these categories do not remain separate, but for the purpose of this exploration I am not attempting a unity of perception in all things, but rather to see whether the assumptions given on either side find resonance across the gap between the two fields.

My method, then, might best be summed up as an attempt to track the experiential manifestations of traces of an Orthodox metaphysic in two main areas, as stated above: that of being qua being (which I extrapolate to an exploration of psyche qua psyche on the depth-psychological side) and that of the energies of eros. I have chosen these two areas because they correspond well to areas of important emphases in depth psychology (as will be shown in Chapters 3 and 4), as well as to well-articulated structures of ontological reflection in patristic thought—specifically (for this endeavor) of St. Maximus the Confessor: that of the *logoi* (principles) of being, and that of the *tropoi* (modes) of being.[41]

This emphasis on experience, of course, does not allow a more common systematic approach of comparative discourse, but such an approach would also be fairly fraught in attempting to put into discourse two fields of reflection that are separated by over a millennium, vastly different historical and religious contexts, and difference in language. While it is also an imperfect method to put experience in conversation with experience, I have chosen this because both depth psychology and Orthodox theology emphasize *experience as the locus of transformation*, not just intellectual knowledge or dissociated belief.[42] Of course, how one interprets a given experience is influenced by any preexistent paradigm, but it is nonetheless helpful to bring similarities of experience and observed phenomena together so that as work in this field continues, we may seek further understanding of their connection. It is my hope, as well, that by choosing the route of reflection on experience, I might bring the reader closer to the realities of transformation. It is, after all, by its fruits that transformation is truly known.

Such deep levels of perception, and healing, deserve, in my view, an opportunity for constructive engagement with each other. Both depth psychology and Orthodox theology disavow false binaries, and both engage with levels of being that go beyond the tragic poles of everyday human experience. Their insights seem both dynamic as well as grounded in objective reality, and—as already noted—borne out of entering into an experience directly. Both, to echo Orthodox philosopher Christos Yannaras, are borne out of "encounter."[43] Yet this is not only an encounter of intersubjective "mutual influence" but also an encounter with an objective reality, reality with an "R," resulting in deep structural transformation.[44]

Writing as an Orthodox scholar, I write with the assumption of the existence of God and, in light of this assumption, follow Metropolitan John Zizioulas who has stated that, as the world is not just a product of our consciousness, ontology rather than subjective psychology "must be given priority and ultimacy in our theological considerations."[45] Thus theology is privileged over psychology in its defining of our ontological roots and telos, but depth psychology brings the greater possibilities of enfleshment of those roots, filling out, including, receiving all the experiences of the psyche and creating the space for deep human flourishing.

While this gives rise, in this paper, to an Orthodox Christian theological and ontological bias, with subsequent consequences, to my method, I believe it also gives it an inherent capaciousness of foundation. Having established the creative presence of God as omnipresent and ultimately "existent," the ontological hierarchy is—I hope—ultimately also one of a deep rootedness of existence and generativity, and not just "authority" as colloquially understood.[46] God's existence, prior to and defining ours, is not oppressive or restrictive of our humanity, unlike Freud's concept of God as projection of our superego.[47] God is of a different category of reflection, entirely, than as a narrow, moralistic, authoritarian cosmic figure who narcissistically demands compliance or condemns with punishment.

While Orthodoxy deeply respects the commandments of God, the level of theological discourse is primarily ontological, not superficially moral.[48] Because God exists, we exist. And, because this is so, our own ontological grounding is secure; *we do not create it ourselves*. Although perhaps a departure from current trends of thought and narrative, this basic assumption is irreducible if the rest of this exploration is to make sense.

Embedded in this assumption, and in the Orthodox apophatic tradition, is also an important self-critique: We may not conflate our subsequent theological reflections with God, or even with the ontology established by our reflections on God. This serves as a warning against creating idols of our own understandings. This also gives rise to freedom, as we do not carry the burden of creating what is ultimately real; we relate to it, are related to by it, and can reflect on our engagement with it. Perhaps, then, there might even be unexpected room to play.

Goals of Discourse

My interest is in healing, and—as stated early on—my hypothesis, having embarked upon the explorations entailed in this work, is that deep healing is possible. There is a vivid and compelling *hope* that permeates and energizes both fields. My emphasis on ontology in this discourse comes out of the theological postulation that healing arises from being itself.[49] Just as—as we will see later—morality arises out of being, so too does healing. There is thus a *dynamis*, an energy, of hope embedded in creation and it is accessible to all, bringing healing not just at the level of narrative but in the deepest ontological structures of the person.[50] This hope is—ideally— engaged with, encountered, recovered, in the work of depth psychology, but it does not belong solely to the analyst's office, nor to those who can afford the time or cost of analysis. However obscured it may have become, however much in need of restoration, it belongs indelibly to being, and to all creation, and is part of the beauty of creation.

The main audience of this book may be Orthodox Christians, Christians of other traditions, those engaged with the field of depth psychology and those simply wishing to learn more about psychology and religion. They may be scholars, students, or practitioners. That said, I have written this book with two other audiences in mind: those of faith for whom the faith has become empty because it can no longer reach in to their deepest sufferings (or indeed, deepest desires), and those for whom the very concept of faith has becomes empty, whose understandings of Christianity are composed of well-trodden paths of deconstructed Western Christianity experienced through postenlightenment and postmodern lenses, often combined with the necessary disavowal of a very Freudian superego type of god and concept of sin, from whom liberation can be the only fitting goal. The common notion that faith and psychology don't actually belong together belies a particular split between theology and anthropology, Creator and creation, spirit and matter, that does not belong in Orthodox discourse. As Bishop Kallistos Ware has written: "Authentic humanism and faith in God are interdependent variables."[51] In Chapter 2, I will briefly discuss the various strands of reflection on the "atonement" that arose and that perhaps easily lent themselves to the critique that Freud, and others since, have offered concerning the "tyrannical" place of God and religion in the psyche. But as I hope to show, these understandings of God, and of human relationships to God, were not foremost in the patristic era, nor do they continue to hold place of primacy in modern Orthodox thinking.[52] Hence I hope this book may open, or reopen, some doors that may have been prematurely closed, or closed of necessity for a while but that might now be reopened.

Lastly, I also write in this area in the hopes of contributing to the larger field of Western psychiatric treatment that has become severely alienated from spiritual, sacramental, and ontological language and context (as well as increasingly alienated from depth-psychological wisdom and accrued experience).[53]

In my work as a chaplain in a psychiatric hospital, I many times heard devout people speak sincerely of their faith in God, and then disparagingly of their own struggles with depression, anxiety, or general feeling of alienation from self, as though these things were not related to the life of faith or taken up—in a meaningful way—into our lives in God. Usually, rather, they were spoken of as failings—failures of faith, failures of self, and sometimes as failures of God to help them. They prayed desperately for healing, to be shown what to do, and felt they received no answer.

Sometimes the greater personal, relational, and communal/societal contributing context was recognized, but often the patients had to struggle with their illness independent of context or in spite of it.[54] To honor this interior space as contextually conditioned would require the ongoing difficult conversations about external contexts begging for social justice, such as poverty, racism, sexism, and broken and abusive relationships.

There did not seem to be an integral correlation between their innermost selves, God, and their wellness; one area was treated largely biochemically (with no individual psychodynamic treatment offered at all, even in a dedicated psychiatric hospital), and the other area left to the realm of pastoral care. That may be necessary in acute care settings, but it speaks too, in my view, of a broader cultural tendency to overlook the complexities of the inner world: the powerful relationships of psyche and soma, heart, mind, and soul, God and the person and their relationships.[55] Any perceived possible telos or communication of the unconscious, being expressed symbolically in symptom formation, is regularly discounted in favor of pathologizing, diagnosing and symptom adjustment. The sufferer's consciously available projections, fantasies, and anxieties about God mostly portray God at a far remove from the intense psychic suffering, as though disinterestedly holding—or withholding—the power to heal like a magician.[56] The innermost depths go untouched and from most angles, one senses the crushing absence of agency. As Ulanov has articulated: "The person feels caught, estranged from the God they pray to and from any ability to rescue themselves from the emotional distress that captures them."[57] At most, one might hear of a willingness to offer up the suffering to God and accept one's cross, but this—I believe—is dangerous if arrived at prematurely and preemptively. If it is a stance demanded by a sense of conscious "piety" that does not allow into consciousness the uncomfortable prompts of the unconscious, it runs the risk of not opening up to the suffering person the deeper possibilities for authentic healing that are not at odds with a life of faith but that might—perhaps—be found in new and unexpected ways in an even deeper encounter with God, the Existing One.

This is an area of especial delicacy and importance. I believe strongly that any theologies that seek to address mental (and physical) illness must engage with the findings of depth psychology, with the potential telos of symptoms and illness that can be seen as communications, expressing the problem and a possible path to healing the problem.[58] In this way, such theologies may further illuminate the great and mysterious workings of God's creation in the human person from this unusual perspective. If they do not, they risk giving theologically authoritative voice to an unnecessarily limited understanding of psychological suffering, and inadvertently perhaps foreclosing on the deep hope that is embedded in creation; this, I believe, does justice neither to the fullness of God's mercy, the glory of His creation or the beauty of the human person.

I therefore hope that the insights of depth psychology can reward Orthodox reflection with an even broader and deeper appreciation of the lived experience of the enormous potential for healing at depth levels—both psychological and also sometimes physical—when conscious and unconscious, psyche and soma, and the transcendent (as well as quotidian) are respectfully engaged with in psychotherapeutic work.

This may be especially important for Orthodox theologians as they engage more generally with the findings of modern science; the increasingly overlooked realm of depth psychology may well show the transformative power of embodied, enfleshed engagement with the transcendent for which modern psychiatry seems to have little patience, perhaps of especial interest when considering the role that psychological suffering plays in somatic illness. As Orthodox theologians reflect on scientific research, while still also recognizing and honoring sometimes extraordinary miracles made possible only by God's grace, I wish also to highlight this third ground of healing—perhaps made less popular because of the work, time, and cost (psychological and often financial) it entails—which, as noted above, may illuminate the deep possibilities for healing that exist in the alive space between body, psyche, and spirit.

Background Literature

Fairly recently within the Orthodox Church there have been numerous publications, translated into English, dealing with both mental and spiritual illnesses, of varying etiologies (organic, sinful, and demonic), such as the well-known works by Jean Claude Larchet on spiritual maladies as well as mental illness,[59] and also works on "Orthodox psychotherapy" and spiritual healing by Hierotheos Vlachos, as well as Archbishop Chrysostomos.[60] These works have brought into clearer relief the laser insight of our ancient tradition into the intricate relatedness of the passions to sin, to the demons, and to the will and spiritual life of the person.

Additionally, there have been some fairly recent interdisciplinary publications, by clergy who are practicing clinicians as well, such as the very well-received study by Alexios Trader on cognitive behavioral therapy and patristic wisdom;[61] the compilation on integral healing by various Orthodox therapists, edited by Stephen Muse;[62] and two compilations, one generally dealing with the concept of personhood, and the other with spiritual discernment and differential diagnosis, both edited by John Chirban, containing essays from medical practitioners as well as clergy and therapists.[63]

In the realm of depth psychology, of great note is the recent work of G. C. Tympas, Orthodox priest and scholar of depth psychology, on Carl Jung and St. Maximus the Confessor[64]—the work with which my own research has perhaps had the most in common. This book comes from a different premise, as outlined above, and also—while heavily engaged with both Jung and St. Maximus—is less of a systematic comparison of the two and more—as emphasized throughout this introduction—an exploration of what their understandings might mean experientially. I am indebted as well as to the writings of Vasileios Thermos, Orthodox priest and psychiatrist; perhaps most well known is his wonderful work on Winnicott and St. Gregory of Palamas titled *In Search of the Person: "True" and "False Self" According to Donald Winnicott and St. Gregory Palamas*.[65] Vladeta Jerotic, a Jungian analyst and theologian from Serbia, has written prolifically, including a book entitled *Individuation and (or) Theosis* (*Individuacija I [ili] Obozenje*) but is sadly not much translated into English.[66] Occasionally, psychoanalytic theory finds its way into Orthodox conversations in other ways as well, for example, showing up in the Orthodox philosophy of Christos Yannaras as will be discussed, as well as in the theological works of Nikolaos Loudovikos as will also be discussed.

I believe it important to attempt to continue in the footsteps of those who have gone before me in stepping out into this terrain of depth psychology and Orthodox theology. The depths of the psyche, however deep or unconscious and—at times—even frightening—where one might find, as St. Macarius famously said, both dragons and poisonous beasts as well as God and the angels[67]—these depths are also part of our created nature and as such, as he lifts up, are also meeting places with the living God, capable of being healed. *At such a level of healing we are no longer talking about symptomatic adjustment but of transformation.* The possibility of transformation makes the journey worthwhile.

1

PSYCHE AND CREATION: INITIAL REFLECTIONS ON ORTHODOX THEOLOGY AND DEPTH PSYCHOLOGY

God's word is not separable from God's being. God's action is not separable from God's being. So where God's word and action are, there God is, invading us as an event, invading human will and human imagination, rearranging all the ways we see and picture who we are, who others are, who God is. This invasion is no violation of our integrity but a liberation. This advent is no mere proffering of possibilities, among which we will then decide. It is not a well-mannered offering of choices. No, this invasion of power alters the entire force field in which we live, making a new creation for us, not a small change of direction.

—Ann Belford Ulanov, *Picturing God*

In this chapter, I wish to make the case for the inherent connection between reflection on the workings of the psyche and Orthodox theological reflection. As I noted in the introduction, I am privileging theology and ontology over psychology, but with the full expectation that depth psychology further enfleshes—gives substance and texture—to the ontological insights of Orthodoxy.

I will therefore, in this relatively brief chapter, highlight Orthodox understandings of creation as sacramental and posit the inclusion of the psyche in this understanding. I will also spend some time on areas of diverging goals and possible conflicts so as not to overlook substantial difference in the disciplines. These conflicts will not form a core part of my reflections, as I am more focused on tracking energies and experiences than comparing specific values and ideals, but there are areas of specific import that deeply inform the unfolding of our own innate natures—namely, around sexuality and gender—that need to be named and the differences held in appropriate tension.

Creation as Sacrament

In Orthodox Christianity, as well as more broadly in the Christian tradition, the Holy Spirit, as one of the Persons of the Holy Trinity, is proclaimed as the "Lord and Giver of Life."[1] Orthodox daily prayers offer worship to "the Spirit of Truth, who [is] present everywhere, filling all things Treasury of Good and Giver of Life."[2] God is recognized in the Divine Liturgy as "the Existing One."[3] In these utterances, it is taken as a matter of truth that there is no life, nor indeed any engagement with any of creation, without God. God is present in all being; without God's ever-existing presence we would vanish into nonbeing. We have, of our own, no existence. This was profoundly articulated by St. Athanasius in the fourth century: "Evil is non-being, the good is being, since it has come into being from the existing God."[4]

This statement, stunning in both its simplicity and its ramifications—if we let it take hold of our imaginative capacities—already serves to dismantle the perceived possibility of "splitting" the conversation between theology and psychiatry, or between religion and science, as though God were present in one sector but not in the other. If we define sacrament, or *mysteria*, overarchingly as a locus of encounter with the presence and energies of God, then indeed, wherever those energies are present we have the possibility of sacramental encounter.[5] As cited earlier, Ecumenical Patriarch Bartholomew of Constantinople has said "all of creation is a sacrament."[6] Additionally, as Orthodox theologian John McGuckin has noted:

> Orthodox thought resists a dominant aspect of Western religious philosophy that has tended to elevate so-called supernatural revelation over and against "natural religion." For Orthodoxy the two things are so intimately woven together in the very substrate of creation, and most particularly in the constitution of the human creature, that there can never be anything, in relation to either the human or angelic orders, that is simply "natural."[7]

There is thus *no ontological split within the person between the natural and the spiritual* and, following on the above, the experiential. We see this in the theology of St. Maximus the Confessor in his articulation of the doctrine of the *logoi* of being (to which I will return in Chapter 3), the "principles" of being that form the basis of *all* creation as divinely known and willed by God. This natural, innate potential is then manifested in how we experience, as well as self-determine, our *tropoi*, modes, of being.[8] Orthodox theologian Elizabeth Theokritoff sees the *logoi* of St. Maximus as the place of "interface" between God and creation.[9] She makes the important point that these *logoi* "never form an autonomous realm *between* God and actual creatures. They are divine *energies*—God himself active in the world. They therefore place no restriction on God's creative freedom, or on creatures' absolute dependence on him."[10]

Our existential trajectory is hence never capable of full dissociation from our ontological roots and potentialities, however much it may become distorted away from what is naturally created and life-giving. As we will also see, through the lens of St. Maximus, our ability to experience, and hence perceive, is a critical part of how we come to true knowledge, which is union, with God. This faculty of perception and experiencing of the sensory world, *aisthesis*,[11] is a locus of healing rather than something to be dissociated.

Thus, psychology, with all of its relatively recent clinically based revelations about the inner workings of the psyche, is also held in this greater reality. The presence and influence of the unconscious, the importance of relationships in our personality formation and basic sense of self and other, our eros, aggression, envy, fear of destructiveness, conflicts, narcissism, neuroses, and even psychoses, as well as the engagement with dreams, images, and fantasy or symptom as communications from the psyche—none of these fall outside the realm of God's creative and life-giving presence. I argue they are all, in some way, "assumed" into the life of God.

It is important to clarify here that I do not intend that sin is condoned by God. But if we understand sin as resulting in a negative distortion of that which is originally good, then my argument is that the preexisting psychic faculties, which can then tend toward sin or toward life, are assumed by God in Christ. In Christ our natural faculties find their proper telos. Without that assumption, there would be no possibility for *transformation* of sinful states; we would be left attempting to simply split them off, to the detriment of our psyche's integrity, an attempt akin to Freud's notion of repression resulting in a God image also akin to Freud's superego. (More on this in the next chapter.)

As St. Athanasius (from whom we will also hear more in the next chapter) proclaimed, God, though not previously distant, "for no part of creation is left void of him . . . he has filled all things in every place" now, out of love, "comes into our realm."[12] He comes to "recreate the universe,"[13] taking on the body of a human, dying in order to abolish death, that we might be rescued from death and corruption and not fully perish.[14] *God recreates us from within.*

This is important because it means that the healing that can be found in the engagement with psyche must also part of a life of faith, though not its totality. Orthodox theologian Olivier Clement wrote beautifully of such a grand and generous vision of the Church:

> The Spirit abounds most plentifully in the sacramental body of Christ, but wherever the Spirit is at work in history and in the universe, the Church is secretly present. There is not a blade of grass that does not grow within the Church, not a constellation that does not gravitate toward her, every quest for truth, for justice, for beauty is made within her (even if the prophets and great creative spirits have sometimes been persecuted by the ecclesiastical institution), every scrap of meditation, of wisdom, of celebration is gathered in by her.[15]

Additionally, akin to much of depth-psychological reflection, Orthodoxy emphasizes that which is "experience-near" in spiritual praxis rather than speculative or primarily constructed through narrative. The life of faith is lived out sacramentally, through fasting, bodily and sensory engagement during prayer and worship, beauty-filled liturgies aglow with candlelight and incense, community, repentance, confession, and, centrally, participation in the Eucharist—all with the joyful expectancy and deep desire of increasing union with God and love for others. At present, there is also a great deal of use of language around becoming one's "true self," becoming a "person," also used in Orthodox circles.[16] Regular spiritual direction is an integral part of this process.

To put ontological reflection as found in Orthodox Christianity in conversation with depth psychology means to take the sacramental nature of creation, and our place in it, very seriously as part of that dialogue. The sacramental reality of Orthodoxy must engage the symbolic discourse of depth psychology. Ann and Barry Ulanov touch on this, in their classic text *Religion and the Unconscious*:

Another way to understand this difference is in terms of the distinction between the symbolic life—a life that can move simultaneously among several zones of meaning—and the sacramental life, where the symbol and the reality symbolized are the same, not flattened into literal univocal meaning, but transmuted into a radiant whole that defies logical analysis.[17]

Orthodox tradition, while fluent in symbols[18], is sacramental above all and lives out of this "radiant whole." Orthodoxy, as McGuckin writes, is not a "system of doctrines. . . . Orthodoxy is the living mystery of Christ's presence in the world: a resurrectional power of life. It cannot be understood, except by being fully lived out."[19] He continues: "Our God is the One Who Is. When the disciple is in ontological harmony with this God, the disciple also comes into life."[20]

The "One Who Is" grounds and defines the terms of existence, out of which constructive reflection on that existence can flow. Ulanov and Ulanov are also clear on the limits of psychoanalysis in this regard: "It is not part of any school or movement in depth psychology to unite or attempt to unite the psyche and the ground of all order and being."[21] Psychological work can clear confusing thickets away in order to help a person more fully find the ontological harmony that McGuckin describes, but it is not a substitute for it any more than subjective experience can find its true origin and telos outside of ultimate reality.

Yet, in the space of attention to the psyche and its workings, there is possible the meeting between the Creator and created, and of the transformation of creation through this ongoing exchange. This is possible because Orthodox theological anthropology proclaims the image of God inherent in every person. As McGuckin writes so beautifully:

> At the end of the day, Orthodoxy insists on the perennial freshness and beauty of the human being, even in the fallen condition, not for the sake of human pride or self-confidence but in order to ensure that the essential truth of the human person is never forgotten: their luminous *energeia* as a song of God's mercy and philanthropy and, because of that, a mysterious entity who is innately beautiful, glorious, and alluring.[22]

As seen, we are never fundamentally disconnected from God. If we were, we would—following the earlier ontological argument—immediately cease to exist. This does not mean that sin does not abound, but the ontology of the person is rooted in the image of God, corrupted but never destroyed, and hence in goodness. It is this referent that informs all Orthodox understandings of healing and salvation of the person. Out of this comes boundless hope.[23]

Psyche

Subjective experience, as I have shown above and will return to again later, is part of creation and as such, participates in the dynamic energies of God. Pantheism is anathema to Orthodoxy—the ontological distinction between Creator and creation can never be crossed. But God is nonetheless present in and to creation. Similar to what I noted above in Theokritoff, concerning God's energies in the *logoi* of being, is the concept further elucidated by McGuckin: "God's divine energy, the reflected image of his action of loving outreach (and thus an accurate image of his own presence), is within the very fabric of material and rational being, as its ontological foundation and (for the ensouled creation) its destined goal (telos)."[24]

The notion of a God who exists "up there" while we are "down here" is alien to the streams that inform Orthodox thought.[25] As stated earlier, there is no being at all without God, so we must not fall into the trap of a spirituality or piety divorced from the body, emotions, creative aggression as well as love, and desire. Such a full-fledged conceptualization of God's presence in our fully embodied lives can become the basis for an understanding of transformation that is not only "spiritual" but that brings life at levels of subjective, and—importantly—embodied experience of self and other. The material world matters.

As integral to the created person, the psyche participates in the goodness of creation, of matter, and as such must be seen as having its own good and purposeful telos that can be further realized through attention and respect given to its workings, just as attention and respect given to the workings of the body have always informed the practice of medicine. Depth psychology, of course, has long observed the interplay between the body and the psyche.

If depth psychology claims a kind of scientific neutrality, seeking only to understand what "works" (as Jung said, "*Das was wirkt, ist wirklich*"),[26] then its various findings are forms of "natural revelation" and as such must inform any theological reflection on creation. Depth psychology offers immense insights into the formation, structure, and influences of the psyche, reminding us over and over again of the existence of the unconscious, the adaptive (and maladaptive) and even *teleotic* formation and mechanisms behind what religion often dismiss as sinful thoughts and behavior. Depth psychology proclaims the possibility of structural transformation at the deepest levels, and the seemingly ontological drive toward integration (reminiscent, as I will discuss later, of St. Maximus the Confessor). Of utmost importance is the role of eros, of the drive to seek relatedness, in our earliest and ongoing experiences of self and other, including the formation of our inner moral code.[27] Further discussion of these areas of ontology and eros will form the core of Chapters 3 and 4.

Orthodox theology and praxis offers reflection on the One who heals humanity and defeats death, participation in the Holy Mysteries wherein we find healing and communion with God, and ancient wisdom as to the deep nature—fundamentally good but filled with passions and distortions—of the person, created in the image of God, who seeks to unite their will with the will of God in a *synergistic* effort toward the restoration of the image and likeness of God within him or her. Salvation is transformation, deification, an ascent of the spirit and a descent into the heart; it is infinite and eternal growth toward God, the boundless increase and satisfaction of our deepest desire.[28] Though keenly aware of the dark and the demonic, Orthodoxy proclaims the radiant joy of life that has no opposite. As St. Maximus reflected:

> [The state of divinization] . . . has been rightly described as pleasure, passion, and joy. It is called pleasure, insofar as it is the consummation of all natural strivings. . . . It is called passion, insofar as it is an ecstatic power, elevating the passive recipient to the state of an active agent, as . . . air permeated by light, and iron suffused with fire. These examples, drawn from nature, demonstrate persuasively that there is no higher summit of transformation for created beings *apart from that in which their natural elements remain inviolate.* It is, finally, called joy, for it encounters nothing opposed to it.[29]

Depth psychology, in turn, offers an invitation to explore unknown interior landscapes, sometimes beautiful, sometimes grim. They are places that frighten us, or ensnare us, that we hide from ourselves and others—the life of the unconscious, the shadow, our splitting and fragmentation, and the ravaging of self that can take place through trauma and neglect. Depth psychology brings us to places that are also deserving of assumption into the life of God and that too often are overlooked as annoying, embarrassing, unworthy, reprehensible, morally "incorrect," "antisocial," and just plain frightening.[30] We get there by facing the shadow, not hopping over it, running away from it, or denying it. We peer into the dark, and let what lives in its protective shadow emerge, trusting in the fundamental validity—goodness—of its initial intent even if we may struggle with all our being to contain its current destructive manifestations. Depth psychology reminds us that the "monsters" often hide the gold, and the healing crucible of analytic engagement with the parts of us we would rather leave out (the "shadow," as Jung so aptly termed it) can uncover and unleash zest, desire, creative aggression, love, and joy—all seeking, and deserving of, fullness of life. We ignore this truth at our own peril, whether for religious and psychological reasons, or for reasons of societal expediency. If the "natural elements" of the person are to remain inviolate, as St. Maximus says above, they must be integrated and transformed, not annihilated.

A Case Study

Let me give, here, a very striking example given by psychoanalyst and medical doctor Medard Boss, in the 1960s, in his book on daseinanalytic psychoanalysis. Without digressing overly much into the specificity of his technique, I will just say that it entailed allowing the psychological phenomena experienced by his patient to have phenomenological legitimacy as psychologically meaning-disclosing, that they might disclose their own meaning to him and the patient, rather than being coerced by the meaning (or dismissal of nonmeaning) imposed by common medical understandings. In other words, rather than dismissing the patients hallucinations as symptoms of pathology, he became convinced of the necessity of looking to them on their own terms, exploring the *meaning* of the images being presented and holding out for the possibility of the psyche attempting to heal itself through their communications.

In this particular case, perhaps also of especial relevance to the life of faith, he was working with a woman in her mid thirties who had been raised by parents of a severely ascetic and fundamentalist faith, where any expressions of spontaneous bodily joy or desire were strictly condemned. This talented woman had grown up to be a medical doctor and director of a psychiatric institution, but at the time she sought analysis was on the verge of a psychotic break.

During the initial course of her analysis, she began to experience "hallucinations" in the form of what she termed "anemic theologians" and "church ladies," visions filled with grotesque mask-like representations of such people, always frowning, spying, condemning her, calling her a harlot, preparing to turn her in to the authorities. She lived in constant terror of the world ending, hyperattuned to all noise and sensation, and unable to trust in anything around her. Initial attempts on the part of the psychiatrist to reason with her, encouraging her to dismiss her hallucinations as organic by-products of disease or even psychological projection, failed. She reasoned back and demanded, in a sense, that her hallucinations be given their own voice. Unexpectedly, the analysis took off when this was finally allowed. Together, the doctor and patient took seriously the job of these figures (to spy on her and condemn her). She began to give face to them in drawings (Figures 1 and 2).[31]

She soon after experienced a severe clinical regression to an infantile place, a place not for the faint-of-heart analyst, but her analyst was able to maintain a steady holding environment for her. In her particular case, it began to emerge that she was psychotically defended against her own existence as a fully embodied, erotic woman. As she reexperienced an infantile dependency within the analysis (it seems she was able to function to some degree normally outside of her sessions), she was also able to begin to experience spontaneous well-being—for the first time in her life—rather than a constant anxiety of self-holding (the attempt to provide security for herself that she did not experience from her environment or caregivers at critical developmental stages).

Her analyst was able to "hold her" and care for her in a way that enabled her to begin to trust in the availability and provision of external love. From this place, she began to grow up—again—but this time bringing all of her bodily instincts and eros with her. It is moving to read, at this point, of how her drawings began to show the emergence of healthy young children, rather than frightening and condemning figures (Figure 3).

Although she continued to struggle with psychotic lash-backs, defenses, whenever she approached the developmental level of mature sexual eros, eventually she was able to express herself not as a child but as a young and attractive woman (Figure 4).

Figures 1 and 2. Persecution.

Ultimately, she was able not only to achieve an authentic female adulthood, but also to claim her artistic talent. She became a talented sculptress. The two sculpted figures here show the inner working out of herself as a woman in two different modes that she vacillated between for a while: the "crucified" feminine (Figure 5), and then the alive and spontaneous feminine (Figure 6).

As Boss concludes the extraordinary study, he notes that from the point of this achievement and for seven following years of observations (to the point of writing the case study), she had had *no further psychotic episodes.*

I chose this case to highlight the possibilities perhaps hidden even in extreme cases. The images spontaneously produced by her psyche[32] in the hallucinations and drawings (and also in her dreams) pointed to the reality of her inner world and its harsh attempt at repressive continuity in the face of instinctual growth, through the arrival of condemning authoritarian figures—reflecting actual people who had formed her outer world and informed her inner world as a child. Her panic at the world ending did, in

Figure 3. Newness.

fact, have some truth to it. Her inner world, as she had created it, was end-ing. But her psyche also produced images that pointed the way toward her recovery. What—to our notions of "normal"—looked like a severe break-down at every level of functioning contained within itself the seed of new growth. This growth, nourished without judgment by the analyst, led to

Figure 4. The beginning of healing.

Figures 5 and 6. Feminine past and present.

an experience of radical transformation as she was released from the brittle shell and psychosis of her accreted self, regressed to a place of met dependency, and from there began to regain what Winnicott would call "true self" experience, a self capable of authentic, spontaneous, and creative self-expression.[33]

Her symptoms eased and eventually disappeared and she, in greater wholeness, emerged forth into her life. Intrinsic and essential to her growth was psyche manifesting its aim toward fuller living, inclusive of areas she had left out—body, spontaneity, eros.[34] This growth showed itself in psyche "speaking" in images—first, of who was oppressing her, and then of a new (baby) healthy growing, then of a feminine sense of eros.[35] This is a level of healing, seemingly little appreciated in either modern medical or theological worlds, that I hope can come to be further known and considered through the work of this exploration.

Psychiatric illness ravages people. It lives in borderline settings, at places of internal and external distortion so severe that the truth is no longer recognizable, the self no longer able to answer to the call of an other, let alone to experience freedom or joy. Depth psychology invites Orthodox theology and pastoral praxis to find ways to engage with that which has been left out, by pointing to ways that that which is often unconsciously excluded actually does participate in the goodness of creation. These parts and bits of psyche, which come creeping in from the highways and byways, can communicate in psychic images that ultimately can yield their own gifts and a fullness of life, or else deliver what feels like the vengeful curse and deathless sleep of the thirteenth fairy in the Sleeping Beauty fairytale, if left out and ignored.[36] Here, too, is the psyche tending toward healing out of its own created nature—though sometimes in ways hard to recognize and through what we might call distortion of their original purpose.

Diverging Goals and Values

While it is my hope that the use of an ontological basis for discussion will open up both theological reflection and depth psychology to mutual illumination via an experiential engagement with what is true and with what heals, it cannot be overlooked that there are also other existent assumptions in each discipline that may cause conflict.

Orthodoxy not only reflects on ontology and eros as implied and offered in the Incarnation, but also draws its self-understandings from Scripture, tradition, liturgy, iconography, spiritual praxis, and the wisdom of centuries of theological reflection and distillation on topics ranging from the Persons of the Holy Trinity, to marriage, to the practices of fasting during Great Lent. It seeks the *phronema Christou*, mind of Christ, in all things. Hence an engagement with Orthodoxy is not only a conversation with a metaphysic but with a tradition born out of a faith in Jesus Christ as Lord. God is *personal*, not just metaphysical. As Metropolitan John Zizioulas writes, the revelation of God in the particular has elevated the personal and particular to the level of the ontological.[37] This, by definition, bounds the discussion in a particularly Christian way, which is not the native assumption of any depth-psychological discourse.

Most depth-psychological discourse functions without any presupposition of the existence of God, though numerous depth psychologists have engaged with religion.[38] Thus, depth psychology might be considered— apart perhaps from the nuanced explorations of Carl Jung and those who work with his theories—anthropocentric rather than theocentric.[39] Depth psychology is concerned with the healing of the person, not theology qua theology, or even morality qua morality.[40]

Additionally, in the Orthodox Christian *consensum patrum*, there is also a sense of what constitutes sinful behavior, as rooted in the passions.[41] The commandments, given by God, give life; sin and lawlessness bring death. In the next chapter, I hope to underscore that—perhaps surprisingly for many—in Orthodoxy, ontology *precedes* morality, not the other way around. Patristic tradition, as I will discuss, teaches that our human nature (*ousia*) is assumed in Christ, as well as our physicality and its limitations, but not our sin. It is important to reiterate that sin arises out of a misuse of free will, and distortion of the passions and appetites. It is not, in Orthodox patristic tradition, endemic to our human nature. It is not correlated to the "flesh" and its limitations or needs, but to the distortion arising out of a misuse of natural desires, appetites, and needs.[42] As I will discuss in detail later, the problem of sin lies in the faculties of mind, heart, and soul, but not in the body qua *physis*.[43] As Orthodox philosopher Christos Yannaras insists, "For this reason the Church rejects morality (which pertains only to conscious will) and insists on the *askesis* (which aspires to the total mode of existence, conscious and unconscious)."[44]

To be truly "natural," therefore, in Orthodox thought, is to be without sin.[45] It is not to be without body, desire, or limitation. This is also not to say that Orthodox imagination generally envisions a person being free from sin in this life. The greater the clarity of perception, the more aware of our sins we become.[46] The optimism that extends to the indestructibility of the image of God in humanity does not preclude a clear-sighted acknowledgement of the devastation that sin, both individual and environmental, wreaks in the deepest levels of the interior life and the exterior world.

Orthodoxy holds, very deeply, a "tension of the opposites" precisely here, mirrored—in my experience—only by that of some depth psychologists in terms of the profound faith in the possibilities for healing embedded in creation, given by God, indestructibly, while still fully recognizing the impact of evil, sin, death, and corruption. At its best, I believe this ability to hold the tension of the opposites becomes yet another amplification of the salvific theological image of empathetic assumption of the human condition by Christ—an image I will use throughout this book.

Orthodox spirituality is concerned with a person's very mode of existence. As noted earlier—but which cannot perhaps be emphasized enough—*theocentric* morality, in Orthodoxy, is concerned with the *freely* willing desire to do God's will, with the rerouting of our most natural energies, the "undistortion of the passions," and the ongoing recovery and infinite growth of the "true self" and "true life" (a la Winnicott) rather than the "superego" imposed repression of particular instincts such as sexuality and aggression, as Freud postulated. As St. Gregory of Nazianzus observed, God persuades rather than "manhandles."[47] This may all resonate with many depth psychologists, but there is still the potential for conflict.

Different schools of depth psychology also hold different positions with regards to the "original goodness" of the person, with some like Freud and Klein seeing an inherent instinct toward destruction (the "death instinct"), and ambivalence as organic to the person, and others like Winnicott, Donald Fairbairn, and Harry Guntrip holding forth the possibility of a true self whose instincts toward eros, spontaneity, creativity, and even aggression are fundamentally constructive and only become distorted in light of environmental impingement.[48]

Excursus on Sexuality

There are two additional areas of potential conflict that need particular attention: sexuality and gender.

Although depth psychology has evolved in myriad ways since Freud first put forth his theories on the relationship of neuroses to repressed sexual and aggressive instincts, there is nonetheless a continued respect for the desires and instincts of the "body-ego," including the role of the famous Oedipal complex, in most schools of depth psychology. Generally speaking, I also experience—and not just among depth psychologists—a continued stereotype concerning Christianity in general that these very desires and instincts are overlooked in the "spiritual life," or worse, that the spiritual life colludes in their repression.

While I will spend a good deal of time on eros in this work, I will not be overly focused on its sexual expression. This is not to diminish its importance, but rather to allow the possibility of going even *deeper* than bodily sexuality to find the roots of transformative ontological eros that fully embrace, integrate, and then also transcend human sexuality. My postulation is that healing at this level also brings healing, even release from repression, at the sexual level; one is not exclusive of, or even a sublimation of, the other.[49]

However, at the level of physical expressions of sexuality, it is true that sexual expressions that are considered sinful in the Orthodox Church, such as premarital sexual activity, homosexual sexual activity (not orientation), and solitary sexual activity, are not considered pathological or problematic by modern depth psychologists unless they present as part of a larger issue. This difficult dissonance, in particular concerning homosexual sexual activity, will unfortunately not be resolved in any way in this discussion. It is territory beyond the scope of this work. But it is important to name this gap as existing, and in need of ongoing care, especially because it should not be the case that anybody feel by definition excluded from the broader processes I do wish to explore.

The Orthodox Church, as noted above, teaches that homosexual sexual activity is a sin, as is any sexual activity outside of the sacrament of marriage. One hopes to, and does, find compassion and love in the giving of pastoral care to gay members of the Church who struggle with this deep issue of irreconcilability, but the Church officially is unequivocal in its stance and interpretation of tradition.[50] It remains an area of great pain, tension, necessary ongoing discussion, and deep pastoral care and concern.

Yet, even here (especially where culture-war proponents from all sides land like vultures on the vulnerability and struggle of others) it may be reminded that "sinfulness" has again to do with a *tropos* of existence expressed, in this instance, sexually; one may equally be concerned, for example in a heterosexual relationship, as to whether it is oriented toward the "other" in love, or toward one's own narcissistic gratification. It is not *desire* that is sinful in the Orthodox Church (as we will see); on the contrary there can be no vividness of spiritual or psychological life without desire. The problem lies in the potential arc and usage of it (or indeed damage to the capacity for expression of it at all).

Excursus on Gender

The question also arises, if salvation hinges on human nature being fully assumed by Christ—as noted in the introduction and as will be returned to in the next chapter—how then do we consider that Christ assumed a male body, and not a female body? Are females thereby left somehow "unassumed"? What about those who identify as transgender?

Since the focus of my own research is how traces of Orthodox ontology and soteriology show up in the life of the unconscious, and therefore how the psyche and mental illness are related to, and healed by, Christ's assumption of our humanity, I will not overemphasize this particular area. But I will provide here some background material on gender in patristic thought, in part because it is important of its own merit, and in part because it is inextricably linked to issues that arise in the course of an analysis—we cannot hop over our own gendered experiences or sexuality when engaging with the unconscious, psychological well-being, or with the religious life.[51]

As Orthodox theologian John Behr has written: "The significance of the fact that human beings exist as both male and female . . . together with its societal and ecclesial ramifications, is . . . being vigorously debated today, not least within Orthodox theology."[52] Lately, even this named significance is seemingly diminishing altogether from modern cultural discourse in favor of claims about gender constructs and gender fluidity, as though paradoxically there is a need to neuter all human interaction,[53] even while proclaiming greater sexual and gender liberation than ever before.[54] As Behr notes, this is also a tension held within the debates in Orthodoxy. There are two main strands:

> The first position holds that God did indeed create human beings as "sexual" beings, differentiated into male and female, that this is integral to God's vision for His creation, and as such is an enduring feature of ourselves. Within this position there is no full consensus regarding what dimensions of a human being are differentiated in this manner . . . the second position within modern Orthodoxy argues that sexuality, and sexual differentiation, was only provided by God in his foresight of the Fall; prior to this we would have multiplied "as the angels."[55]

Behr refutes the second position as dissonant with Scripture, citing, for example, early rabbinic literature that celebrated the consummation of Adam and Eve's marriage in Paradise, and also Christ himself in the New Testament answering the Pharisees, saying: "Have you not read that He who made them from the beginning made them male and female" so that they could be joined together.[56] Behr acknowledges that the proponents of the second position derive their position from patristic literature, but equally rebuts the assumptions entailed in the exegesis of patristic literature to support modern concerns, where the writings are decontextualized and used to support anachronistic argumentations.

Perhaps of more immediate import to this discussion is the next level that Behr addresses, which concerns how we conceptualize sexual differentiation. Citing Orthodox theologian Valerie Karras, who writes forcefully against an inherent, God-given differentiation between male and female, he outlines the problem in terms that will perhaps strike modern readers as unfamiliar, but that concern the patristic approach to human nature—the question is whether male/female differentiation is located at the level of nature (*ousia*) or of personal identity (*hypostasis*). It does not seem rightly allocated to either, and so Karras contends that theologians who do write from an assumption of sexual differentiation, such as Paul Evdokimov and Thomas Hopko, introduce an "intermediate level of ontological existence between that of essence . . . and hypostasis"[57] that does not rightly belong in the conceptual schemata of patristic thought.[58] This argument Behr sees as an attempt to tame existence itself into preexisting modes of conceptual thought.[59] That we do not have a preexisting category for something should not negate the reality, or import, of its existence.

Lastly, Karras contends that to introduce such an intermediate ontological category of existence is to negate the personal freedom of each individual to relate to God and other persons, as now "each human being expresses himself or herself within the bounds of his or her sexual nature . . . we cannot be restricted by our biological hypostasis, for we are called to transcend biological necessity."[60]

Behr's clarifying response here, a response that I experienced to be stunningly beautiful in its ramifications, is to point out that Karras is actually setting up freedom as a property of the person (*hypostasis*) in relation to their nature (*ousia*). But, he refutes, this is an inversion of the patristic perspective, especially as expressed in the Sixth Ecumenical Council and by St. Maximus the Confessor (as we will see in Chapter 4); our *freedom is a property of our nature*, rather than a *property of our person with respect to our nature*.[61] One is left wondering whether our modern concerns and expectations regarding our subjective personhood, although eloquent in their claims, have not actually shrunk far below the joy-filled expectation of the ancients regarding the restoration and healing of our true nature.

It is not that Behr doesn't understand the ramifications of possible abuse of existential differentiation between male and female. As he writes:

> To argue that a human person is not intrinsically either male or female allows for a supposedly theological argument in favor not only of equality, but also of identity. Inasmuch as sexual difference has often been abused to legitimize almost anything, one can sympathize with the motivation—but is the conclusion, denying the givenness

and divinely intended reality of our biological existence, the best way of attaining the desired goal? . . . The Origenist/Alexandrian theologians (and their modern counterparts) who condemned, as being mere lovers of the body, those second-century Christians who held literally to the resurrection of the flesh in an earthly kingdom . . . are as culpable as the modern writers who dismiss the patristic anthropological and ascetic thought as being body-hating, other-worldly fanaticism.[62]

The Fathers were not arguing that salvation only applied to men. That they spoke out in defense of women at other times, but seemed totally unconcerned that their soteriology might leave out the "female," indicates to me not a universal lack of concern for women, but a utilization of an understanding of human nature that was considered to be self-apparently universal.[63] As we will see discussed later, the principles of being, the *logoi*, inherently willed, created, and held in being by God, and the "natural will," *thelema*, whose expression in the "deliberative will," *gnome*, informs the personal and unique trajectory of each person in their individual context, are both assumed in the healing energies of God, regardless of the gender of the person.[64] They are properties of the human *ousia*, nature, which is common to all.

For this reason, whether male, female, or transgender, no one is left out of this conversation, and—more importantly—no one is left without meeting place with God. This, as we have seen in the above discourse, is coherent with a patristic understanding of the *ousia* of the person. Additionally, I think it important to point out that our sexual and gender identities as *consciously* known, constructed (or deconstructed), and experienced in a modern Western context, with the influences exerted by familial and cultural expectations, in our daily lives, can be very different than how they may be experienced as making their presence known at an unconscious level. Is it not possible, then, that our experience of ourselves and God, at the very deepest levels of self and spirit, may be fully sexually informed, without being sexually circumscribed in ways we think we ought to understand and avoid in advance of actually experiencing them? In other words, perhaps we still need to be curious about what is really *there*, and look to its healing, rather than predetermining what ought not to be there.

While Behr's article mainly delineates the discourse and does not provide a final answer as to where exactly sexual differentiation is located, perhaps we may open to the possibility of the *influence* of differentiation between male and female in the *process* of each person's transformation in Christ, while not falling into the error of thinking that it is being "male" or "female" that is itself assumed.

2

"THAT WHICH IS NOT ASSUMED IS NOT HEALED"

When, therefore, we see in him some things so human that they appear in no way to differ from the common frailty of mortals, and some things so divine that they are appropriate to nothing else but the primal and ineffable nature of divinity, the human understanding with its narrow limits is baffled, and, struck with amazement at so mighty a wonder, knows not which way to turn, what to hold to, or whither to take itself.

If it thinks of God, it sees a man; if it thinks of a man, it beholds one returning from the dead with spoils after vanquishing the kingdom of death. For this reason we must pursue our contemplation with all fear and reverence, as we seek to prove how the truth of each nature exists in one and the same [subject], in such a way that nothing unworthy or unfitting may be thought to reside in that divine and ineffable existence, nor on the other hand may the events of his life be supposed to be the illusion caused by deceptive fantasies.

—Origen, *On First Principles*

To return to the exploration at hand, I would like to now offer a central patristic image of salvation to hold in heart and mind as we proceed. This chapter will briefly run through some of the main theological influences that have formed this image, and in so doing will hopefully help flesh out the image so that it may accompany the reader into the next chapters.

For those deeply familiar with the Orthodox Christian tradition, this chapter will simply highlight what is likely already well internalized. For readers who are less familiar, I offer a brief tour through of early Church theology (and theologians) in order to glean some central themes, images, and dynamics. In order to catch a real sense of the tradition that I am attempting to put together with depth psychology, and to ward off unnecessary (and faulty) assumptions about Orthodoxy, it is also necessary to clarify some differences between Eastern and Western Christian soteriological emphases as well. Lastly, in the next two chapters as I explore specific traces of Orthodox ontology and soteriology in depth-psychological healing, I will be drawing on the vast wealth of insight contained in patristic theology, most often refracted through the work of St. Maximus the Confessor. Thus it is important to get a sense of the context in which this theology arose, and of the rich and lively streams of reflection that pour into the deep river of theology I will be traveling upon.

In the latter part of this chapter, I will spend some time discussing a conceptual understanding of the Orthodox concept of salvation as *theosis* more generally. But the Orthodox way is not, finally, a concept; it is an experience. And so to talk about the faith that informs this experience, I would like to start by using an image.

John Behr describes theological reflection of the earliest Church Fathers as being greatly concerned with "how and why Jesus is called the 'Word of God.'"[1] The focus of the question was Christ Himself, not a desire to simply exegete Scripture or illuminate ultimate reality in ontological terms, but to answer Christ's question that he himself posed: "Who do you say I am?"[2] The reality of the person of Christ retains priority over any theological endeavors. And yet, those endeavors sought to faithfully describe the reality He embodied and disclosed. In this collective endeavor, "the most important soteriological model that nourished this increasingly focused theological reflection was that of *healing and salvation through sharing, solidarity, and exchange.*"[3]

Out of this basic soteriological premise arose a patristic maxim, first recorded by Origen in *Dialogue with Heraclides* and made famous by St. Gregory of Nazianzus: "*That which is not assumed is not healed.*"[4] In this pithy phrase was summed up the profound perception of the reality of healing to be found in the Incarnation of the Lord, a reality of assumption and co-inherence, of empathy and divinely interpenetrated life, which transfigures and transforms the human creature. I have referred to this phrase already as a model for the premise that the life of the psyche must be included in Orthodox reflection, and this is the central theological image I would like to use going forward in continuing to reflect on how traces of Orthodox ontology and soteriology show up in the life of the psyche. Thus, as already mentioned in the introduction, in a sense my work in the next two chapters will be a kind of exegesis of some of the psychological possibilities proclaimed in this statement.

In the late fourth century, St. Gregory of Nazianzus famously wrote in his *Letter to Cledonius*: "The unassumed is the unhealed, but what is united with God is also being saved."[5] In this particular instance, he was arguing for the reality of Christ's fully human mind, as well as the divinity of his Godhead, such that we may be assured that our human minds in their fullness, are assumed, are being healed, in Him.[6] It was an argument for the completeness of Christ's fully human nature, in addition to His divine nature. Without a human mind, and as he further elaborates, without a human soul, how can the human mind and soul be healed? Thus, he posits, it can only be the case that Christ has a fully human nature and a fully divine nature; two natures, one person.[7]

This was in further keeping with the common patristic understanding that God became human so that humans could be healed of corruption and "become god."[8] There is, in a sense, an "exchange" of natures, where our human nature is fully penetrated by God in order to be restored to its original beauty.[9] We will see more on this in various forms in this chapter. One might postulate, therefore, that such healing also includes the deep reaches of the psyche as we have come to understand it through modern depth psychology. As St. Gregory writes: "Keep then the whole [person], and mingle Godhead therewith, that you may benefit me in my completeness."[10]

Although this central theological maxim was made famous by St. Gregory, this image did not arise in theological isolation. It is an image that condenses some of the most profound understandings of the salvation of humanity enacted by God, which arose in the earliest theological reflections of the Church.

I will therefore spend some time in this chapter looking at the roots and theological antecedents of this image in the works of St. Irenaeus, Origen, and St. Athanasius (in the second, third, and early fourth centuries AD respectively). I will then look at the words and thought of St. Gregory himself in the fourth century, and from there proceed onwards to the evolution of this image as it was exegeted and defended by St. Maximus the Confessor in the Monothelitic controversy of the seventh century, as he expounded on the teachings of St. Gregory of Nazianzus and further developed his own radiant conceptualization of how the Lord's Incarnation assumed and healed our human nature.

I will delve into depth-psychological reflections in the next two chapters but in this chapter I wish mainly to set up a strong and lively sense of some of the foundational theologies that inform Orthodox theology. These explorations will give us a collage of various but deeply connected theological imagery of salvation, life, and healing. Again, my hope is that this, in turn, will make richer and more intuitive my usage of the theology in the two following chapters. As will be shown, as we briefly journey back to these theological ancestors of modern Orthodox thought to amplify the image and let their words speak to us through the centuries, in this short maxim is summed up an extraordinary beauty. It is the beauty of salvation, perfuming all of creation with its fragrance of life, hope, healing, and transfiguration.

St. Irenaeus of Lyons

Irenaeus sought a unity amongst the bewildering varieties of primitive Christianity, a basis which became the accepted framework for normative Christianity thereafter. . . . This was the most significant transition in early Christianity. Hereafter Christians were committed to a common body of Scripture, including the apostolic writings . . . the canon of truth, apostolic tradition and succession . . . in a unity of faith which marked out the "Great Church" from the various sects.

John Behr, *The Way to Nicaea*

St. Irenaeus of Lyons, the earliest "systematic theologian" of the Church, is famous for his fully extant work of the late second century, *Against Heresies*. His systematic exposition against Gnosticism "affirms the sacramentality of the world . . . and sets out the theory . . . of the recapitulation of human destiny in the person (and body) of Christ. . . . His system is a major patristic elaboration of the theology of deification."[11]

I will touch here, only briefly, upon some of the aspects of his theological vision most salient to an exploration of depth psychology and theology, and to highlight the early strands of a theology of "assumption."

His exposition of salvation, lengthy and interwoven throughout his work as a many-threaded tapestry, famously uses a multifaceted concept of "re-capitulation"; the concept that Christ recapitulated in its entirety the life of fallen humanity—which had been wracked by disobedience and had fallen subject to the power of death—thereby "assuming" and healing human life.[12] As he wrote:

> For in what way could we be partakers of the adoption of sons, unless we had received through the Son participation in himself, unless his Word had not entered into communion with us by becoming flesh? Therefore he also passed through every stage of life, restoring all to communion with God. . . . It behooved him who was to put sin to death and redeem the human being under the power of death that he should himself be made that very thing which he was, that is, human, who had been drawn into slavery by sin and held bound by death, so that sin should be destroyed by a human being, and that the human being should go forth from death. . . . But if he seemed to be flesh, not having been made flesh, his work was not true; but what he seemed to be, that he also was: God, recapitulating in himself the ancient formation of the human being, that he might kill sin, deprive death of its power, and vivify the human being; and therefore his work are true.[13]

D. V. Twomey, citing Irenaeus, continues: "Had not man conquered the enemy of man, the enemy would not have been properly conquered. On the other hand, if God had not given us salvation, we would not have it for certain. . . . He had to live through all the ages of man to heal them . . . this includes his real death."[14]

Not only is it emphasized that Christ recapitulates and, in a sense, re-integrates creation, summing "the whole cosmos in his divine and human person"[15] but also that in His full divinity and full humanity, God and humanity are reconciled fully. "That God can do all things was always clear," Hans von Balthasar interprets Irenaeus, "but that man together with God can also do all things had to be proved. The mediator came to exercise this power together with man, in order 'by his own affinity with both lead both back to mutual love and harmony, to introduce God to man and man to god.'"[16] Here we see the critical emphasis on his *enfleshed* being. Von Balthasar underscores this: "In this the flesh is crucial: if the flesh had not had to be saved, the Word of God would on no account have become flesh, and *flesh is really saved only by flesh*."[17]

Through his divine assumption of all stages of life, Christ also calls forth the truest nature of each creature. In Christ, all things achieve their natural telos implanted in them from the beginning: "In Christ's reality, Adam's reality comes to its own truth, in Mary Eve, in the Church the Synagogue."[18] The person is created *in* the image of God; Christ *is* the image of God.[19]

It is clear that for Irenaeus, at an individual level, this creative becoming is a matter of process. It entails the free will of the person, formed and educated through *experience*, and the creative activity of God. I will return to this notion later, but at this point it is important to recognize that for Irenaeus,

> becoming is the mode of creaturely existence. For Irenaeus every moment of that becoming is significant—and so every moment of the history of salvation where everyone in his or her assigned place does the will of God and so either anticipating the fulfillment in Christ or living out of its fullness subsequent to Christ's coming.[20]

Irenaeus spends a goodly portion of his treatise arguing against the gnostic heresies, in particular the teachings of Valentinus. Of particular interest to this study is how substantial differences in thought between the two have been elucidated concerning the roles of the psyche. As Basil Studer notes, Gnosticism as a general school of thought encouraged the belief that by recollecting one's own affinity to God through gnosis, one could attain liberation from this world and salvation.[21] Rather than read the Scriptures through the lens of the historically crucified and resurrected Christ, Scripture was read as an allegory of a kind of "psychodrama," where the highest concern is the personal subject, or self.[22] With regards to Valentinian Gnosis as described by Irenaeus of Lyon, von Balthasar comments: "Never have man, his structure, his sufferings and his tragedy, been more plainly projected on the screen of heaven in order to fascinate him and, professedly, to redeem him by contemplation of this magnified image of himself."[23] Contrary to this vein of thought, for Irenaeus, "theology begins by seeing what is. This is revelation understood as a process. . . . Truth is *discovered, not manufactured*."[24] As Studer adds:

Contrary to the dualistic tendencies of his gnostic opponents Irenaeus outlined a soteriology which is completely founded on unity. The themes of the unity of God, the creator and invisible Father, the unity of Christ, true God and true man, as well as the unity of material nature and spiritual man feature among the most prominent.[25]

Here again, we see an emphasis on the assumption and integration of creation.

Creation was meant for *life*. Irenaeus spends a great deal of time on the notion of the vivification of the person through the Spirit of God. His emphasis on the importance of the flesh offers a classic patristic paradox when held with his emphasis also on the eternal vivification of the person through the Spirit—a life that is different than the simple animating life as originally breathed into each soul by God.[26] While the created "breath of life" living within each person until death is dependent upon the life-creating Spirit for its existence, it is not the same as the ultimate vivification of the person by the life-creating Spirit itself. Paradoxically, this life is achieved through the creature dying, with Christ, to receive the new life given in Christ.[27]

In a sense, we have a very particular icon of assumption in simply looking at the relationship between the breath of life that animates the person and the life of the Spirit that vivifies them with the Spirit's own life. One is contingent on the other, and hence—in a sense—always and already related to it. At the same time, the full expression of life only takes place through those who willingly yield to receive the Spirit. Irenaeus writes:

> When this Spirit, commingled with the soul, is united to the handiwork, because of the outpouring of the Spirit the human being is rendered spiritual and complete (*perfectus*), and this is the one who was made in the image and likeness of God. But if the Spirit is lacking from the soul, such a one, remaining indeed animated and fleshly, will be incomplete (*imperfectus*), having the image, certainly, in the handiwork, but not receiving the likeness through the Spirit.[28]

Rather than suggesting that humanity had this life of the Spirit prior to the fall, and then lost it, Irenaeus suggests that although humanity became subject to death by turning toward evil, the Spirit has prepared humanity first through the "breath of life," and then through increase to receive life from God alone through his life-creating Spirit.[29] It is never the case, for

Irenaeus, that the flesh is discarded but rather body and soul, together, receive the life of the Spirit. In one of his most famous passages, expounding on life as communion with God, he wrote: "The glory of God is a living [human], and the life of [the human] consists in beholding God."[30]

Lastly, I wish to briefly comment on the soteriology of Irenaeus as viewed from a more modern emphasis on "atonement" theology. This was picked up by Gustaf Aulen in the early twentieth century. He underscored the categories of life and death—as mentioned in the introduction—as integral to Irenaeus's understanding of sin and salvation. He wrote:

> The truth is . . . that Irenaeus' organic view of sin as a state of alienation from God [and hence death] saves him both from a moralistic idea of sin and moralistic idea of salvation. . . . [We may also look to] the Pauline and Johannine epistles, where we find the most definite statements that salvation is life, in direct connection with the thought of Christ as victor over sin and over death.[31]

Aulen outlines the work of Christ: in His obedience through which He "recapitulated and annulled the disobedience"; in His teaching and preaching as means of knowing the Father; and in His death, using the ransom image, paid to the powers of evil—hence God is both reconciler and reconciled.[32]

This is not the substitutionary atonement common to Latin Christian thought; God is not receiving Jesus's offering on behalf of man, but is using man to liberate man from bondage and thus reconcile him back to God.[33] In Christ's death on the Cross, death itself meets defeat. Aulen highlights a favorite patristic paradox: "The power of evil ultimately overreaches itself when it comes in conflict with the power of good, with God Himself. It loses the battle *at the moment when it seems to be victorious.*"[34]

Christ instead is victor, and salvation is the restoration of life and progressive deification. Thus we might conclude this section with the words of Irenaeus himself: "The Word of God, our Lord Jesus Christ, through his transcendent love, became what we are, that he might bring us to be even what he is himself."[35]

Origen of Alexandria

In all the twists and turns of his telling the great tale, the kerygma of the divine salvation of the cosmos, Origen never lost sight of the

one single thread that holds it all together: the restless and un-
swerving love of a God who is determined to bring back the cosmos
to the unity of the circle of love that was its original conception and
reality.

John A. McGuckin, *The Westminster Handbook to Origen*

Born in Alexandria, Egypt, in the late second century, Origen follows
closely on the chronological heels of Irenaeus. While he was ultimately condemned as heretical in the sixth century, his influence on Christian
thought from the third century onward, with a deep and vast range from
speculative theology to allegorical exegesis to ascetic practice, can hardly
be overstated.[36]

His theology would come to influence (as well as come under refinement from) St. Gregory of Nazianzus, Pseudo-Dionysus the Areopagite,
and St. Maximus the Confessor—all of whose works inform this work.[37]
McGuckin salutes him as the first great mystic of the Christian Church,
"describing the divine Word's quest for the soul through the recesses of
time and space, and the soul's fearful search for its lost Lord, in terms
drawn from the Song of Songs, where the bride seeks her beloved in the
starlit garden."[38]

Much of Origen's theology centered around the usage of the preexisting concept of the Logos. Studer notes that, like Irenaeus before him,
Origen was opposed to the gnostic movement and embarked on the
task of defending an ecclesiastical Logos Christology as well as a true
Christian gnosis.[39] As Behr observes, for Origen, "the veiled content of
Scripture is identical to the truth taught by Christ, which is Christ
himself."[40]

Through this work he elucidated the center of connection between God
and humanity: "It was the genius of the Logos scheme to be able to connect the eternal (immanent) life of God with the economy of salvation."[41]
It was also a meeting point of Scriptural tradition, Hebrew thought, and
Hellenistic philosophy. It was to become profoundly influential:

After Origen the schema of Logos theology entered so profoundly
into the mainstream that it formed the substrate of all Christological and Trinitarian thought thereafter. It takes its point of origin from
the (very few) references in the Fourth Gospel prologue to the Logos
of God, which was "with God in the beginning." (John 1:1) and which

"became flesh and dwelt amongst us" (John 1:14). The connection of the idea of Logos (reason, inherent structure, creative pattern, or spoken word) with the biblical tradition of the Word of God (see Isaiah 55:11), particularly that word, as uttered throughout the Wisdom literature, for the ordering of the cosmos in wisdom and grace struck the early patristic writers as a highly useful term of reconciliation between the Greek philosophical traditions of cosmogony and the biblical understanding of God as personal creator.[42]

It is a beautiful paradox. The Logos of God is personal, and also both the link between God and the created world as well as the soul of the world that establishes its ordering.[43] The Logos could be seen in contemplation of creation as well as in contemplation of Scripture, it being the one and same Logos who created them both.[44] Through the Logos, the person is able to progressively ascend toward Christian gnosis, as the Logos descends in accommodation to the spiritual needs of each individual.[45]

Of particular import to my reflections here is the importance of Jesus's human soul in the theology of Origen. C. Kannengiesser, in his article on Origen's Christology, elucidates that for Origen, the Incarnation could not have happened without Jesus having a human soul, for the spiritual Logos could not be directly united with a human body. In Origen's understanding, of all the souls (preexistent, in his thought) ever created by God, only the soul of Jesus never turned away from God and so was prepared to receive the Logos fully. The Logos had to descend from the purely spiritual realm to become Incarnate in the material realm. Only a pure soul could mediate this union, and Jesus was the soul chosen by the Logos to effect this salvific undertaking. What this understanding allowed for, in part, was an overcoming of the Alexandrian dualistic mentality—a splitting between spiritual and material.[46] The soul of Jesus becomes the linking possibility between the two. As Studer writes:

> As this [human] soul was always attached to the Word, it did not fall from God like the other spiritual beings. Thus it always remains attached to the Logos *like iron penetrated by fire*. In this way Origen not only sought to explain the deep union of the divine and human in Christ, but also made a decisive soteriological statement. On the one hand he makes out the soul of Jesus to be the model for any union with the Word, on the other he anticipates the later principle: *quod non assumptum—non sanataum*.[47]

Thus, for Studer, Origen's Logos theology comes to define his soteriology, and we see here, intrinsic to that soteriology is the maxim of "what is not assumed is not healed." While Origen does not pass over the traditional themes of the victorious and sacrificial death of Christ, it is above all in the Incarnation that He leads humanity back to Himself, fully accommodating Himself to humanity and so fully perfecting prior theophanies.[48] In Christ's accommodating Himself to humanity, the Logos creates the possibility of true meeting with God for each person, with an emphasis on the importance of the free will of the person in turning to God voluntarily and seeking further communion with Him.[49]

One gathers from the above that the emphasis in Origen is on what Kannengiesser calls "soul-communion" rather than "enfleshment."[50] This is in striking contrast to Irenaeus for whom, as we saw above, the soul was intimately bound up with the animation of the body, the very body that would receive eternal life. Origen's soteriology was, Kannengiesser proposes, largely pedagogic. He writes:

> The Soul-joined-with-the-Logos operates in the flesh by addressing other souls. . . . His message dissipates ignorance. He rekindles the spark of noetic transcendence that enables human souls to become again irradiated with the divine Logos, in order to recover their original integrity as images of the image of God who is the Logos himself.[51]

As Kannengiesser continues, this lent itself well to a Christian asceticism[52] which sought purification of the inner state and the development of noetic perception. It lent itself rather less well to an embodied, pastoral theology of everyday life—a situation that Kannengiesser observes St. Athanasius addressed in his refinement of Origen's theology. We will turn to Athanasius in the next section; however, while retaining a sense of caution about the degree to which reading Origen might lead one to a "disembodied" or otherworldly theology, I think it important to also hear Behr's comment on the proactive reach of Origen's emphasis on the transcendent immanence of the Logos. In not overly emphasizing the enfleshment, while still emphasizing the union of the Logos with the human, Origen seems to make a plea for the wondrous hope found in the accession of the transformative power of the Logos to all humanity, past, present and future:

Origen is concerned that the Word of God should not be reduced to the flesh which he assumed to make himself known, through his salvific death, nor that his presence should be restricted in this way to the past . . . : *"According to the coming of our Lord Jesus Christ as narratively told, his sojourn was bodily and something universal, illumining the whole world, for the 'Word became flesh and dwelt among us' (John 1:14). . . . However it is also necessary to know that he was also sojourning prior to this, though not bodily, in each of the holy ones, and that after this visible sojourn of his, he again sojourns in us. . . . It is necessary for us to know these things, because there is a sojourn of the Word with each, especially for those who would benefit from it. For what benefit is it to me, if the Word has sojourned in the world and I do not have him?"*[53]

As Behr further notes, "the significance of the Incarnation is thus not limited to the coming of Jesus Christ, but is extended to all those in whom the Word sojourns."[54]

The notions of assumption and union, and of healing and transformation, have here become inseparable. The soul of each person, containing an irreducible spark of divinity, is capable of being transformed and healed, restored to its original integrity, through turning to and receiving the Word that sojourns with us throughout eternity.

St. Athanasius of Alexandria

Athanasius' insistence that Christ was God . . . compelled him to assert that the incarnate Lord was not merely the means of salvation (that is his life and teachings had exemplary force) but was also its goal (*telos*) and dynamism (*energia*). Following on this insight . . . he described the incarnation of the God-Logos (in terms reminiscent of the earlier theologian Irenaeus) as a two-way transaction: one that involved the deity's enfleshment but also the simultaneous divinization (*theopoesis*) of the flesh of the God-Man Jesus.

Later writers have often described this as the "physical theory of Atonement" and are correct in so far as the analogy is rooted in the image of God's assumption of flesh (incarnation) being at one and the same moment a deification of matter (*theosis*). However, Athanasius takes the idea further and uses the radiant instance of the divination of materiality (the flesh of Christ the God) to be the indication for his readers that in making this divine transformation of part of the material world (his own body) the Lord has initiated a transformation of the entire cosmos.

John McGuckin, quoted in D. V. Twomey,
Salvation According to the Fathers of the Church

The fourth century AD was a pivotal time in the history of the Christian faith. The Council of Nicaea, held in 325, famously established the full divinity of the incarnated Logos as *homoousion toi theoi* in an effort to clarify the orthodox theology in light of the challenges presented by the theology of Arius of Alexandria. However, while this faith was established at Nicaea, it was not until the Council of Constantinople in 381 that it truly became entrenched. The years between the two councils are portrayed as tumultuous years, both theologically and politically, and there are a few theologians whose work stands out during this time as having been critical to the maintenance of the Nicene faith. One of these is St. Athanasius, bishop of Alexandria from 328–73.

A young Athanasius was established as bishop of Alexandria in 328. For the next five decades until his death in 373, Athanasius would dedicate his career to upholding the Nicene faith in spite of and against both theological and political challenges, as well as numerous periods of exile. By the time the Council of Constantinople was held in 381, heralding the final triumph of the theology established at Nicaea, Athanasius had passed on from this world but his legacy in defending the orthodox stance against the Arian strains of Logos theology would resonate for the next two millennia.

Athanasius was of the utmost conviction that there was something deeply existential at stake in these deliberations. The issue of the full divinity of the Logos in Christ was, for Athanasius, an issue of salvation effected by a real transformation of humanity. His argument hinged on one pivotal conviction—only God Himself could deify humanity, and it is for the deification of humanity that God became man. If we understand salvation as both transformation and creation of the new, then Athanasius indeed makes a compelling argument for the divinity of the Logos, as only God is capable of true creation ex nihilo.

Living in Alexandria in the early fourth century, he was primarily influenced by Clement and Origen and made Christian use of Platonic cosmology and ontology.[55] His theology also shows Irenaean elements. As with other Church Fathers, his theology was a product of his own internal spirituality that in turn was a product of "personal experience, social culture and communal belief."[56] It is interesting to keep in mind whether Athanasius's focus on the transformative power of the Logos perhaps does not arrive as a sheerly dogmatic theological answer to the questions posed by Arianism and others, but also arose out of his own encounter with the Living God.

Like Origen and Irenaeus before him, he is concerned with the existential consequences of the ontological relationship of God to His creation. His is a dialectic between the "being-ness" of God and the created-ness of humanity, which comes from nothing and tends toward nonbeing—it stands over an underlying emptiness by its very created nature. Yet, as part of its creation it has been given grace by God, who reaches across out of His great love to uphold our being-ness. For Athanasius, the human as created by God participates in both nature and grace, with "'nature' referring to the whence of creation's being . . . also an intrinsic orientation to nothingness, and 'grace' the reality of its establishment in being through the Word."[57] The contingency of the person's existence constitutes that existence as gift. "Precisely because its whole being is gifted, humanity has no hold on being apart from that irreducibly radical gift."[58] This hearkens back also to Irenaeus's emphasis on the dependency of the human upon God, and the realization of this dependency on God and receptive acceptance of God's creativity activity in the person as a state of thankfulness.[59] These themes of dependency, gift, and creation and gratitude will be central to the later reflections of this exploration as well. This relatedness is, for Athanasius, central, and is taken up into his soteriological vision:

> His conception of the relation between God and creation may thus be considered as the architectonic center of Athanasius' theological vision; his account of this relation provides the overarching framework in which his various doctrines acquire their distinctive resonance. Yet it must be remembered that this central focus on the relation between God and creation is at the same time always a Christological focus. . . . His account of the relation between God and creation is thus ultimately a Christology conceived in the most universal terms.[60]

Let us turn then to the words of St. Athanasius himself, and very briefly look to his fully extant treatise *On the Incarnation* to see how he describes the transformative power of the Logos within the context briefly outlined above.[61] He begins by emphasizing right away that "it is first necessary to speak about the creation of the universe and its maker, God, so that one may worthily reflect that its recreation was accomplished by the Word who created it in the beginning."[62] Thus he immediately establishes that it is God Himself in Jesus Christ who is at work for our redemption.

> In the act of divine incarnation, the Logos . . . came again to re-create humanity in its original dimension: this time restoring immortal life through the communion with God he restored in his presence. As the Logos was made flesh for the salvation of the world, so Athanasius sees the deification of the world as taking place by a progressive assimilation to that salvific principle.[63]

He also establishes a basic—and psychologically profound—understanding of God: "God is good, or rather the source of goodness, and the good *has not envy for anything. Thus, grudging nothing its existence*, he made all things from nothing through his own Word, our Lord Jesus Christ."[64]

He then outlines the predicament of humanity in having fallen away from knowledge of God:

> For the transgression of the commandment returned them to the natural state, so that, just as they, not being, came to be, so also they might rightly endure in time the corruption unto non-being. For if, having a nature that did not once exist, they were called into existence by the Word's advent [*parousia*] and love for human beings, it followed that when human beings were bereft of the knowledge of God and had turned to things which exist not—evil is non-being, the good is being, since it has come into being from the existing God—then they were bereft also of eternal being.[65]

It is apparent that God's intention toward us is life. Death, or any kind of begrudgement of existence, is contrary to God's abundant generosity in bestowing being. Rather, it was "by envy of the devil death entered into the world."[66] But humanity, having chosen transgression, is subject to death "according to nature, and no longer live[s] in paradise, but thereafter dying outside of it, would remain in death and corruption."[67]

We can see, from various angles, how Athanasius is primarily concerned with issues of life and death, rather than simply morality as an extrinsic issue. Here again it should be emphasized that what Athanasius believed was effected in the Incarnation was an ontological transformation for all humanity and not just a moral reawakening. He addresses this, saying:

> Nor does repentance recall human beings from what is natural, but merely halts sins. If then there were only offence and not the consequence of corruption, repentance would have been fine. But if, once the transgression had taken off, human beings were now held fast in natural corruption, and were deprived of the grace of being in the image, what else needed to happen?[68]

Thus he surmises that only the Word of God Himself, who had in the beginning also created all things out of nothing, would be able to bring again the corruptible to incorruption. This ontological rescue is effected in two main ways. The first one he discusses is the abolition of death through the death and Resurrection of Jesus Christ. He writes:

> For the Word, realizing that in no other way would the corruption of human beings be undone except, simply, by dying, yet being immortal and the Son of the Father the Word was not able to die, for this reason he takes to himself a body capable of death in order that, participating in the Word who is above all, might be sufficient for death on behalf of all, and through the indwelling Word would remain incorruptible, and so corruption might henceforth cease from all by the grace of the resurrection.[69]

The consummate problem facing humanity is corruption and the turn toward nonbeing; the finality of death through participation in nonbeing rather than being. The Logos voluntarily takes on the shroud of death, so that it may be defeated from within. As McGuckin comments: *"His design is to work his energies of life in the primary locus of the sickness of the race."*[70] It is the paradoxical descent of life into death, which overcomes death through unconquerable life: "If he died for the ransom of all, yet 'he saw not corruption' (see Acts 2.31; 13.35; Ps. 15.10). For he rose whole, since the body belonged to none other but Life itself."[71]

The second theme in Athanasius is that of restoration to humanity of the knowledge of God, thereby bringing healing and return to grace. God had given humanity a multitude of ways of knowing Himself—namely, though contemplation of the knowledge of the Word given to all by grace of being created in His Image, through contemplation of the created order, through discourse with holy men, and through following the law and the prophets whose wisdom Athanasius maintained was not only for the Jews though it came through the Jews.[72] Yet because of mankind's increasing slide toward corruption and away from grace, humans "beaten by the pleasures of the moment and the illusions and deceits of the demons, did not raise their gaze to the truth."[73] As Behr comments, "evil does not belong to God's creation, but rather it exists when human beings turn from what is truly real to insubstantial fantasies, so giving evil some kind of phantasmagorical existence."[74]

This left God with no other recourse, according to Athanasius, than to renew His Image in mankind so that "through it human beings might once more come to know him"[75] This emphasis on the transformative impact of the Incarnation allows Athanasius to once more drive home the point of the divinity of the Logos as he surmises "The Word of God came himself, in order that he being the image of the Father [see Col. 1.15], the human being 'in the image' might be recreated. It could not . . . have been done in any other way without death and corruption being utterly destroyed."[76]

It is clear that, for Athanasius, all transformation and healing follows on and from the destruction of death and corruption. For if the devil holds the power of death,[77] then perhaps the power of all evil spirits is related to the power of death, and hence so is all that veils knowledge of God from the hearts of humans. When the power of death is broken, the power of the evil spirits to confound humanity in its knowledge of God is also broken, as is the fear of the death that bound us, making what once were iron chains of bondage into cobweb-like tendrils that may linger but no longer have the power to bind.[78] Perhaps that which is evil, nonbeing, can only pervade where being itself is somehow obscured, and so the dual action of both conquering death/nonbeing and restoring life/being to humanity is the most complete way to sense the trajectory of Athanasius's thought.

It is a fascinating dual-edged soteriological blade of pedagogy and re-creation. Athanasius famously describes the Cross as the locus of the exorcism of the devil who, having been cast out of heaven with his demons, "wanders around these lower airs and . . . works illusions in those who are deceived and attempts to prevent them rising upwards."[79] But in Christ's death on the Cross, which stands "in the air," He has "purified" the air and opened up a way for us to heaven, *"through the veil, that is, His flesh"* (Heb. 10.20).[80]

Of particular salience to this discussion is also, once again, that humanity found itself in a situation from which it could not rescue itself. The saving activity of God, as "Other," was required:

> Since even the best of men were confused and blinded by evil, how could they covert the souls and minds of others? You cannot put straight in others what is warped in yourself . . . wherefore . . . desiring to do good to men, as Man He dwells, taking to Himself a body like the rest; and through His actions done in that body, as it were on their own level, He teaches those who would not learn by other means to know Himself, the Word of God, and through Him the Father.[81]

Key to understanding Athanasius, and in keeping with his emphasis on the simultaneous distinction and relationship between God and the world is that for him, the subject-object distinction between humanity and God is never lost, even in the process of deification (which I will discuss further later in this chapter). He differentiates between *identity* and *likeness*.[82] Vladimir Kharlamov elaborates:

> Identity presupposes the oneness of nature or consubstantiality, while likeness is more like resemblance to some quality of the nature that is not necessarily the predicate of the nature of those who demonstrate such resemblance. Here, Athanasius methodologically makes a distinction between the object of participation and the subject that participates. The subject that participates does not become equal or identical with the object of participation.[83]

While Athanasius keeps the distinction between subject and object with regards to humanity and God, it is precisely this distinction he seeks to abolish between the Logos and God. It is this absence of difference that allows us to become reconciled to God through the Logos, and continues the basis for theologies of assumption. Norman Russell writes:

> The incarnate Word took our nature into himself in order to save it. Thus . . . Athanasius understood redemption "as taking place within the mediatorial life and person of the Incarnate Son. Just as he thought of the Logos as internal to the being of God, so he thinks of our

salvation as taking place in the *inner relations of the Mediator*, and not simply in Christ's external relationship with sinners." Or, as Anatolios puts it, "our whole salvation and deification are rooted in our human condition's being 'ascribed' to the Word, for that is what essentially constitutes our own being 'Worded.'"[84]

Athanasius also describes how the resurrected Christ continues to impact the lives of those who are living. It would seem that his emphasis in this case is not so much on the transformation of the individual as it is on making the point that the Resurrection really took place and that Christ lives—as is seen by His ongoing power to cast out demons and altering the lives of the individuals by continuing to bring them back to knowledge of God. In an impassioned passage, he argues:

> Is it like a dead man to prick the minds of human beings so that they deny their father's laws and revere the teaching of Christ? Or how, if he is not acting—for this is a property of one dead—does he stop those active and alive so that the adulterer no longer commits adultery, the murderer no longer murders. . . . How, if he is not risen but dead, does he stop and drive out and cast down those false gods said by unbelievers to be alive and the demons they worship? For where Christ and his faith are named, there all idolatry is purged away . . . and no demon endures the name but fleeing, only hearing it, disappears. This is not the work of one dead, but of one alive, and especially of God.[85]

Again, we see a dual action of defeating that which brings death, and restoring to humanity that which brings life. We also see an emphasis on living experience.

To conclude, we see the culmination of several richly woven threads—Irenaeus's saying that God became what we are so that he might bring us to be what he himself is; Origen's emphasis on the paradoxical nature of the union in Christ of the deathless nature of God with the human nature, vulnerable to death (in what, according to Behr, would later come to be known as the *communication idiomatum* "the exchange of properties"[86])—in Athanasius's famous exhortation:

> [Let us] marvel that through such a paltry thing things divine have been made manifest to us, and that through death incorruptibility has come to all, and through the incarnation of the Word the uni-

versal providence, and its giver and creator, the very Word of God, have been made known. For he was incarnate that we might be made god; and he manifested himself through a body that we might receive an idea of the invisible Father; and he endured the insults of human beings, that we might inherit incorruptibility.[87]

St. Gregory of Nazianzus

Seeing as Christ had set in the human body a piece of heaven, when he saw it blasted with heart-gnawing evil, and the twisted dragon lording it over men, he did not . . . send yet other aids to treat the disease (for a little cure is inadequate against great illnesses); but, emptying himself of his glory . . . he appeared for me himself . . . so that the whole of him might save the whole of me. . . . Therefore, humanly, and not after human custom, in the hallowed womb of a maid inviolate he took flesh (amazing! to washed-out minds incredible!) and came, both God and man, two natures gathered into one: one hidden, the other open to mankind; of these, the one is God, the latter was created later with us. He is one God out of both, since the human is mixed with the Godhead, and, because of the Godhead, exists as Lord and Christ.

St. Gregory of Nazianzus, *On the Two Covenants*

Chronologically, we are returned now to St. Gregory of Nazianzus, Cappadocia, who (though younger than St. Athanasius) also lived in the fourth century. John McGuckin describes him as "the finest Christian rhetorician of his day, and the most learned bishop of the early Church."[88] He is perhaps most famous for his writing on the Trinity, which, as McGuckin writes "was never rivaled, and he is the undisputed architect of the Church's understanding of how the divine unity coexists in three coequal hypostases as the essential dynamic of the salvation of the world."[89] He is one of only three saints in the history of the Orthodox Church to have been awarded the official title of Theologian (along with St. John the Evangelist and St. Symeon the New Theologian).

We encounter him, here, mainly through his *Letter to Cledonius*. This brief section can do no justice to the immensity of his thought or impact; I will simply focus on his use of Origen's maxim and how it relates to the concerns of this discussion.

In his *Letter to Cledonius* (*Epistle* 101), St. Gregory was concerned with a school of thought called Apollinarism. This theological stream had come gushing forth from a theologian named Apollinaris, as a strong anti-Arian response, at the time of Athanasius.[90] It was primarily concerned with presenting a "mystical Christology" emphasizing a God who had remained impassible in the Incarnation while still remaining the subject of all of Christ's action.[91] In order to make this argument, Apollinaris proffered that the Word had assumed *only* human flesh in Jesus, inhabiting his body as a kind of "vessel," rather than in fact becoming himself human. On the one hand, this ascribed infinite value to all that Jesus did, since he was, in fact, solely God in all of his actions including his death.[92] However, "the flaw in this strong theory of the Word of God's direct and unmediated subjectivity in the life of the incarnate Christ was the question of psychological subjectivity."[93] Was there any humanity, as we recognize ourselves, in this image? If there is not, could any of what we know ourselves to be, or what we experience of life, be of value to God?

Apollinaris understood the Word of God as the immediate source of all human wisdom. Each person was given by God an "icon" of his own divine wisdom, which constituted the "image and likeness of God" in the person.[94] However, in the body of Christ, God "instilled within it his own Wisdom and Nous. . . . There was no need for a soul (Psyche) or for a human Mind (Nous) in Jesus since the Word of God supplanted them. . . . What need was there for a small imagistic prototype when the archetype himself was present?"[95]

Understandably, this could be seen as a highly reverent theology. It certainly was a staunch disavowal of Arian claims that the Word of God was less than absolutely divine. Yet, as McGuckin continues:

> Others were less sure of the wisdom of [Apollinaris's] scheme. If the divine presence so supplanted the characteristics of human soul and human mental consciousness, was it not tantamount to suppressing the very essence of Jesus' humanity? Were human soul and human mind so peripheral that an idea of humanity could survive at all without them?[96]

We see, then, embedded in this discussion a concern for what is of value in humanity. There is also, as we saw in the other Fathers, a concern for what is capable of transforming and healing—or rather one might say, capable of *being* transformed and healed—in the person.

Gregory sees the mind as that in need of greatest healing in the person, because it was the mind that had transgressed against God.[97] As he writes:

> Mind not only fell in Adam, but it was the "protopath," to use the term the physicians use in the case of first ailments. The very thing that had accepted the commandment did not keep the commandment. The very thing that did not keep it ventured its transgression. The very thing that transgressed stood in special need of salvation. The very thing that needed salvation was assumed. Therefore mind was assumed.[98]

McGuckin clarifies that if Christ is without mind, or without human soul, "he has accepted an incarnation that is deprived of the very factors in human life that stand most in need of redemption: the moral and spiritual lights in a human existence."[99] Yet one does not read, in Gregory, a concern only for a disembodied morality or spiritual purity of existence, as though the "mind" exists in schizoid conditions of its own. And it is not only in this letter that Gregory insists on this trajectory of healing and assumption. In his *Theological Oration 37*, he reiterates this theme with a poignancy that belies, perhaps, his own desire to know Christ's solidarity with his own humanity and human struggles—a theme one can find in his beautiful poetry as well. For example, he writes:

> As I said then, He is made a Fisherman; He condescends to all; He casts the net; He endures all things, that He may draw up the fish from the depths, that is, Man who is swimming in the unsettled and bitter waves of life. . . . He teaches, now on a mountain; now He discourses on a plain; now He passes over into a ship; now He rebukes the surges. And perhaps He goes to sleep, in order that He may bless sleep also; perhaps He is tired that He may hallow weariness also; perhaps He weeps that He may make tears blessed. He removes from place to place, Who is not contained in any place; the timeless, the bodiless, the uncircumscript, the same Who was and is; Who was both above time, and came under time, and was invisible and is seen. What He was He laid aside; what He was not He assumed; not that He became two, but He deigned to be One made out of the two. For both are God, that which assumed, and that which was assumed; two Natures meeting in One, not two Sons (let us not give a false account of the blending). He who is such and so great—but what has befallen

me? I have fallen into human language. For how can So Great be said of the Absolute, and how can That which is without quantity be called Such? But pardon the word, for I am speaking of the greatest things with a limited instrument. And That great and long-suffering and formless and bodiless Nature will endure this, namely, my words as if of a body, and weaker than the truth. For if He condescended to Flesh, He will also endure such language.[100]

In the language of hallowing even the most mundane of human experience, weariness, sleep, tears, there is a tender embrace—reminiscent of Irenaeus's emphasis on recapitulation—what one might call true empathy, with the human condition. Divine-human empathy has become the healing balm to which we may open our deepest wounds. Thus it is not solely a pivotal conceptual argument for the importance of the human mind and soul, though it became that. And—though theologically profoundly noteworthy—it is not solely a moment where Christology and soteriology become inextricably linked in a "landmark of Christological development,"[101] and in his "insistence . . . that a real acknowledgement of the full humanity of Jesus was is no way detrimental to the mystical force of a true and direct incarnation of the person of the divine Word himself."[102] It is also a perception of a dynamic "initiated not because God needed it, but because God was determined to use the incarnation as his healing medium for the salvation of humanity."[103] It is an impassioned plea for an understanding of salvation as *healing.*

St. Maximus the Confessor

Even in the densest of his theological treatises, Maximus' concern for the life of prayer and engagement with God is still uppermost. *The purpose of theology is to safeguard against misunderstandings that frustrate a Christian life of prayer.*
       Andrew Louth, *Maximus the Confessor* (emphasis mine)

Approximately two centuries later, St. Maximus the Confessor was born in the late sixth century in the Byzantine Empire.[104] I will not spend too much time with St. Maximus's theology here, only a brief overview and context, as his is the theology that I will return to exploring in the greatest detail in the following chapters.

McGuckin writes of Maximus that he is "one of the most subtle of all the Byzantine theologians."[105] He wrote theology that ranged from basic steps in the spiritual life-understandings of love, of sin, of the passions, even of images and how they come to be represented to the mind conceptually, as well theology of glorious cosmogenic insight, luminous meditations on the nature of Christ's salvific work, and the glorious destiny of the cosmos as transfigured by God to its original nature through the mediating function of the person as "microcosm" of the "macrocosm."[106] As Orthodox theologian Andrew Louth writes, Maximus

> draws together a metaphysical analysis of being that places the human person at a kind of central crossing-place in his understanding of reality, and then relates that to the renewal of nature through the Incarnation, and the celebration and recapitulation of that renewal in the Eucharistic Liturgy.[107]

In the intervening years between St. Gregory of Nazianzus's death and St. Maximus's birth, the Council of Chalcedon of 451 had been convened and established an articulation of the dual natures of Christ that became official Church dogma:

> We all with one voice teach the confession of one and the same Son, our Lord Jesus Christ the same perfect in divinity and perfect in humanity, the same truly God and truly man, of a rational soul and a body; consubstantial with the Father as regards his divinity, and the same consubstantial with us as regards his humanity . . . acknowledged in two natures which undergo no confusion, no change, no division, no separation . . . the property of both natures is preserved and comes together into a single person.[108]

Louth notes that Maximus, who was deeply influenced by Chalcedonian Christology, is fond of using the terms of confusion, division, change, and separation in meditating on the effects of the fall, so that while the fundamental *logoi* of beings (which I have already briefly mentioned and will return to in Chapter 3) remain as originally willed by God, in the way "fallen natures act and interact . . . confusion, division and fragmentation obscure the fundamental reality, disclosed by the *logos* of each creature, of what God has created." Maximus saw the restoration of creation as a succession of integration and unification—though without confusion—of five levels of being that had become subject to division, that created and uncreated, the intelligible world and sensible world, heaven and earth, paradise and the inhabited world, and male and female.[109] Love, for Maximus, was the only force capable of bringing this integration.[110]

Part of Maximus's work then, which deeply embroiled him in the Monothelitic controversy,[111] had to do with his insistence that Christ had a fully human will (*thelema*). In the lineage of St. Gregory's maxim and Chalcedonian logic, Maximus was clear that if Christ had only a divine will, and did not also have a fully human will, then *our* will could not be healed.[112] At stake, in addition to a defense against an understanding of God that was more akin to Hellenistic impassibility than an Incarnate God of compassion, subject to the woes of life—as mused upon by St. Gregory above— was also a defense of nothing less than human freedom.[113] McGuckin writes:

> The incarnation, which Maximus sees as the high point of all human history, is for him the dynamic method and means of the deification of the human race; a spiritual re-creation of human nature that allows individuals the freedom needed to practice virtue, since all humans before the advent of the Logos into human flesh, and will, and mind, were wholly enslaved by the passions.[114]

As I will discuss in much greater detail in Chapter 4, this concept of will is more closely aligned with desire than with "choice" as colloquially used. (And it is compelling that the virtues, for Maximus, correlate more closely to integration than to any superficial overlay of "morality.") So in a sense, it is Christ's *desiring* (as noted also earlier in the excursus on death) human will that reconfigures our own, through our participation in His ontological energies. As I will show later, this links willing closely to eros and to love, grounded, unexpectedly, in *beauty*. As McGuckin continues:

> What is special to Maximus in fighting so vigorously for this high patristic doctrine of soteriological incarnationalism, is that he sees more clearly than many other before or after him, that this . . . is at root a doctrine of the perception of the beauty in God's ordering of the *Cosmos* (the place of beauty). He has seen the link between the doctrine of the ascent of human consciousness from material forms to immaterial perceptions (*aisthesis*): from the earthly creation to the divine realities: and understood most clearly that this ascent is also synonymous with a comprehension of the beauty of love as the ex-

planation of all that God does in Christ. Maximus has kept faith with the ultimate reasons Chalcedonianism had insisted on the full Humanity of the Lord: he sees how necessary it is to protect the moral teleology at the heart of a true Christology. He keeps faith as a philosopher-theologian with the ever present call to ascend to truer and more beautiful perception (*aisthesis*), rising to Beauty from a beautiful life, and thus into the embodied experience of Beauty Hypostatized (the *Logos* made flesh). In a word, Maximus' theory of the Ascent to Beauty is not a separate treatise from his dyothelite Christology of deification. It is simply his teleologically moral expression of it.[115]

It is creaturely participation in the divine assumption of human will, in Christ, that manifests the beauty of God through the reconfiguring of our warped and wounded desiring wills, and that recreates the human faculty of *aisthesis*, perception, such that it is released from the delusion of the finality of the material and created order and released to seek and join with the author of Beauty and of Love.

Maximus was a profound theologian, sweeping and visionary, but—as the above indicates—he was also very much concerned with experience. He movingly wrote:

> Hence nothing, according to sacred Scripture, will shift him who truly believes from the ground of his true faith, in which resides the permanence of his immutable and unchanging identity. For he who has been united with the truth has the assurance that all is well with him, even though most people rebuke him for being out of his mind. For without their being aware he has moved from delusion to the truth of real faith; and he knows for sure that he is not deranged, as they say, but that through truth . . . he has been liberated from the fluctuating and fickle turmoil of the manifold forms of illusion.[116]

It is perhaps a telling statement of the kind of faith that was necessary to willingly undergo the trials that his convictions would bring him. In 655 he was brought to trial in Constantinople for consistently and publicly refuting the Monothelitic heresy. Steadfastly refusing to stand down from his position as virtually the sole remaining resister of Monothelitism, he was first exiled.[117] He refused even then to remain quiet, and so he was called back to Constantinople in 662 for a second trial after which he was tortured, with his tongue brutally cut out and his right hand severed so that he might neither speak nor write of the faith, and exiled once again.[118] He died of his wounds, aged over eighty, unrecognized and abandoned by all but two disciples, and though his theology would be vindicated twenty years later at the Sixth Ecumenical Council, there would be no mention of his name.[119]

Salvation and the "Atonement"

The preceding sections have offered some of what one might call the "raw material" of continuing Orthodox soteriological reflection. The themes of life and death, being and nonbeing, truth and illusion, separation and reconciliation, deadness and re-creation, all stand out vividly. The healing balm of divine assumption, exchange, descent that enables ascent, recapitulation, integration, and transfiguration holds and nourishes a creation torn apart by idolatry, isolation, fragmentation, suffering, and grief.

How might we consider briefly, from a modern perspective, this soteriological emphasis? Since I write this in a Western context, I think it important to elucidate where the Orthodox soteriological emphasis lies generally, otherwise there is the risk of mis-understanding by those who might assume that these ancient patristic images speak out of the same extrinsic legalistic soteriological framework that came to be dominant later in much of Western Christianity.

This issue has to do with the particularly patristic, and particularly Byzantine (as opposed to Latin/Western) emphasis on particular swaths of what would later come to be termed as "atonement theology," meaning theological reflection on how God has reconciled humanity to Himself through Jesus Christ. It is not uncommon, especially in the West, to hear the saving act of Christ described in transactional or legalistic metaphors—e.g., "Christ died for me," or "Christ died for my sins"—thereby using transactional, or what one popular blogging priest often terms "forensic,"[120] metaphors for the opening up of a path of grace and reconciliation to God. McGuckin writes:

> In the West the idea of substitutionary sacrifice, to appease the anger of God, remained the dominant and most vivid idea of the atonement. The idea was prevalent in the North African writers Tertullian and Cyprian, and when it was restated by Augustine (in more balanced and philosophical terms) it was set to enter the Western church

as the primary motif of atonement theology for centuries to come. It is conveyed in Augustine's statement: "Since death was our punishment for sin, Christ's death was that of a sacrificial victim offered up for sins" (*De Trinitatae* 4.12.15).[121]

This leads to one reason why *theosis*, even at a conceptual level, is of import to any discussion on healing, having to do with its difference in emphasis from these particular understandings of the atonement. The commonly held Western view of the atonement as having to do with the appeasement of God's wrath through the demanded sacrifice of His son in order to justify those who come to believe in Him, has come under sharp critique from modern, and perhaps especially feminist, theologians, as leading to a glorification of violence and suffering in ways that have perpetuated abusive systems.[122] It also represents an interesting shift in theological assumption: namely, that salvation can be understood somehow apart from the nature of Christ. We saw, underscored by Behr early on in this chapter, and again in the section on St. Gregory, that for the early Church this was not possible. According to Twomey:

> In Western theology, there is one specific factor that colors our general understanding of salvation, namely the way Christology and soteriology parted company over the past few centuries. The reasons for this are complex, but one major and generally accepted contributory factor is the way St. Anselm's expiatory theory of salvation came to dominate soteriology since the dawn of the Middle Ages. . . . It was a theory that lent itself to the depiction of a wrathful God injured by the sins of humanity demanding not only his own Son's pound of flesh but his entire immolation. . . . [While medieval scholars show this doesn't do justice to the full theories of Anselm] . . . the effect was to reduce soteriology to the question of atonement, with emphasis on the Cross, and to separate it from Christology, which in turn tended exclusively to concern itself with the conundrum of two natures of Christ.[123]

But as we have now seen, such a separation between Christology and soteriology does not represent the patristic, or the Orthodox, view. As seen through the so-called "physical view" of the atonement, salvation is not primarily forensic, it is *dynamic*. The emphasis, in the patristic and Orthodox view, is on the *victory* of Christ, not a redemptive *suffering*. This tension between the tragedy of Christ's death and the glory of his victory is found in the Anaphora of the Divine Liturgy of the Orthodox Church when the priest proclaims: "On the night he was given up, or rather gave himself up, for the life of the world."[124] Christ is seen as both betrayed and having had full agency. Both are true. St. Athanasius addresses this directly:

> The Life of all, our Lord and Savior Christ, did not contrive [the mode of] death for his own body, lest he should appear fearful of some other death, but he accepted and endured on the cross that inflicted by others, especially by enemies, which they reckoned fearful and ignominious and shameful, in order that this being destroyed, he might himself be believed to be Life and the power of death might be completely annihilated.[125]

This agency is linked to the joyful celebration of victory in the Orthodox understanding of salvation, not victory over God in having persuaded him to look upon us kindly once again, but victory over death and all that separates us from life. And this is accomplished in all the works of God in Christ. As Studer writes:

> This theology of victory . . . was not restricted just to Jesus' death, but rather comprised all his mysteries: the virgin birth, the temptation, the proclamation of the gospel, the passion as well as his work in the Church and finally his second coming. Everywhere the Logos revealed—and still reveals—his *dynamis*.[126]

As Athanasius notes with great satisfaction: "That devil, who formerly exulted in wickedly in death, '*its pangs having been loosed*' (Acts 2.24), only he remains truly dead."[127]

In the West, this particular atonement emphasis on the victory of Christ has come to be known as the Christus Victor model, brought particularly to the fore by Gustaf Aulen in the early twentieth century.[128] But, to get an idea of how central this has been to Eastern Christian thinking historically, one can look at one of the primary symbols found in the Orthodox Church (Figure 7).

This ancient symbol, which stands for Jesus Christ Victor, can be found throughout the world in Orthodox churches.[129]

As was shown in the section on St. Athanasius, this "physical theory" of the atonement, including the emphasis on victory, emphasizes the inner

Figure 7. The symbol for Jesus Christ Victor.

relatedness of Christ to God, rather than external relations. As Christ is directly related to God internally, so entering in to the life of Christ is transformation through participation in the life of God, rather than salvation through a legal justification enacted externally. The atonement, or at-one-ment, is not simply about changing how God views humanity, but how humanity relates to God, and thereby regains life. It is generation of new life at the deepest level of the person, because the life of the person, in Christ, has been assumed into the life of God.

This briefly sketches the relationship of a soteriology of *theosis* to an understanding of Christology and the atonement that expresses God's deep love for humanity in a way that can be understood as not only justifying but revivifying humanity through defeat of the "principalities and powers" that separate humanity from life in God. I would also propose that this particular understanding of the atonement lifts up the in-breaking of God's redeeming love in creation in a way that can become relived in the individual as a form of healing and transformation, as opposed to perpetuating models of sacrificial suffering and guilt, which some theologians have argued actually prohibits the possibility of healing.[130]

I believe it is largely for the above reasons that the Eastern Orthodox emphasis on *theosis*, or deification, is gaining interest among Christians of various denominations.[131] The promise of salvation as communion and transformation, rather than legalistic expiation, offers up the possibility for participation in this life, in this very moment, in the grace-filled joy of God's energies and radiant creation.

Theosis

Theosis, also sometimes called *theopoesis*, divinization or deification, is the ancient understanding of salvation most closely associated with the Eastern Orthodox Church. While the concept of *theosis/apotheosis* was also existent in various pre-Christian Greek, and some Jewish, thought, it obtained its more commonly held understandings in early Christian theological reflection.[132] *Theosis* is the transformation of the believer into divine likeness. In spite of the usage of the term divinization or deification, in the Orthodox Christian understanding of this concept, the implication is never that the believer become merged with God entirely, or become God, but rather become *like* God, growing infinitely *toward* God. *Theosis* is often cited in conjunction with the passage from the New Testament concerning becoming *"partakers of the divine nature"* (2 Peter 1:4), implying participation in the life of God.

Norman Russell, in his impressive work *The Doctrine of Deification in the Greek Patristic Tradition*, offers a helpful discussion of the many nuances of the usage of the concept of deification throughout the writings of the early Church Fathers. As no formal definition of deification occurs until the sixth century when Dionysius the Areopagite wrote *"Theosis* is the attaining of likeness to God and union with him so far as is possible,"[133] and as it is not discussed as a theological topic in its own right until the seventh century by St. Maximus the Confessor, there can be no easy conceptual explication of what is meant by *theosis*.[134] But we have now seen its antecedents clearly in the words, for example, of St. Irenaeus and St. Athanasius concerning God becoming human so that humans might become what God Himself is. And Russell creates a useful framework within which to explore the various nuances of the term as used throughout history. He starts by describing the main usage of language around deification as being nominal, analogical, and metaphorical.[135] These categories constitute part of a continuum, but they are helpful in sketching a broad understanding of how the term deification was applied.

In this discussion, it is metaphorical usage that concerns us most, and this category has in turn two approaches of which it is characteristic; the ethical and the realistic. The ethical approach discusses the attainment to likeness to God through reproduction of divine attributes by imitation of virtues, ascetic and philosophical endeavor. The realistic approach is based on the conviction that humans are transformed in deification, in some very real sense, by participation (*methexis*) in God. The realistic approach itself has then two aspects, the ontological and the dynamic.[136] The ontological approach, substantiated by the salvific economy of God in the Incarnation, is concerned with the Incarnation and Resurrection as grounds for ontological transformation of humanity—as we have seen, through divine/ human coinherence in Jesus Christ, the restoration of the life of God to humanity through the in-breaking of the Spirit, and the defeat of death and corruption in the Resurrection. The dynamic approach has to do with participation in this economy through appropriation of "deified humanity through the sacraments of baptism and the Eucharist."[137] It is language and discussion of *theosis* from the realistic angle—namely, *ontological* and *dynamic*—which has characterized all I have so far explored, and will continue to explore, in this book.

Russell describes the realistic angle as of particular concern to the Alexandrian school, particularly for Athanasius and Cyril, engaged as they were in Christological debates.[138] As we have seen, for Athanasius the debate around the divinity of Christ turned on the ability of the Incarnate Logos to deify humanity. Famous for the sentence "[God], indeed, assumed humanity that we might become God,"[139] the core of his argument was that the Logos must be one in divinity with God, for only God could deify humanity.[140] As we have also seen, this "exchange formula" brought the divine and the human together, trading the corruption of humanity for the incorruption of God, entirely through the grace of God, and based on the internal relatedness of Jesus Christ to God rather than on an external act of propitiation.[141]

Jules Gross, in his famous study *The Divinization of the Christian According to the Greek Fathers*, concurs:

In brief, Cyril with Athanasius and Gregory of Nyssa form the group of the most brilliant representatives of the physical conception of divinization. . . . [According to Cyril] our Savior had to be both perfect God and complete human: God, in order to divinize, and human, in order that in Him the entire human nature might be deified; for "what has not been assumed has not been saved." In this, once again, the interdependence of soteriology and Christology is manifested.[142]

Here we find again the theological maxim that I have chosen as the central theological image for this work. The realistic angle is deeply bound up with a strongly Christological, rather than primarily philosophical or Platonic, approach.[143]

Theosis as Promise and Image

In an essay on the "The Problem, Promise and Process of Theosis," Michael J. Christensen offers a brief overview of some additional perspectives from which to consider *theosis*.[144]

He first outlines some of the scriptural bases from which patristic theologians have surmised that *theosis* can be associated with divine intention.[145] These include the aforementioned 2 Peter 1:4, as well as Matthew 5:48 where Jesus says to his disciples *"Be ye perfect as your Father in heaven is perfect."* It is notable that the word translated as "perfect" in English is, regarding the disciples, the Greek word *teleoi*, and regarding God, *teleois*, both of which are rooted in the word "telos." Thus it would seem that here Jesus is not giving a moral command, but rather describing a destiny of "completeness" or even "wholeness" as what constitutes "perfection." Christensen writes: "Perfection and deification in patristic soteriology are often seen as closely related if not synonymous terms, though individual writers vary on how they understand deification, and careful, nuanced use of the terms and symbols of *theosis* is important."[146] While humanity cannot become what God is by nature, it can become God-like, through participation in the divine, and through restoration of the image and likeness of God in the person. Christensen also cites 1 John: *"Now we are children of God, and it does not yet appear what we shall be. But we know that when he appears, we shall be like him, for we shall see him as he is"* (1 Jn 3:2), and further he cites Paul: *"We all, with unveiled faces, beholding the glory of the Lord, will be changed into his likeness, from glory to glory"* (2 Cor 3:18). These passages give a sketch of the types of New Testament passages that have been used to "point to the divine promise of *theosis* as the fullness of salvation."[147]

Christensen then turns to the process of *theosis*. He describes Origen's understanding of deification as being made possible because of God's prior humanization in Christ: "[Origen's] vision of *theosis* is one of education of souls, transformation of nature, and unification with God. Progressively the soul is perfected in time until all is reconciled and time is no more."[148] He also describes Gregory of Nazianzus's contemplation of the Trinity, wherein he likens the process leading to deification as akin to the polishing of a mirror, so that the *imago Dei* within humanity can become a perfect reflection of the "divine source of light."[149] Gregory of Nyssa writes that this process of movement toward God is without limit in the degree to which one can progressively achieve "perfection, knowledge of God, or Godlikeness."[150] Maximus the Confessor understood the process of *theosis* as one of *perichoresis*, "an 'interpenetration' of God and humanity."[151]

In concluding the section on the process of theosis, Christensen offers a summation of images of the process of *theosis* gleaned from various patristic writers. It is perhaps helpful to hold them in mind and heart when considering the writings, to be discussed in the next section, which reflect on the way of *theosis*:

> Likeness to God as far as possible, climbing the ladder of divine ascent, crossing the chasm that divides, learning to fly, putting on the robe, interweaving threads of God and humanity, interpenetration, the wax of humanity and divinity melting together, the polished human mirror reflecting its divine source, the red-hot iron receiving heat from the divine fire, fusion into a new Divine-humanity—these are the common images and symbols of deification.[152]

The Way of *Theosis*

In his well-known book *The Mystical Theology of the Eastern Church*, twentieth-century Orthodox theologian Vladimir Lossky describes the way of union leading to *theosis*. It is a synergy between the saving act of God and the cooperation of humanity. He sees the sole end of the Christian life as the acquisition of grace, which is given without merit and yet which finds its home in the person through meritorious acts, for both reside together in a synergistic bond.[153] The beginning of the process is an act of conversion and repentance, yet this is also an ongoing act. Repentance is necessary to receive grace, and yet repentance knows no bounds for even the most perfect perfection falls short of the perfection of God.[154] He writes of the stages distinguished by St. Isaac the Syrian in the way of union as being: penitence, purification, and perfection, "that is to say, conversion of the will, liberation from the passions, and the acquisition of that perfect love that is the fullness of grace."[155]

Prayer is a central component of union with God, for

> prayer is a personal relationship with God. Now this union must be fulfilled in human persons; it must be personal, conscious, and voluntary . . . in prayer man meets with God *personally*—he knows Him and he loves Him. Knowledge (*gnosis*) and love are closely connected in Eastern asceticism.[156]

Asceticism is also foundational to *theosis*. Andrew Louth writes:

> This reconstitution of our human nature is therefore something beyond our human powers . . . but on the other hand it is something that involves the most profound commitment of our human powers; it is not a change in which we will be passively put right . . . it is a change that requires our utmost cooperation, that calls for truly ascetic struggle. No theology can call itself Orthodox in the true sense that does not embrace such as ascetic commitment.[157]

Louth elaborates that the struggle to allow the soul to be returned to its original state of beauty involves an emptying of the self, a *kenosis:* "This self-emptying of the passions, of all distortions and corruptions that lay waste our nature, cannot take place without *serious ascetic struggle*, because it involves a real change in our nature: a change that restores it to *its truly natural state*."[158] As we have seen already, it is of strong theological anthropological import to note that that the passions that are to be overcome are considered, by many Fathers including St. Maximus the Confessor, to be those "impulses of the soul contrary to nature":[159]

> What is envisaged is a transformation, a transfiguration, of human beings . . . [involving] a kind of reconstitution of our humanity, a reshaping, a straightening out of all the distortions and corruptions that we have brought upon our humanity by misusing—abusing—our human capacities. . . . This reconstitution of human nature is something impossible without the grace of God, without everything implied in God the Word's living out what it is to be human.[160]

It is not human nature itself that is the problem, but the *misuse* of natural God-given instincts, appetites, and faculties. I will return to this again later.

Lossky further elucidates: "For the ascetic tradition of the Christian East, the heart is the center of the human being . . . of the intellect and of the will, and the point from which the whole of the spiritual life proceeds, and upon which it converges." While the heart is a "vessel" for all the vices, God is also to be found there. He continues:

Grace passes by way of the heart into the whole of [the person's] nature. The spirit, the highest part of the human creature, is that contemplative faculty by which [the person] is able to seek God. [It is] the principle of his conscience and of his freedom . . . it might be said that it is the seat of the person . . . this is why the Greek Fathers are often ready to identify the *nous* with the image of God in [the person]. [The person] must live according to the spirit; the whole human complex must become "spiritual" . . . it is in fact the spirit which becomes united with baptismal grace, and though which grace enters the heart, the center of that total human nature which is to be deified. "The uniting of the spirit with the heart," "the descent of the spirit into the heart," "the guarding of the heart by the spirit"—these expressions constantly recur in the ascetic writings of the Eastern Church. Without the heart, which is the center of all activity, the spirit is powerless. Without the spirit, the heart remains blind, destitute of direction.[161]

This beautiful passage elucidates the movement of grace within the person, not splitting off the heart as an area of possible vice from an intellectualized faith of attempts at virtue, but rather seeking to express a conjoining of grace to spirit, spirit to heart, and heaven to earth.

Thus, the qualities of conversion through baptism, as repentance and illumination in the Spirit, and active Sacramental participation in the new life of Spirit, through the Eucharist, prayer, confession, and life lived in community, are regarded as indispensable to those who seek the way of *theosis*.

Modern Thinking on *Theosis*

As noted earlier, in recent years *theosis* has come to the forefront of both Eastern and Western theological thinking. It has surfaced especially in discussions around personhood, and theological anthropology.[162] Russell highlights this angle on *theosis* at the conclusion of his study, where he cites the more modern iteration of *theosis* as "our destiny is not that we might be made divine but rather that we might at last become truly human."[163]

Russell considers the work of Metropolitan John Zizioulas and Christos Yannaras. Zizioulas maintains that the individual is not a static or self-contained entity, but rather that personhood implies "openness of being" and as such is a relational category expressed through love and freedom.[164] For Zizioulas, Christ is the paradigm for true personhood, which is restored to the human being by entering into the same filial relationship that constitutes Christ's being. And, as personhood is relational in nature, this unity with God implies real "difference without division, as well as communion with him without confusion."[165]

Yannaras takes this theme and develops it along with an understanding of eros (to which topic I will devote Chapter 4). God as the Triune God does not have love as an attribute, but *is* love. Human beings have the potential to participate in the love that is actualized in God. They have the potential to stand across from each other as true "other," addressing the "I" to the "thou." The true function of the erotic impulse is the "overcoming of this otherness." This also pertains to the person in relationship to God. As Russell observes: "Because we are in the image of God, we can either respond to the erotic call of God, which is life, or reject it, which is death."[166] He continues, citing a powerful quote from Yannaras:

> For [the person] to be an image of God means that each one can realize [their] existence as Christ realizes life as love, freedom and not as natural necessity. Each can realize [their] existence as a person, like the Persons of the triadic Divinity. Consequently, [the person] can realize [their] existence as eternity and incorruptibility, just as the divine life of triadic co-inherence and communion is eternal and incorruptible.[167]

Russell writes that the alternative is "an autonomy and existential self-sufficiency that *imprisons us in our own inadequacies*."[168]

Yannaras elsewhere writes that "the human person is born in the space of God. The impetus of desire for a fulfilling relationship with Him is His life-giving summons, which establishes and constructs the human person as an existential event of erotic reference."[169] He elaborates that the nature of the human person lies in the freedom to "realize or reject" existence as mutual relationship.[170] As we have seen repeatedly, it is not a moral issue that is at stake, in the eyes of the Orthodox Church, but our entire mode of existence. A denial of love means "curtailment, maiming, diminishing of existential potentialities of desire."[171] And here Yannaras bridges into depth-psychological territory, writing of the refusal to actualize existence as an event of relationship that "the disruption of desire into narcissistic egocentric objectives is only self-punishment: the torture of an existence that actively denies itself without, however, being capable of nullifying its hypostatic composition."[172]

In these more recent reflections on *theosis* and personhood, the return to immortality and incorruptibility, so important in the writings of the early Church, takes place through the transcendence of death in personal communion with God. That this is contiguous to the birth of the possibility of real relationship with other people as well, and self as well, is a theme to which I will return later.

As can be seen, especially in the work of Yannaras, these sketches of modern understandings of *theosis* offer an additional lens through which to view the meeting places between Orthodox ontology and soteriology and the healing to be found in depth psychology. To a reflection on these meeting places I will now turn.

3

AN ONTOLOGY OF HEALING?

God . . . completed the primary principles (*logoi*) of creatures and the universal essences of beings once for all. Yet he is still at work, not only preserving these creatures in their very existence . . . but effecting the formation, progress and sustenance of the individual parts that are potential within them. Even now in his providence he is bringing about the assimilation of the particulars to universals until he might unite creatures' own voluntary inclination to the more universal natural principle [*logos*] of rational being through the movement of these particular creatures toward well being . . . and make them harmonious and self-moving in relation to one another and to the whole universe.

—St. Maximus the Confessor, *Ad Thalassium 2*

The previous two chapters have given us a basis for this exploration, and a plethora of theological imagery and experience filled with exchange, assumption, vivification, healing, and transformation. In the next two chapters, we will consider how these may relate to the depths of the psyche and the workings of the unconscious.

Earlier, I referred to the juxtaposition of the radiance of Orthodox spirituality with the frightened, desolate, and despairing places that depth psychology regularly encounters. I offered that, for our human nature to be truly "assumed," it must be the case that even places of gut-wrenching anxious upheaval, emotionally frozen schizoid terror, or dull depression and inner deadness must be somehow assumed and offered the possibility of healing in the life of God.

Without this possibility of assuming even the most dissociated parts of our experience, the experiences we would often much rather avoid acknowledging, salvation as healing—as was discussed in the last chapter—can only remain a one-sided concept apprehended by the "functional" parts of ourselves at the cost of dissociating the "dysfunctional," a striving toward which induces splitting rather than an on-going experience of integrative healing and transformation available to all who seek it.

In the next two chapters, therefore, I would like to return to the hypothesis I laid out in Chapter 1—namely, that traces of the ontological and soteriological truths put forward by Orthodoxy, many images of which we have now been given, ought to be discernible in how we heal from a depth-psychological perspective. In the case of this discussion, the hypothesis of Orthodox truth is that our human nature has been assumed, and is being healed, in Christ. Put another way, if we hearken back to the reflections of the various theologians in Chapter 2, we must be able to find "meeting places" between the depths of psychological suffering and God as the Logos, in order that those places of suffering might begin to heal.

I believe that this is possible, that there are "traces" of such meeting places to be found, and that they can be strongly seen and experienced from two vantage points—that of the healing experienced in engaging with "being" in our self qua creature; and that of the healing experienced in accessing the ontological energies of eros, the eros of God and the eros of the person, connected to the free willing and desiring of the person. This chapter will concern itself with the former, and the following chapter with the latter.

Preliminary Reflections on Ontological Discourse

Ontology, as discussed earlier, is reflection on the nature of being, of reality itself. More specifically, it has to do with the structure and relations of being.[1] This chapter will look at the possibilities of healing embedded in being itself, from both an experiential depth-psychological level, and from an Orthodox/patristic level of discourse about the very nature of being.

G. C. Tympas suggests that, given the complexity of the matrix of relations in being at all levels, only a transdisciplinary approach can "propose a hermeneutical line able to permeate all realms of life."[2] Previous discussions that favor ontology over experience, or else phenomenology over ontology, have dominated theological, philosophical, and depth-psychological discourse.[3] In Tympas's work, and also the work of Nikolaos Loudovikos (both of whom engage primarily with the theology St. Maximus), there is what seems to be an emerging approach of finding the connections between theological ontology and psychological experience, *without losing the distinction between the two.*[4]

Although Loudovikos's work is not primarily psychological, but focuses rather on becoming-through-communion and hence has an eschatological emphasis, he is still concerned to locate the manifestation of this theology in our concrete daily lives, as well as in our psyches, and so psychology is drawn into the discourse.[5] Vasileios Thermos, as well, brings ontology into discussion with depth psychology, looking, for example, at the connection between an ontology of communion, the necessity of forgiveness, and Winnicott's understanding of the "other" who must withstand our destructive impulses in order to fully establish him or herself as an Other available for real relationship: i.e., communion.[6] Here he sees psychological insights as further confirming deep truths about the structure, and even necessities, of our being as already known to ontological reflection.

It is largely in this vein of thought that I continue my own reflections in this area. But it must be owned, of course, that such an exploration as I am about to undertake in this chapter, even while based in theological and psychological reflections that have preexisting structure and tradition grounding them, must also represent some element of imaginative and intuitive extrapolation from the one to the other, in terms of how the ontology manifests psychologically. It is hard to know, *experientially*, what is true about the deep structures of being qua being. Thus I turn to the ancients who concerned themselves with such reflection. Such reflection also took place in the context of, and as such was deeply informed by, theological reflection and prayer. This forms a richly interwoven tapestry of wisdom, as those gifted with spiritual insight were able to perceive that the very ways in which we perceive being and ultimately perceive God are affected by our spiritual lives. As St. Athanasius offered, we are like silver mirrors, created to reflect the light of God, to perceive God inwardly, as McGuckin writes, "radiant, and instructive."[7] Yet, we have lost consciousness of this divine image in our interiors, just as silver becomes tarnished. It is not destroyed, but covered over and unrecognizable.[8] Hence the need for restoration and redemption through the healing made available to us in the Incarnation. And so, in part, the goal of *askesis* is to restore the mirror to its former clarity, thus restoring to ever-increasing clarity our perception of God and being. One can perhaps more clearly see why, in Orthodoxy, there can be no theology without prayer.

In patristic and hence Orthodox thought, ontology and theology are deeply linked, both of which in turn inform pastoral care and understanding of the person. That the ontological structure of the person is transformed and healed through the healing offered in the Incarnation is a core assumption in Orthodox theology. As McGuckin writes, "The creative Logos himself came into history as Incarnate Lord, to reconfigure the inner structure of humanity's being."[9]

We see this clearly in the profound theology of St. Maximus the Confessor, to whom I will turn a great deal in this chapter and the next, and whose structure of reflection I have attempted to participate in, in dividing these two chapters into one dealing largely with the *logoi* (principles) of being and healing, and the second looking at the *tropoi* (modes) of being as impacted by eros and desire. His concept of a foundational, *given*, "being," as well as a "well-being" that must be appropriated *willingly* by the person becomes the locus of expression of the premise "that which is not assumed is not healed," for *both* our being as *given* and our being as *self-determined* must open up out into the possibilities of well-being.[10] If it were any other way, we would only be able to will against ourselves, otherwise our notions of self and God must certainly default to the neurotic. And, as I have proposed, this coherence must show up in traces in our psyches, at the very least at the deep level, if we are to be able to fully live into it in this life and appropriate the healing possibilities therein. But it is inevitable that some amount of extrapolation is involved, particularly in this chapter that deals with the structure of beings and experiences of the unconscious. Hence why I limit myself to possible "traces" of ontology in psychology. It does not work to fully import one set of theories into the other; we are working—as I noted earlier—across vast differences of time, culture, language, and context in terms of the goal of discourse.

Logos as Substrate of Being

As was shown in Chapter 2, particularly introduced by Origen, the Logos is both the "organizing principle" of the world, as well as the Person of God. And as the "substrate" of being itself, the possibility arises that whatever healing is to be found simply in engagement with being itself, is in fact borne of a truth of the Logos Himself.

This is echoed at the personal level in the concept of the indestructible image of God found in each person, as discussed above in Athanasius's image of the mirror. This *image* exists as irreducible potential. The potential made manifest, for many patristic thinkers such as St. Irenaeus, becomes the *likeness*.[11] Restoration of the *image to the likeness* of God becomes the fullness of the process of transformation and, ultimately, transfiguration, as was discussed in the section on *theosis*. This process of divinization was examined in great deal by St. Maximus the Confessor in the seventh century. Maximus explores in depth the created and potential nature of each person, their *logos*, and as well as their *tropos*, the developmental arc, mode, and telos of being. As I discussed in Chapter 1, and as we have seen, initially, in the citation at the beginning of this chapter, he sees each work of creation as containing an essential *logos*, the original "principle" and divine willing of its being as well as the seeds of the telos of the created nature of each creature, all of which derive their innate potential, being and ultimately fulfillment, from the Logos.[12] These he terms the *logoi* of being.[13] I will return to this later in this chapter. But for now it is important just to note what Orthodox theologian Elizabeth Theokritoff underscores: "[What] strikes us here is that 'essence' or the truth of the thing itself is inseparable from God's providential guidance of it, from its origin in his will, and its ultimate resting place in him."[14]

The movement from *image* toward *likeness* entails, in Orthodox thinking, a restoration, education, and utilization of the free will of the person. This forms, for example, an integral strand of the theology of St. Irenaeus.[15] Centuries later St. Maximus also wrote extensively on the need for the healing of the will,[16] and his understanding of its importance is also intimated in the earlier citation. I will look at this extensively in the next chapter. In this chapter, however, I am interested in looking at what happens at the level *below* conscious willing, but which is a kind of willing nonetheless, and how it may still be connected to the goodness of being, even when—from a conscious perspective—it seems to be the very opposite of that.

If we take seriously Christos Yannaras's admonition, cited earlier, that Orthodoxy eschews simple "morality" in favor of a healing of the entire *hypostasis*, conscious and unconscious, of the person, this is a fundamentally necessary on-going exploration.[17] To do this, we must descend into these uncomfortable places and inquire as to what depth psychologists have learned that may be somehow linked to Orthodox ontology.

The life of faith often entails a great deal of sincere and conscious effort, particularly in the Orthodox faith where the understanding of the process of *theosis* entails an active synergy between the ascetic efforts of the believer, and God's dynamic grace-filled energies. However, without a working knowledge of the unconscious and its particular concerns, there can also be a baffling dissonance between what we attempt, and where we actually land. To simply view this as a failing, or to feel bereft of God's assistance, does not—to my mind—offer a full enough view of the kind of contrary, hidden, and sometimes even life-seeking, willing that can be taking place in the person.

The unconscious psyche, as will be discussed, seems to have a telos of its own as it reaches for the fulfillment of—what I believe to be—its God-given capacities. But exploration of this territory can feel fraught. Where the suffering unconscious erupts into our lives in a protesting way, bringing disorientation, confusion, sabotage, physical symptoms, or a sense of alienation from self, it can be terribly painful to even reflect on, touching off in each one of us recognition of our own despair, depression, futility.

Not all suffering within us has language, though as Ulanov writes, it always seeks recognition, be it through bodily or psychological symptom.[18] But if we can begin to listen for its communications and trust in its telos, we might find not only a trace of Orthodox ontological truth in depth psychology, but a freeing hope that is built into the structure of existence.

When the Unconscious Prays

How then, do we begin to consider such areas outside of our daily ways of knowing? We may know our places of unarticulated, stuck, suffering from the areas where our thoughts become obsessive, beset with a repetitive litanies of anxieties.[19] We may find ourselves awakening to stare at the ceiling in the darkest hours of the night, captive to a convincing, though futile, narrative of abandonment by God that only masks a deeper energetic reality of our having turned sadistically against ourselves.

We may feel our stomachs seize up, the same clenching or uncontrollable heaving reaction of suppressed fear or resentment every time we must complete a certain task. Our hearts, even our skin, may carry the feelings not admitted to consciousness, erupting instead in excited or anxious palpitations, unexplained severe protesting allergies, or in rashes and flare-ups that match our hidden rage.[20] We may maintain a serene façade while our dreams speak of earthquakes, tsunamis, turmoil, indicating an inner up-heaval that has become distant from our consciousness.[21]

In our inability to forgive a deep wound rashly or deliberately inflicted by another—an inability so distressing for those of sincere faith attempt-ing to follow Christ's command to forgive—may hide a willful and health-filled innate insistence that *someone recognize* the suffering inflicted on our innermost selves, so that our very claim on being is not also annihi-lated as part of the necessary sacrifice that forgiveness, or indeed being for-given, so often entails.[22] Instead of seeing embedded in this issue a mute cry for recognition of being, the person is all too likely to "double-down" on their self-condemnation as failing "religiously" and thereby collude with the self-annihilation. This only leads to a dissociated piety fraught with pockets of pain and untended "passions."[23]

And surely we all know the havoc that our wounds, our struggles to love and receive love, can play in our relationships, in our ministries, in our creative pursuits. Our unconscious envying of others, our unconscious sab-otaging of ourselves so as to avoid the persecuting envy of others,[24] our complexes, the "frozen heart"[25] of our schizoid fears of our own love as well as our own hate—all these primal energetic orientations, when deeply unconscious, can create enormous dramatic upheavals in our lives while the roots remain deeply hidden from our consciousness and hence unavail-able to transformation.

As Ulanov writes: "The hardest thing to grasp about the unconscious is that it exists, and that it is unconscious."[26] It is not simply a question of putting our best foot forward, pulling ourselves together, or getting "over it." We do not have direct access to the life of the unconscious, and yet its life directly impacts ours. Indeed, at times it may feel as though the un-conscious has a prayer life of its own, willing and desiring against our own conscious desires, hindering us despite our best attempts at "progress" in a given area. I have come to wonder if God doesn't respect our unconscious pleas as much as our conscious pleas. Perhaps all the more reason why we must articulate a faith that can reach, can assume, even this level of our being.

This can all sound rather overwhelming. It is understandable that, from an ego perspective, we most often would rather simply disavow such parts of ourselves. A depth exploration can strike even deeper chords of dread. Some of us come to know experientially the often barely conscious exis-tential anxiety of constantly trying to "hold ourselves" together, to maintain a platform of our own making over a terrifying abyss of nonbeing.[27] We live on the frantic surface of our lives, uncertain whether there is anything holding us in being, particularly anything other than our own thoughts. Our hearts submissively turn their instinctive sight away from this basest of despair to avoid its deadly attack, while never losing sense of its threatening location and always living in fear of its awakening.

Religion, unfortunately, can also collude with us in all these levels of splitting, when it promotes so called "positive thinking," or even discussions of spiritual warfare that engage with the unconscious as though it were demonic, seeking to split off, repress, and disown the passions rather than transform them back to their natural state.[28] We can live as though our ego ideal is commanded of us by God, rather than letting God meet us in the deepest places of our broken humanity and heal us.[29] We try—as St. Irenaeus trenchantly observed almost two thousand years ago—to become God before we have even become fully human.[30]

Such collusion between ego ideal and religiosity would be dire indeed, but it may be that God has been more generous with us than we even dare to imagine by not fully allowing such a collusion to continue.

I say this with two things in mind: The first, as I touched on at the beginning of this chapter, is that it seems we may live in a *cosmos* that, as ontologically given, is far more generous than we imagine at most times. We may speak of the grace of God rather freely in religious settings, but how often do we *truly* consider the grace of God built into the structure of existence? Do we turn toward being in awe? Do we receive it? Dare we rest in it? Can we feel held by it and understand our own lives and those of others through this lens? The second is that—as also noted above—from a depth-psychological perspective, we seem to have been created with an enormous capacity to heal and transform, given conducive circumstances.

Ulanov observes that the psyche insists "that all its feelers be included, all its legs, all its feathers. It repeats and repeats and repeats, trying to gain admittance for the parts of us that belong to us yet remain unintegrated."[31] There is what one might call a pressure to heal, indicated by the unconscious communications that arrive through our symptoms, pressing for recognition of suffering parts that want inclusion in our living.[32] We must grasp their meaning in order to become more fully the being we are given to be in and with the Existing One.[33]

What becomes immediately relevant is that the drive to heal, the drive to wholeness,[34] what some might even begin to suspect is the image of

God—known psychologically—within us, does not easily succumb to our narrow ego perspective, or even our religious collusions. This impetus toward life can be consciously worked with, in which case it becomes an ally, or if negated, it can make itself known in the negative—when symbol drops into symptom. To play off of Carl Jung's famous inscription, "Bidden or not bidden, God is present," one might say bidden or not bidden, depth psychologists have observed that the psyche seems to have, embedded in its created nature, an impetus toward healing.

The question, both psychological and spiritual, becomes: Do we have the awareness and openness to receive into consciousness the beckoning possibilities for new life, even when they arrive in the guise of the crumbling of our favored religious (or other) persona? It is not always enough to rely on our conscious attitudes, however prayerfully informed, to lead us to the levels that need healing. As Jung observed: "Every analysand starts by unconsciously misusing his newly won knowledge in the interests of his abnormal, neurotic, attitude."[35] And as Ulanov compassionately notes, "The passage to openness always means feeling psychic pain, and we must build up stamina and the hope, based on experience, that the pain is not the end point. It leads somewhere we desire to go, to dwell."[36]

Hence we must go deeper, at times, than our conscious attitudes and see what is coming toward us from our being itself, from the place we wish to dwell. A good part of the early work of analysis can lie simply in the cultivation of this sturdy ability to receive the unknown, and faith in its merit. The deeper question it begins to pose, which is implicitly addressed in this chapter, becomes whether there is sufficient goodness in our created nature, in its being, that we can trust the life impetus contained in it? Is there an indestructible link between the good, ordering, life-giving Logos of God and our own being, such that we may trust in our own inherent telos as we experience it psychologically, albeit unconsciously?

A Healing Ontology?

Twentieth-century Orthodox theologian Olivier Clement, wrote: "Nothing exists—anger or lust—that does not have some share in what is good. That fact is the basis of metamorphosis. Good in the Greek sense, is, of course, the fullness of being."[37]

This is supported, for example, by his reading of Pseudo-Dionysus the Areopagite, a patristic theologian who reflected extensively on the ontology of being, of evil, and the attributes—knowable and unknowable—of God. Over a millennium ago, he wrote:

> All beings, to the extent that they exist, are good and come from the Good and they fall short of goodness and being in proportion to their remoteness from the Good. . . . However, that which is totally bereft of the Good never had, does not have, never shall have, never can have any kind of being at all. Take the example of someone who lives intemperately [other translations clarify "lustfully," "covetously"]. He is deprived of the Good in direct proportion to his irrational urges. To this extent he is lacking in being and his desire is for what has no real existence. Nevertheless he has some share in the Good, since there is in him a distorted echo of real love and of real unity. Anger too has a share in the Good to the extent it is an urge to remedy seeming evils by returning them toward what seems beautiful. Even the person who desires the lowest form of life still desires life and a life that seems good to him; thus he participates in the Good to the extent that he feels a desire for life and for what—to him at least—seems a worthwhile life. Abolish the Good and you will abolish being, life, desire, movement, everything.[38]

Approximately 1,500 years later, D. W. Winnicott, pediatrician and psychoanalyst of the British object-relations school, sought insight into the nature of "the antisocial tendency" in children. While behaviorally a delinquent child may not present as anything other than "a nuisance," perhaps bed-wetting, or stealing, or destructive aggressiveness, Winnicott saw in this behavior a kind of reaching out for life. In stealing, the child was seeking replacement for something (a someone) it had lost. In being destructive, the child might be attempting to regain a stable environment that could contain their aggressive impulses and not be destroyed by them. If the reparative environment could manage to provide for the child the need that these behaviors were attempting—in however a distorted manner externally seen—to communicate, the behaviors stopped.[39]

Winnicott also came to perceive that the breakdown obsessively feared by some patients was the breakdown that had already occurred, like an incessant echo of lost suffering clamoring for healing.[40] Rather than dismissing the fear as unfounded, he saw in it a clue to a suffering that had not yet found conscious experiencing, and hence voice. Yet, it lives in the person nonetheless, making itself known obliquely. This hearkens back to the earlier observation by Ulanov that all suffering seeks recognition.

More generally, he saw in patients an often necessary drive toward regression and dependence, at odds with their adaptive functional self. While the conscious drive would be toward functional adaptation, there could also be an unconscious drive pushing back to the place of rupture from one's given connection to spontaneous life, what he termed the "true self," and where such a rupture birthed the creation of the "false self." While this regressive pull could manifest as a "creative illness," perhaps a kind of nervous breakdown, it too had a healing telos.

He saw how regression to a place of dependence where the rupture might heal could result in a new fusion of eros and aggression—a life where aggression, perhaps akin to the incensive faculty of the soul in patristic thought, becomes available to serve love rather than oppositional destructiveness (I will discuss this again in the next chapter). Such a regression, and reexperiencing of the vulnerable states of dependency, when met by reliable presence and steady care on the part of the analyst, leads to a strengthening and growth of the true self and dismantling of false self constructs.[41] It is as though the unconscious knows where it needs to return to find the possibility of life that was left behind.

In a similar way, at the far reaches of human exploration of evil, Sue Grand writes movingly about those who have experienced the self-annihilation of devastating trauma. They live, she posits, in a place of "catastrophic loneliness," imbued with hate, fear, shame, and despair. The self lives on an excruciating cusp of life and death, for the victim has survived her own annihilation. Grand writes; "Death has possessed her in its impenetrable solitude. But life makes [the victim] desire to be known in that solitude."[42] While "the survivor's resurrection requires that she be known by another in this solitude," she is simultaneously unknowable in this place, and also refuses to be known, for that very knowing threatens her with new annihilation. Thus, an excruciating problem is raised. This insolvable paradox can find no way of expression other than to enact itself out on others—hence leading to the enactment of evil on another. In this destruction of another, the Other comes to experientially know the inner annihilated state of the perpetrator. While this is a complex area and requires continued explication, for the purposes of this example I think what is important is to see the conviction Grand holds that there is a distorted seeking of life even in the horrific ejection of one's own experience of self-annihilation onto an Other.[43]

These are perhaps somewhat startling examples of the instinct toward life and goodness that can be deeply present even in the most abhorrent behaviors. Yet taken together with the theological and ontological postulations put forward by Pseudo-Dionysus, it seems that these psychological examples point to an engagement with an ontological truth, if you will, of participation of all creation in the fullness of being, even when seemingly seeking the annihilation of self or other.[44]

Reliance upon such engagement in clinical practice implies a possible implicit metaphysic in depth psychology, and gives experiential credence to the more explicit one in patristic thought. In turn, the psychological insights elaborate, in an embodied and perhaps startling way, upon the idea of the distortion of energies, known to theological reflection on the corruption of the *imago dei*. A relationship emerges between an ontology of all things participating in the Good, in however a distorted fashion, and the processes of the psyche's unconscious attempts to heal itself.

Such theories, in my view, give far more credence to the patristic and Orthodox conceptualization of the human person as fundamentally good, albeit distorted, rather than fundamentally cut off from the goodness of God. This disparity of views is summed by McGuckin:

> The Greeks never favored that streak of pessimism that dogged the steps of Latin Christian thought, culminating in Augustine's severe North African view of the wholesale corruption of the world and human nature after the fall, such that only the supernatural grace could repair the extensive structural damage. The Greek patristic tradition never fully accepted Augustinian grace theory, and thereby resisted the implications of a scheme that inserted a radical division between nature and supernature. In Greek patristic thought all of nature was a divinely graced mystery, even if fallen, and one in which the symbiosis of the divine presence with the material form was frequently and luminously manifested (most sublimely and archetypally in the incarnation of God himself as man).[45]

Let us take the exploration of this symbiosis further.

St. Maximus the Confessor, in contemplating the insights of Pseudo-Dionysus and St. Gregory of Nazianzus, as well as refining those of Origen, reflected extensively on the connection between the one Logos and all of creation. His was an understanding that was not only speculative but also experiential, linking the origin of the person to their ultimate telos of deification. He utilized ancient metaphysical concepts, but in a distinctly Christian way, and connected God and creation through the presence of what—as we saw earlier—he called the *logoi* of beings. Perceiving the presence of the Creator in all creation, Maximus articulated:

> Who . . . [would] fail to know the one Logos as many *logoi*, indivisibly distinguished amid the differences of created things, owing to their specific individuality, which remains unconfused both in themselves and with respect to one another? Moreover, would he not also know that *the many logoi are one Logos, seeing that all things are related to Him without being confused with Him, who is the essential and personally distinct Logos of God the Father, the origin and cause of all things.* . . . From all eternity, He contained within Himself the preexisting *logoi* of created beings. When, in His goodwill, he formed out of nothing the substance of the visible and invisible worlds, he did so on the basis of these *logoi*. By His *word (logos) and His wisdom He created* and continues to create *all things*—universals as well as particulars—at the appropriate time.[46]

The *logoi* of every created being represent both the essence of that being as divinely *known* by God before creation came to exist, as well as the divine *will* of God for that aspect of creation to come to be.[47]

The creature, while fully contingent on God for its being, is not simply an "emanation" of God, but receives its own existence:

> A creature, for instance an animal, does not emanate from God. The creature is made from nothing and as made it participates in God as Life, Being, Goodness. It does not participate in a portion of Life, Being, Goodness, but in the whole of these gifts. Its capacity to receive, however, is limited by the logos or divine idea that defines its essence.[48]

I will return very shortly to the importance of the posture of "receiving" from a depth-psychological perspective as well, but first I wish to highlight that for Maximus, we can therefore see that it is simply an impossibility for any aspect of creation to be disconnected from God, because anything that exists not only exists because God *knows* and *wills* it to exist, but in its existence it is fundamentally participating in the Logos that is, metaphysically, the center of the *logoi*. As Torstein Tollefson notes, "He is present in each of them."[49]

But the *logoi* are not static. As noted earlier, like seeds they also contain the potential telos of beings, the goal and fulfillment of each created nature. And so there is, in Maximus's thought, an assumption that "no being in principle is devoid of motion" for no being is self-created.[50] Only the ultimate end—that is, God, who is self-caused—"exists for the sake of nothing else" but "nothing that has come into being is perfect in itself, for if it were, it would be devoid of activity, having no want or need of anything" and so

> in the same way, nothing that has come into being is impassible . . . and therefore no created being which is in motion has yet come to rest, either because it has not yet attained its first and sole cause, to which it owes its existence, or because it does not yet find itself within its ultimate desired end.[51]

There is an assumption that a fundamental aspect of being is to be in motion, and more so that there is a latent teleotic drive toward fulfillment in God. This, too, comprises an aspect of our deepest created being. As Maximus continues, "For the end of the motion of things that are moved is to rest within eternal well-being itself, just as their beginning was being itself, which is God, who is the giver of being and the bestower of the grace of well-being."[52]

Self-determination and desire, as we will see, play a great role in the trajectory of this motion, but the motion is there nonetheless, the movement born of innate desire seeking fulfillment, whether it be what Maximus calls "natural" or whether it be distorted. It is possible, though not life-giving, to seek ontological fulfillment elsewhere than God, and the implication is that either way, our being is still in motion. As he points out:

> For having reckoned up the costs, the saints may have asked themselves what it profits a man who is not the author of his own being to remain in motion around himself, or around anything else but God, if neither from himself, nor from anyone else apart from God, can he add even the slightest interest to his principle of being?[53]

This lead us to an answering of the question, which arises out of the assumption of the innate connection of all livingness to God, as to whether all expressions of life are equally "good"? Is there no essential distinction between sin or disease, and fullness of life?

As has been outlined above, Maximus saw the *logoi* of beings as distinct conceptually from the *tropos* of being, the mode of being, which each

creature—in particular those endowed with freedom of will and desire—
embarks upon.[54] As Melchisedec Toronen remarks, "Sin and virtue are a
matter of what one makes of one's natural capacities; they are the *tropoi* of
the application of one's *logos*."[55] That we are created with an indestructible
connection to God, one that gives rise to the very possibility of *theosis*, does
not mean that we live out this potential without fail. Toronen pithily observes: "In Maximian terms, the 'mess' is in the *tropos* rather than in the
logos."[56] Fallen nature is no longer able to accurately perceive the *logoi* of
beings, having turned from contemplation of God to an idolatry of the
created and sensible world.[57]

> Maximus regards passions as an end result of confusions: "Every pas-
> sion always comes about by mixing some perceived object, a sense
> faculty and a natural power, diverted from the natural—the incen-
> sive power, desire, or the intelligence, as the case may be."[58] Thus the
> intellect's wrong move causes a disorder in the human architecture.
> This leads to the distortion of the natural state of the individual
> parts of the soul, which in turn is expressed in unhealthy and sinful
> activity. . . . The mind which has abandoned its correct way of relat-
> ing to the world . . . cannot retain its wholeness and unity. It be-
> comes like someone who is constantly dragged in different directions
> at one and the same time. "Sin is ever scattered," Maximus says "and
> with itself it ever scatters the mind which has committed it. It cuts
> the mind off the singular identity of truth and sets up the irrational
> habit that disperses the mind about many and unsteady imaginations
> and opinions concerning beings."[59]

Depending on the direction of the will, humans—who always participate
in being itself by virtue of their existence, and in eternal being by virtue of
God holding them existence—nonetheless are agents of their own trajectory toward well-being and eventually eternal well-being, or ill-being and
even eternal ill-being.[60] Everything hinges on free will.[61] Additionally, as
can be glimpsed from the above citation, while sin fragments the individual, love and virtue bring integration.[62] I will return to these issues in the
next chapter.

In Maximus's thinking, the *logoi* come to serve not only a sweeping, if
potentially speculative, metaphysical understanding of creation but also a
very tangible aspect of the process of deification: For Maximus, the *logoi*
are the faculties of the soul capable of virtue, for "the essence in every vir-

tue is the one Logos of God."[63] *Participation* in virtue is "[participation] in God, who is the *substance* of the virtues."[64] Through free will and ascetic endeavor, as well as the deifying grace of the sacraments, the person's *tropos* is brought into line with their *logos*. Using other words one might say the person begins to develop from the indestructible *image* of God (*logos*) to the *likeness* of God (*tropos*).[65]

Movement in the Depths

Returning to the depth-psychological side of this reflection, if we look to other theorists as well as those mentioned earlier, might we see the traces of the symbiosis, or more specifically of the *logoi* perceived by St. Maximus, in their God-willed and God-given good and connected essence, and in their inherent motion, manifested in the natural workings of the psyche toward healing?

Carl Jung is noted for his work with archetypes, the collective unconscious, and objective psychic reality. He saw the possibility for transformation, and drive toward individuation,[66] as latent in the psyche and its workings and its relationship to objective reality.[67] For example, he observed that, even in the throes of agonizing psychic turmoil, an image might spontaneously arise from the unconscious that—if consciously engaged with—begins to yield meaning and symbolic context for the feelings being experienced.[68] A telos of psychical energy, what he called libido, can be observed and engaged with.[69]

This direction of reflection led Jung to the awareness that the unconscious contains not only a personal level, but a collective, archetypal level.[70] What he found was that the unconscious, as though answering to an invisible guiding point, seemed to be developing in its own direction, pulling the psyche toward a deeper telos of wholeness, rather than just symptom resolution through basic Freudian analysis.[71] He called this innate process "individuation."[72] Reliance on this process came to serve as both a "model and guiding principle" in his method of treatment.[73]

In a case study he describes finding himself stymied as to how to resolve the dilemma of a patient's transference, a charged set of feelings and attachments projected upon the analyst by the patient, the analysis of which is often critical to the treatment. This particular patient seemed to be so dependent upon Jung as to make the possibility of resolving the treatment seem unattainable. He decided to make use of the unconscious and see if it might lead somewhere. He turned to her dreams. He wrote:

> Now, since the psychic process, like any other life-process, is not just a causal sequence, but is also a process with a teleological orienta-tion, we might expect dreams to give us certain *indicia* about the ob-jective causality as well as about the objective tendencies, precisely because dreams are not less than self-representations of the psychic life-processes.[74]

Eventually his analysis of the patient's dreams, many of which included him as the doctor, with tinges of the patient's father as well, portrayed in terms of superhuman importance and primordial imagery,[75] led him to conclude that the patient's unconscious "was trying to create a god out of the person of the doctor."[76] He pondered as to whether the longing for a god could be a "*passion* welling up from our darkest, instinctual nature, a passion unswayed by any outside influences. . . . Or was it perhaps the highest and truest meaning of that inappropriate love we call the 'transference'?"[77]

As he wrestled with this possibility, startling for his culture and "scien-tific" context, he wrote, "No one will doubt the passionate longing for a human person; but that fragments of religious psychology . . . should come to light as an immediate living reality in the middle of the consulting room . . . seems almost too fantastic to be taken seriously."[78] And yet he did take them seriously, and as he continued to work with this patient, he also noticed the development of what he called a "guiding function" in the psyche that gathered and redirected the energetic charge of the patient's transference to him, now slowly manifesting the internal growth processes that allowed the patient to grow out of her transference to him as the doctor.

This "transpersonal control-point,"[79] as he termed it, expressed itself "symbolically in a form [in the dream] which can only be described as a vision of God."[80] Elsewhere, he wrote:

> It is always a difficult thing to express, in intellectual terms, subtle feelings that are nevertheless infinitely important for the individu-al's life and well-being. It is, in a sense, the feeling that we have been "replaced" but without the connotation of having been "deposed." *It is as if the guidance of life had passed over to an invisible centre.*[81]

This was of particular note in this patient, since consciously she was "critical and agnostic" toward religion and her self-directed seeking would not have been in this direction.[82] Yet her unconscious seemed to require a "religious" solution.

Of the utmost importance to Jung is that the god-image arose from within her; it was not imposed externally by tradition and acquiescence to a set of doctrines, but rather was experiential and had immediate impact. While this poses immediate questions from an Orthodox perspective as to whether this is truly an experience of God, what is of note is that what gave it the power to heal was that it arose organically from deep within the patient, was experienced, and the experience of it acted as a catalyst for the reorganization of her psychic processes around a deeper center. It is for this reason, perhaps, that for Jung an experience of the "Self," the entirety of the person, and an experience of God were indistinguishable.[83]

I am not making the point here that this image, or Jung's concept of the Self, is an image of God, as God is approached, known, received and reflected upon in the Orthodox tradition. I am, however, highlighting a function of the psyche that requires that a person engage with what Jung calls a religious instinct, and with their deepest selves, in order to become whole. It is this opening up to our deepest levels of being, and a trust in their spontaneous ordering toward a telos of wholeness, that marks a distinctly Jungian approach to faith. It does not seem amiss to notice the possibility of a trace of the *logoi* known to St. Maximus as being part of the innate faculty of the psyche to undergo such a transformation, hinging on an experience of, and a desire for, the transcendent.[84]

> [As] the dreams . . . began to materialize . . . [they] brought up bits of the collective unconscious, and that was the end of her infantile world and of all the heroics. She came to herself and to her own real potentialities. This is roughly the way things go in most cases, if the analysis is carried far enough. That the consciousness of her individuality should coincide exactly with the reactivation of an archaic god-image is not just an isolated coincidence, but a very frequent occurrence which, in my view, corresponds to an unconscious law.[85]

To make the brief case that this observation of an innate drive toward that which is healing and transformative is not simply a Jungian approach, one can look to Christopher Bollas too, who speaks implicitly of an innate drive toward transformation that drives us to seek what he termed the "transformational object," seeking healing for our deepest sufferings—sufferings that display themselves obliquely in our innermost aesthetic structures of being.[86] Not only would our very aesthetic of being in some way communicate our sufferings, but the attempt to transform will be unconsciously repeated in futility over and over again using various objects, cohering with his sense that patients are often involved in the kind of repetition compulsion that feels like a doomed fatedness, until they are released through the healing analysis into a life of rooted belonging that lives with a sense of destiny, a life that flows freely out of deep roots from within, rather than fatedness that feels like constant and externally imposed despair.[87]

Lastly, Karen Horney also speaks of a naturally created "real self" that can actualize under the right circumstances, just as an acorn naturally develops into an oak tree under the right conditions, or—having been disowned through the neurotic creation of an idealized self—be returned to in the work of analysis, through the rerouting of energies and the finding of the capacity to love. Her language around the pride system, the "Faustian" deals we make, the finding of a true conscience and morality, and the central inner conflict between the real self and the neurotic self have already found some resonance in the Orthodox world.[88]

Although the emphases and investigations of each theorist are different, each one relies on, indeed has faith in, something innate in the workings of the psyche to move toward healing, especially if given assistance *and with an Other*. Each one sees the manifestations of symptoms as indicative of misappropriated energies in the service of, variously, complexes (Jung), the false self (Winnicott), the idealized self (Horney), or a drive for transformation that takes a futile direction and leads to a sense of fatedness rather than destiny (Bollas). Thus, while specifics of theories may come into conflict, there is a consistent theme of engagement with the "real," and hence even the notion of an implied ontology, by which I mean engagement with being, in depth psychology.

Not all schools of depth psychology hold to a notion of "original goodness," but there is a sense that symptoms can be adaptive or representational of an original drive toward the "good," if by good one means fullness of being. This fullness can be distorted or, as every school of depth psychology observes, somehow split or fragmented. Defensive splitting, precisely because of that service of defense that it performs, can be seen as protecting and preserving the "good," even though it may ultimately become destructive, or find that it what it creates has no real basis in ontology and hence leads to existential anxiety.

In fact, while psychology can articulate, and hopefully help build a bridge between, the gaps that exist between neurotic and psychotic subjective experiences of reality and objective reality, theology can point to the basic ontological void in which such perceptions exist, while also *affirming that there remains a connection to that which ontologically has being*. As Olivier Clement observed, this is the basis for transformation, for the undistortion of our natural energies. He writes succinctly: "Truth is metamorphosis."[89]

Symptoms and disease can hence be seen as psyche still participating in the fullness of being, attempting to live, though in a way that causes enormous suffering, distortion and constriction of life. These observations affirms what Pseudo-Dionysus further wrote:

> Disease is a disorder and yet it does not obliterate everything since if this were to happen the disease itself could not exist. . . . For that which totally lacks a share in the Good has neither being nor a place in existence, whereas that which has a composite nature owes to the Good whatever place it has among beings, and its place among them and the extent of its being are directly proportionate to the share it has of this Good.[90]

Such a direction of reflection on the part of those concerned with healing does not allow for the splitting, if you will, of the disease from the person—something that modern psychiatry and its pharmacological emphasis often seems to be intent on, even if at times for the laudable purpose of immediately diminishing excruciating symptoms or the shame that has long been attendant of mental illness.

In daring to press deeper we can see that all of these theorists express faith in the natural processes of the psyche, and in the *possibilities*, however distant or hard-won, for healing emotional distress, releasing and transforming life caught in psychological misery into "livingness," feeling real and with joy—a truly felt sense of life in abundance.[91] This, I believe, actually restores an enormous dignity, and possibility for integration, to the patient if we can be vigilant in avoiding any sense of "blame" or disparaging of the very real suffering they endure.

Encountering the Dragons of the Heart

As the first psychoanalytic case study in Chapter 1 preliminarily put forth, it is possible that even in the cases of seemingly complete dissociation from reality in psychosis, there is still an indestructible link to something purposive, seeking of life, in the total psyche of the person. While seemingly counterintuitive, facing symptoms (and even "sins") as potentially meaning-disclosing, rather than simply pathological, opens up a different avenue of exploration that—from a depth-psychological perspective—may lead to greater life. It should be stated, however, that this in no way underestimates the genuine suffering that the person experiences in such psychological states, or the seriousness of the "sin" when the inner state is expressed in destructive ways.

Part of the tension of the depth-psychological endeavor is to accept all these levels of reality of suffering, while also holding out the possibility for a deeper, purposive, disclosure of meaning seen through the symptoms, which—if followed—can lead to a healing of the person at a core, integrated level. Simply put, healing takes place at the level of the wounding or the illness, not just of its manifestations. As Carl Jung wrote of the therapy of neuroses: "this [treatment] is not a kind of psychological water cure, but a renewal of the personality, working in every direction and penetrating every sphere of life."[92]

Such healing brings a level of transformation where one no longer has to constantly "will" oneself to be well, or functioning, or even virtuous in a specific way (e.g., to be less selfish) because the healing is so profound that one simply *is* different. One doesn't have to forcibly overcome one's sloth, for example, because one is no longer unconsciously bound by a depressive fear of one's aggression or even a schizoid fear of one's love. The energy is released from the split and lives freely accessible to the flow of desire and conscious willing. This is not to say that a depth analysis eradicates sin; on the contrary, if anything it makes one more conscious of it.[93] But to the degree that what one experiences as sin is a infectious festering of clogged life-force and inarticulate suffering, healing in these areas does manifest in greater natural outflowing of love toward others, potentially opening up the person to deeper relatedness to God, others and self.[94]

This kind of depth process entails holding difficult tensions, and requires a suspension of judgment as well as a kind of *askesis* on the part of both the analyst and the analysand, in being able to tolerate that which is upsetting or unfamiliar without succumbing to it, condoning it, or denying it. A preemptively moral attitude toward the symptom or the sin forecloses the possibility of hearing its communication. But it is precisely the unconscious meaning proffered by symptoms and their attendant suffering that beckons to a consideration of the possibility of healing embedded in our very being, and so, perhaps, to an even greater awe at the mystery of being as created by God. We engage with the "dragons" found in our hearts, whose presence St. Macarius recounted, without trying to kill them off (or succumbing to their danger). We ask them what they are guarding and why. After all, as the classic heroic stories tell us, dragons are often found guarding gold, slumbering away until somebody stumbles into their treasure, at which point their fiery ire bellows forth.[95] It would not do to simply dismiss as a "passion" that which guards (however inappropriately) something beautiful and necessary within us. The hidden gold in our hearts is worth facing dragons to find. We relinquish "knowing" and open to "un-knowing."[96] We let the fearsome symptom speak.

Let me give here an example from a case study offered by Ann Ulanov in her book *The Unshuttered Heart*. She worked extensively with a woman in her fifties, married, professional, with children, who had suffered from deep depression for as long as she could remember. Over a period of a great deal of analytic work, a remarkable shift occurred "from long-standing depression as a condition, an entrapping character disorder that medication had helped but did not remove, to its becoming a defense . . . and thence to soften into a helpful symptom alerting her to preventable danger."[97] Central to my reflections here is what Ulanov sees as the pivotal approach: "The shift came slowly through engaging with not knowing, and opening to imaginative encounter with this crushing depression."[98]

Analyst and analysand together peered into this depression, wondering about its permanence, wondering what image it might present with. An image arose from the patient of living in a waiting room, a baseline of being stuck in a transitional place that always leads to no-where, to nothing happening, blankness. Any flickerings of spontaneous desire were swiped away and caught up into a more acceptable narrative of duty. Together, over multiple sessions, analyst and analysand continued to consciously live in this "waiting room," until another image arrived: this time of a Plexiglas wall, endlessly stretching, no way out. They stayed with it, holding it, receiving it, accepting its unshatterable walling off together. But then, a new image occurred, a fascination with the primal primate—the curious, aggressive energy of a group of baboons in a wildlife park. Ulanov saw that this kind of energy was "precisely what was walled off in her and contributed to the sense of deadness afflicting her."[99] From there, an image arrived of treading water in an ocean, despairing, later symbolized by deep purple, a heavily viscous liquid bubble bath. Yet, Ulanov notes that, objectively speaking, the heavy viscosity of bubble bath dissolves in running water, transforming into pleasurable bubbles. Was the analysand's depression slowly "dissolving in the current of feelings and imaginative symbols [bubbles]?"[100]

Then, from deep within, a confession: "My defense as a kid was, I don't need anything."[101] And here Ulanov sees the inhibited desire "announcing itself by confessing her disavowal of it."[102] Her continued work led to access of deep feelings that, when disavowed, pulled her into an undertow of viscous depression, but that—when accessed—began to open her up to new life and living. The final image that arrives, in the form of a painting that so captivates the patient, is a door standing ajar. Ulanov writes:

> It is not what is beyond the door, [the patient] emphasized, but that it opened. What was sealed became unsealed. . . . She sees that . . . this being on hold in the dead waiting room, treading endlessly to keep afloat above the thick but deeply colored, that is passionate feeling-states, is a defense built up over years, helped but not removed by medication. A year later she raised the same issue in a very different way. I want to talk about what gets in the way of my loving, and my feeling the love I know is there (for her husband).[103]

This case study is awash with spontaneous images; the power of simply holding the space; "being-with" the other, the image, the pain, the symptom; and letting emerge what needs to emerge. Of note, to my mind, is also that what does surface is—finally—an intention, a disavowal, a refusal of desire.

This pain-ridden decision, driven by deprivation in early life, becomes the willed intention that led to the depressive defense. It was not, however, consciously willed in the way we commonly think of free will. Nor could the patient be held "accountable" for it, especially having been just a child. But it lived in her, causing violence to her deeper instinctive desiring nature. The depression was both a defense against the desire, and a painful red flag marking the place where something had gone wrong, which needed a returning to and tending to, requiring courage, strength, and love on the part of both analyst and analysand.

Theologically speaking, this is not a paradigm of simply accepting psychological suffering and, however sincerely, offering it back to God, but rather freely using one's agency to turn in toward the suffering, inquire after it, following it to its roots (often trusting in God as well as the analyst or spiritual director with every shaking fiber of one's being), in the faith that there is a life-giving impulse to be found and recovered, healing to be experienced and integrated into living for greater fullness of life. One might say it is a journey to recover more being.

Part of the enormous courage such a journey requires is that it often feels like going against the express wishes of God almighty, when our *own* god-image, constricting as it may be, has taken up residence, and is tormenting us from, the inner throne that belongs only to the Living God. In that sense, such a journey expresses great faith in the Existing One to exist beyond our own "rules" about God. As Ulanov writes elsewhere: "When we let go, we let go into the hands of a living God, not a dead one; otherwise we could not let go."[104]

Receiving Being

We begin to see here how it may be the case that, without terming it as such, depth psychology has come to rely on ontological truths already perceived by the early Church Mothers and Fathers, in particular as such truths extend to the unconscious strivings, and even telos, of the psyche.

What then, becomes of the will in a chapter devoted largely to unconscious willing? I believe that it is in the unconscious drive toward healing that we may see a "trace" of the *logoi*, and hence the connection to the Logos, in every person. Just like God's indestructible knowing of us, and willing of our existence, something in the psyche knows what is necessary to live, and *wills to live*. Yet, this "natural" state can become terribly distorted (to use patristic language) or pathological (to use clinical language). And here lies a great difficulty, because—as Maximus noted—our will is critical to our *tropos*, whether it becomes one of well-being, or ill-being.

In the case study offered by Ulanov, outlined earlier in this chapter, the patient became aware of an unconscious willing that went against her natural faculty—to use Maximus's language—of desire. In essence, to avoid pain, she tried to amputate part of her natural, created self. Her healing entailed a "confession," not as a legalistic admission of wrong-doing, but of repentance as *metanoia*, a turning away from the old way of being toward a new way of being. She had to begin to turn *toward* desire, however painful and fraught that might have felt. She had to turn toward her deep feelings that had previously been disallowed by her inner "architecture." Then the depression abated, returning as a twinge of alarm when she would return to her old ways—as we all do. It cannot be overstated here that this *does not make depression a punishment*, it makes it—in this case—a *symptom* of the flock having lost a precious sheep.[105] The seemingly ontological drive toward wholeness, unity (though with differentiation), and integration shows up in the psyche's unwillingness to let "all be well" when, in fact, all is not well.

The journey of depth-psychological healing often begins with the reluctant admission that all is not well, and we have no idea what to do to make it better. In fact, our own attempts seem to only land us up in the same place over and over again. Again, as we saw in the case study earlier, and as I described in the beginning of this chapter, entering into the unknown, and staying there for some time, may be the first necessary step to receive what we need to heal. But what finally comes to meet us there is a cause for wonder.

As Jung saw, as Ulanov saw, the images spontaneously arising begin to tell us what we cannot consciously articulate—much as the ancients understood the *logismoi* (thoughts/images) as emanations that showed the state of the soul. But deeper than that, *when we are willing to receive what comes*, something else begins to come through: a different way of living altogether, a *tropos* of psychological well-being at the deepest of levels. Ulanov writes: "We can rely on the psyche to display what being does with its communicative resilient capacities, just what God displays in the unceasing generosity of creation. We need only return to the place where we can once again receive what is given."[106] Healing begins.

This movement of receiving what is given, of receiving our being itself, is a movement, in a way, of repentance. When done in a religious context, we consciously let go of our own machinations and yield ourselves up to receive God instead. We confess our "exile," and what Ulanov calls the "snakelike power to exchange our lives with God for a self-originated identity,"[107] where having ruptured our dependence on God, we feel not liberated, but as though we were living in exile, like Adam and Eve banished from the garden. Ulanov observes that, in psychological terms, such exile "perverts our imaginative power into an encapsulating fantasy that protects our true self in embryo form but also traps us in repetitive compulsions that both defend and persecute the unmet, dependent, parts of ourselves."[108]

And yet, thankfully, not only does God's empowering, vivifying *dynamis* meet our willing and desiring efforts to move toward His reality, but the holding, healing, seeking, and wooing energies of God also "[overcome] all our refusals to receive and partake of the bread of life."[109] Our symptoms become our "meeting places" with grace. Ulanov continues:

> Our drinking problem, our food addiction, our reliance on drugs to meet our dependencies, our lusting after power . . . our unrealized hopes, our cruelty to others—whatever looms as our basest fear or despair or hopelessness—now turns out to be just the occasion and place where God comes to us. We are found on our own cross. We cannot get out of that gap to get to God. We do not leave behind our problems to get to God. God comes to find us where we are weakest, in the secret hiding places of our compulsions, in the segregated district of self that we despise and oppress. . . . God comes to us.[110]

The beginning of a new journey commences when the unconscious "no," to being, to God, becomes a receiving, desiring, and willing "yes."[111] We come to know that God can do for us what we cannot do for ourselves—restore us from a turn toward illusion, nonbeing, self-love that cannot see the Other, toward being itself, and more so—as Maximus writes—well-being.

When we return to receive what is given, we confess our ontological dependence on the life given by God. To use the language of St. Irenaeus: "For creation is an attribute of the goodness of God; but to be created is that of human nature."[112] John Behr comments:

> Irenaeus argues against those who display ingratitude by refusing to accept that they are what God has created them to be "men subject to passions" . . . but want to be even as God. . . . They establish their own agenda for becoming what they want to be. To become truly human, to become a god, man must allow God to fashion him, and this requires that he be open and responsive.[113]

Thus, even when working with the unconscious, the will is engaged in the willingness to be responsive, to listen, to be open to what arises, to receive the new, to repent of the old, and to receive healing.

And slowly we begin to experience gratitude for what is coming to us, given to us, *by that which is not us*—be it the loving care of an analyst, the faithful holding of one's life in prayer by one's spiritual mother or father, the healing depths and wisdom of the psyche, or the holding-in-being of God Himself. Goodness flows in from all sides. Citing Irenaeus, Behr further notes:

> "As God is always the same, so also the human being, when found in God, shall always go on towards God" [*Against Heresies*, 4.11.12]. Likewise, God never ceases from bestowing gifts upon the human being, nor does the human being ever cease from receiving these benefits and being enriched. . . . Following on from the basic dynamic of the relationship between Creator and created, is the need for created beings to respond to the creative activity of God by *allowing* themselves to be created, an attitude that Irenaeus characterizes as thankfulness.[114]

Might we, from all of the above, see the manifestation of Orthodox and patristic ontology that even when we experience the deepest levels of psychic despair, we are still connected to the Good and the Beautiful, and that herein lies our greatest hope of healing and transformation?

4

EROS: HEALING FIRE

Without the power of desire there is no longing, and so no love, which is the
issue of longing; for the property of desire is to love something. And without the
incensive power, intensifying the desire for union with what is loved, there can
be no peace.

—St. Maximus the Confessor, *The Philokalia*

Eros is a questionable fellow and will always remain so, whatever the legislation
of the future might have to say about it. He belongs on one side to man's
primordial animal nature which will endure as long as man has an animal body.
On the other side he is related to the highest forms of the spirit. But he thrives
only when spirit and instinct are in right harmony. If one or the other aspect is
lacking to him, the result is injury or at least a lopsidedness that may easily veer
towards the pathological.

—Jung, "The Eros Theory"

In the last chapter, I looked for the possibility of traces of Orthodox ontology in depth-psychological experiences of the psyche qua psyche; I
explored the possibilities of an innate telos in the ordering of existence and
of the movement toward God from an Orthodox perspective, and
conversely, in the ordering of the psyche toward healing from a depth-
psychological perspective.

Toward the end of the chapter, I noted that while these potentialities
do seem to exist, and perhaps in ways that far exceed common understandings
of them, there is also a similarity in that to be actualized, both perspectives

ultimately require a turning of will *toward*, and *desire* for, that which is Good: being itself. The process of healing from both angles seems to include confession,[1] repentance in the form of *metanoia*—a turning around, and the gaining of the ability to *receive* what is being offered by way of healing and growth.

This, I postulated, was a move from not only experiencing a possible telos of existence, but also toward actively willing and desiring to engage with the healing inherent in this telos. In both Orthodoxy and depth psychology, the true agency of the person is evoked, summoned forth, even recovered, by the generosity of life inherent in being itself, and in turn, she or he may discover, receive, and embrace more life from that place of choice and agency. This agency is inseparable from desire. Thus, there appears to be a pivotal link between healing and restoration in Orthodoxy and healing in depth psychology, found in the realm of willingness, in what we shall see is finally a discourse on *desire*, engagement with the Other, be it a person or God, even life itself. In both disciplines, there is an emphasis on the openness and willingness to *become* a self, filled with personal valuing, desiring, perceiving, and responding to the Other evoked by communion, by love between self and Other.

This brings us to the level of the personal and, through questions of agency, volition, and desire, we land in the mysteries of eros and love. Clinicians of different schools of depth psychology have all recognized the centrality of the energy of eros—in its various facets, some of which I will discuss shortly—to analysis.[2] For this chapter, I use eros—as will be seen below—to describe a *drive toward* relatedness (though not the same as actual relationship), *seeking* union and communion, rooted in desire. It includes sexuality, but is not circumscribed by it. It may serve love, or it may serve despair, but it is an instinct that cannot be eradicated. I will discuss various images of eros, as understood psychologically, in the next section.

Is, then, our eros assumed and healed? The later Greek patristic tradition also reflects on the eros of God toward humans, the eros of the person toward God, and the resultant possibilities for transformation and healing of the eros of the person in this ecstatic communion. The healing entailed is deeply linked to the healing of desire as well.

In this chapter, therefore, I would like to consider the possible traces seen in the depths of the psyche of the healing love and desire—the eros—of God as Person toward the creature. We might anticipate seeing that personal eros qua eros is central to healing of any kind (just as we saw the possibility that being qua being both offers the basis for, and exerts a foundational pull upon, the unconscious attempts of the psyche to heal). We might further hope to see that the divine eros known and experienced in the *mysteria*—the living and continuous embodiment of the soteriology of the patristic theologians—should act upon the psyche of the person in such a way as to begin to make possible not only the radiant divinization anticipated by the later Greek Fathers, but also to kindle the dulled embers of personal eros and desire in a way that brings a healing recognizable from a depth-psychological perspective. In turn, perhaps we might even see that desire itself is integral to *theosis*.

It is not only at the level of being itself where we encounter healing, but also at the level of the personal and interpersonal, the related; healing takes place between the person and God, between the person and other persons, and intrapsychically between fragmented parts of ourselves, through eros, *born of love*. Desire, healed by love, becomes the impetus of erotic reunification and healing of fragmentation within the self, and between the self and other. As will be seen throughout the theology of St. Maximus, to whose work I will once again turn, only love overcomes the fragmentation of human nature.[3]

On the depth-psychological side, I will spend some time in this chapter on an in-depth examination of aspects of object-relations theory. While I do not wish to limit this consideration solely to an object-relations perspective, I find that, within the theories of Donald Fairbairn and Harry Guntrip in particular, there is a helpful specificity of the mechanics of development that may point to how we arrive—from a depth-psychological perspective—at the spiritual and psychological sufferings primarily to do with love and eros, rooted in wounded desire. Fairbairn was influenced by the thought of Hegel, and saw the frustration of desire as the root cause for the splitting of the ego.[4] Guntrip, in turn, was deeply influenced by both Fairbairn and Winnicott's work on the "true self" and "false self."[5]

For Fairbairn and Guntrip, the person is known as primarily relationship-seeking, and the *primary locus of wounding is to the capacity and desire for relationship with others*. Such wounding leads to what they call schizoid phenomena, a kind of deep dissociation of the heart from one's lived life, inevitably resulting in both egocentricity and a "splitting" between mind and heart. I have chosen this particular issue because such splitting is seen as the *primary* developmental move toward psychopathology (preceding all others). It is a disorder that manifests itself starkly and tragically in some cases, but is also known at some level along a spectrum to most people. Lastly. the split that this wounding entails resonates with a great deal of Orthodox reflection on the manifestation of sin as a splitting and fragmentation of the person, and—as will be discussed—with St. Maximus's emphasis on the natural desire that constitutes a basic part of our ontology as human beings.

I suggest that we need not take their theories as utterly concrete, but as providing—through their conjecture on the life of the infant—a kind of useful "myth" as to an "original wounding" at a psychological level that, in turn, forms the basis, a wounded and weak core, out of which grow many and various other psychopathologies. It is also a wounding that can be hard to accurately diagnose, and hence all the more of interest if the energies of God bring healing to it even in its mute resistance to being known.

Eros, a "Questionable Fellow"

How do we describe eros psychologically? In this realm, eros is what Ulanov describes as the "*function of psychic relatedness* that urges us to connect . . . be in the midst of, reach out to, get inside of, value, not to abstract or theorize but get in touch with, invest energy, endow libido."[6]

Ulanov maintains that eros is not the same as actual relationship, being consciously engaged with someone or something. But it "may initiate erotic embodiment in connection with another person, with one's God, with what conveys to us the loving of life, and the transpersonal source and value of it."[7] She clarifies the distinction between eros and sexuality:

> The most common understanding of eros is sexuality. Eros in the body is sexuality. Yet the sex drive transforms into eros, the life and love instinct striving for eternal forms of truth and goodness, a force for unity in our self, with another person, with life itself.[8]

Here we have eros as a function of psychic relatedness, as instinct for life and love, and the charge of sexuality. Ulanov cites Freud as describing eros as the energy of all the instincts that concern themselves with love, and linked to the love-force that he called libido.[9]

Jung disagreed that libido was circumscribed by sexuality and broadened the conception of libido to describe psychic energy more generally,[10] though tracing its etymology back to appetitive roots of desire and love,[11] hence staying firmly planted in the close connection of life-force, volitional willing, desiring, movement with attraction and love. He understood eros as the function of relationship[12] and libido as "appetite in its natural state,"[13] an "energy value which is able to communicate itself to any field of activity whatsoever, be it power, hunger, hatred, sexuality, or religion, without ever being itself a specific instinct."[14]

Ulanov brings us back to the connection of libido to eros in saying "the pull of the erotic is . . . wanton, bawdy, lusty, ardent, passionate. It is personified by Cupid shooting his arrows here and there, arousing our libido which we then lavishly invest in objects, others, causes, pursuits."[15] Eros garners and demands libido. And for Guntrip, via Fairbairn, libido and the erotic drive toward the other meet in the definition he offers of libido as *"the object-seeking drive* of the primary natural ego or psychic self . . . the libidinal quest for objects is the source of the capacity to love, and the maintenance of loving relationships is the major self-expressive activity of the total self."[16]

Through self-giving love, we see eros offered also in Heinz Kohut's concept of empathy, the patient "being-with" on the part of the analyst, who remains present to the analysand even when feeling utterly invisible and blotted out by the analysand's narcissism.[17] This empathy love expressed as unconditional presence, over time, becomes the loving solution in which the rigid walls of narcissistic defenses are dissolved. In alchemical imagery, much utilized by Jung, eros is seen as the bringer of the *solutio*, the dissolving of crusty hardness into living streams of life flowing forth, a harbinger of transformation.[18]

Hence we can see that eros is inextricably related to, and sometimes seemingly coterminous with, desire, sexual attraction, love, and libido, but its function as an *energy* pushing toward relatedness and connection is not fully apprehended by any of those terms and so it is not fully synonymous with them. Again, it is not relationship, or communion, itself, as this requires *personal* feeling and valuing of the other, of the "object"; it is rather the energy that drives toward such relatedness.

It is helpful to reflect on these terms from a patristic perspective as well, where we find many similarities. Since I will be primarily looking at the work of St. Maximus, I will consider his reflections on eros, which in turn will draw his theological anthropological understandings into the discussion.

Before continuing on, however, I wish to highlight an important area of possible misapprehension. This has to do with the consideration of religious instinct and impulse, even erotic love, as a kind of sublimation of more primordial instincts, all of which exist within the totality of the psyche. G. C. Tympas sounds a note of caution, which he applies to his reading of Jung's vision of the transformation of psychic material from one form to another yet remaining primarily psychological:

> By treating "love of God" as a transformed libidinal material, Jung is not at all aware of what is the precise impact of such a "love" on Maximus: it is "the inward universal relationship to the first good connected with the universal purpose of our natural kind." . . . It is thus the universal principle of "love" that unites—and not "love" as a psychological shield of repressed desires.[19]

While one might nuance this interpretation of Jung's stance in another discourse, here it is simply important to note that we are not talking about religious eros as sublimation of physical eros. Rather, for Maximus, love connects us to the God that is other and, through this love and our efforts toward it, binds us back to our true selves, reintegrating and transforming our natural faculties.[20]

This works through his principle of the *logoi* of being, the *image* of God in us that we strive to transform into the *likeness* through prayer, asceticism, and participation in the sacraments.[21] Through sin and the fall, we have become subject to illusion and fragmentation, subject to endless cycles of pleasure and pain, because we have "*fallen in love* with what is not real, and so [must] be taught to redirect our power to what really exists."[22] And yet, far from the answer lying in a disavowal of desire, Maximus is clear that it lies instead in the transfer of desire to what does exist.[23] Thus eros for Maximus seems to have a primordial function that runs deep and wide, uniting the most basic appetitive faculties of the soul and body to the highest of faculties of perception and union with God. It is not "sublimated" from one area to the other, but encompasses and unifies the personality, plunging—as Olivier Clement writes—the "opaque, divisive, death-ridden modality" of this world into its "Christ-centered modality, into that 'ineffable and marvelous fire hidden in the essence of things, as in the Burning Bush.'"[24]

Thus, beyond my main goal of exploring the traces of the theological and ontological centrality of eros and desire in depth-psychological healing, there is an additional question. It involves not only whether depth-psychological understandings of eros can be sympathetically aligned with those of Orthodox theology, or whether sexuality informs our spiritual life, or even how our faith ought to inform our sexuality; rather, it asks whether the erotically charged plunging of this "death-ridden" and "divisive" modality into the "fire in the essence of things" might actually *contribute* to the healing of eros and desire from a depth-psychological perspective.

Eros, Desire, and the Ontology of the Person

In the Orthodox theological vision, Jesus Christ as Lord does not simply assume our human nature as the Logos, the substrate of our existence, but as a Person, the Divine Hypostasis. God is not simply defined by the relationship we ourselves establish *to Him*, which can be strengthened or weakened by our efforts or denials, depending solely upon our subjective state. God, as Person, and in complete freedom, "has intersected our existence when we didn't expect it . . . [such that] . . . we are faced with a God who is in relationship *to us*."[25] As Ulanov writes:

> We come up against a hard fact that is right at the center of our faith—that we really do not get to God from our side, that we do not get to God by strictly human effort . . . we always must come up against the hard fact at the center of the Gospel: we do not get to God by our own efforts. *God comes to us*.[26]

This leaves us with the question of our response. Our freedom constitutes our authentic response, and is inviolate by God. This leads us to a discussion of St. Maximus's conception of the person and the will.[27]

For St. Maximus, the person is composed of body and soul, and neither can be understood, or more precisely, known without the other.[28] Further, he worked out of an understanding of the human person that consisted of a tripartite soul and a highly sophisticated understanding of the will, all situated within the context of a basic dichotomy between the intelligible and the sensible world—with humans having the vocation of integrating these opposites within themselves.[29] The mind (*nous*) is capable of relating to "intelligible and incorporeal substances, which it apprehends by its own substance" and sense (*aisthesis*) is "related to sensible and bodily natures."[30] The soul, then, occupies a place between the two, struggling toward the original human vocation of experiencing the divine and yet bogged down in the illusory claim to the ultimacy of the material world.[31] Yet neither level is to be disregarded. Orthodox theologian Andrew Louth notes that, for Maximus, "to be human is to be a creature that loves with a love that integrates the several layers of our being, layers some of which we share with the non-rational, and even non-animal creation."[32]

Louth suggests that Maximus's understanding of the will is largely original, though drawing on precedent.[33] Maximus differentiates between two different kinds of will: a will that he calls a "natural law," and a will that has to do with inclination.[34] He describes the natural will, or law (*thelema*), in saying that it is

> the natural appetency of the flesh endowed with a rational soul, and not the longing of the mind of a particular man moved by an opinion, that *possesses the natural power of the desire for being*, and is naturally moved and shaped by the Word toward the fulfillment of the economy. And this they wisely call the will, without which the human nature cannot be. For the natural will is "the power that longs for what is natural" and contains all the properties that are essentially attached to the nature.[35]

This willing forms an integral part of divinely created human nature, and this desire is inherent to human nature as ontologically given. As Paul Blowers notes:

> With Origen, the two Cappadocian Gregories, and Pseudo-Dionysius the Areopagite, Maximus understands desire, in all its cosmological and psychosomatic complexity, as the principal register of creaturely passibility and affectivity, as integral to the definition of human volition and freedom, and as central also to the subtle dialectic of activity and passivity in the creaturely transitus . . . to deification.[36]

Yet, as Louth explicates, "with fallen creatures, their own nature has become opaque to them, they no longer know what they want, and experience coercion in trying to love what cannot give fulfillment."[37] In the fallen state, creatures have lost an awareness of God and so

> various apparent goods attract them: they are confused, they need to deliberate and consider, and their way of willing shares in all this. Maximus calls this willing in accordance with an opinion, or intention, or inclination (the Greek word for all these is *gnômê*). Such "gnomic" willing is our way or mode of willing, it is the only way in which we can express our natural will, but it is a frustrating and confusing business.[38]

Thus what we normally experience as willing is only possible *because* of the existence of the natural will, and yet does not reflect our desire in enfleshed fullness because our nature has "become opaque to us." We live at a different level of experiencing, one of conscious deliberation and conscience, at odds with our true nature. But freedom, for Maximus, is located in the natural will, not in our ability to simply "choose" to do as we like,[39] or to wrestle with our consciences to do the "right thing," as necessary as both of those may be to our fallen existence. He is at pains to assure that this natural will does not override our power of "self-determination," but rather "affirming . . . [an] unchangeable natural disposition . . . so that from the same source whence we *received our being*, we should also long to *receive being moved*, like an image that has ascended to its archetype."[40]

Nikolaos Loudovikos highlights this freedom we have to live out of our nature—or refuse to—in St. Maximus's conception of the *logoi* of beings, which we encountered in the last chapter:

> The *logoi* are, according the Confessor's expression, "the fire existing in the essences of creatures," but . . . the essences themselves, which are the created results of the *logoi*, although full of divine glory, are also independent, by the freedom of their agents, from the burning, divine source.[41]

Loudovikos argues that it is not enough to claim that relatedness constitutes our ontological reality,[42] because this would negate an even deeper essential freedom to *not* be related; rather, our deepest structures are rooted in *desire*, the *thelema* of Maximus. Desire is foundational to freedom:

> We cannot substitute the personal reality of the gifted with any a-personal relatedness. . . . Relatedness, as a given structure . . . [would be] . . . a passive dictation upon living and desiring individuals as a pre-existing ontological structure. We have strongly denied such a relatedness that ultimately makes givenness void of real otherness, i.e., void of *desire* in its manifold, conscious or unconscious, adventures.[43]

Thus we find desire at the root of relatedness, not predetermined by it but freely giving birth to it.

To return to the trichotomy of the soul, one of the main distinctions found in Maximus is that between "the *rational, irascible*, and *concupiscible* elements . . . a distinction found almost everywhere in ancient Greek philosophical, theological, and ascetic literature."[44] In a discussion of the interior lives of saints, Maximus notes that the saints, "illumined by grace," came to understand that the soul has three movements that "converge into one: movement according to intellect, movement according to reason, and according to sensation."[45] The level of the sensate is gathered up to the intellect through the "medium of reason," and reason in turn to intellect, and intellect offered to God.[46] In this way, they are "wholly gathered into God."[47]

It is interesting, especially from a depth-psychological perspective, to note that two of the main faculties of the soul correspond to desire (*epithumia*) and aggression (*thumos*).[48] This desire is of a different category than the desire of natural will, *thelema*, discussed above. This is the "appetitive" desire that can be swayed by passions toward sin, or be engaged by love of the Good, directing eros toward God.[49] This allows Maximus, for example, to note that the healing of the soul as it turns to God involves a *full transformation and utilization* of both the capacity for desire and the capacity for aggression.[50] In his *Chapters on Love*, he writes:

> When a [person's] intellect is constantly with God, his desire grows beyond all measure into an intense longing for God and his incensiveness [the aggressive faculty] is completely transformed into divine love. For by continual participation in the divine radiance his intellect becomes totally filled with light; and when it has *reintegrated* its passible [prone to passions] aspect, it redirects this aspect towards God . . . filling it with an incomprehensible and intense longing for Him.[51]

Maximus wrote at length about the consequences of the *distortion* of these faculties and the ensuing passions and predicament of humanity.[52] But for now, it is enough to lay out a basic framework of the understanding of the human person so as to better envision how it is that God's eros touches and kindles the eros of the person. Blowers explains:

> For Maximus, to modulate *eros* goes far in redeeming and reorienting a potentially vicious constellation of human passions rooted in *epithumia* and *thumos* . . . *epithumia* the concupiscible faculty, while liable to becoming lust or infatuation with material goods, can be converted into *eros* as well as *agape*.[53]

Of course, if we are to look at the eros of the person, we must briefly look at Maximus's understanding of human sexuality. The role of human sexual differentiation, and hence also sexual interaction, meets with varying hypotheses in the patristic theologians, with—as we saw in chapter one—modern scholars debating how best to interpret their teachings on these subjects, especially given that their concerns and context were not ours and it would be problematic to read our concerns into their writings. Thus, here we come into tricky waters, where it is also important to note that Maximus was a monk, writing not only sweeping philosophical and dogmatic theology, but initially especially, focusing on spiritual and ascetical theology as short treatises designed to provide guidance in the spiritual life.[54]

In Maximus, various writings show a cautioning against "sensual pleasure" that lies at the root of almost every sin,[55] that sexual intercourse is for the purpose of procreation and not sensual pleasure,[56] and a subtle but clear infiltration of the desire for sensual pleasure in the choice of Adam to transgress God's commandments.[57] It seems to be generally accepted that for Maximus, marriage is "providentially" instituted by God in light of the fall—it was not necessarily in the original design for humanity.[58] I think it important to highlight again that Maximus was not writing to address "gender issues" or questions of "sexuality." His forays into these topics are located in his attempt to explicate something much larger—namely, the suffering of the human condition and the healing and return to God, achieved through the virgin birth, the Incarnation, death and Resurrection of Christ. Adam Cooper, in his study on the body in Maximus, asserts that for Maximus the sexual instinct is morally neutral, acquiring its moral valence through the aims and goals of the *mind* that is utilizing it.[59] As Maximus writes: "There is nothing evil in creatures except misuse, which stems from the mind's negligence in its natural cultivation."[60] He further clarifies that: "The trouble therefore is not with sexual intercourse itself, but with the fact that human existence is dependent upon a law that arose out of . . . an unnatural desire for carnal pleasure, a desire whose ultimate root is 'self-love' (*philautia*)."[61]

I will return shortly to the concept of *philautia*, but it is worth noting that the desire is seen as unnatural through its linking to an idolatrous "self-love," which implies a *lack* of eros, if eros is a function of ecstatic (going out of oneself) relatedness to an Other. It is also noteworthy that Maximus elsewhere defines pleasure as "desire combined with sensation"[62] and laments the misdirection of this function as being *solely* directed toward the material world rather than God. He describes that in a state of divinization, the mind would no longer be "moved toward some [created] thing by the desire to know it" for in such a state "all things intelligible and sensible will be enveloped in the ineffable manifestation and presence of God."[63] In other words, contemplation of God suffuses all else. Rather than splitting the person away from creation, all of creation is gathered up in this greater knowing that seems also to be a knowing born of desiring and relating, a knowing through union. And for the saints who proceed not only through knowledge of the "principles of being" and the "principles of virtues," but onward to the source of those principles, and are eventually united with the Word Himself, "none of the original attributes that originally define human beings have been lost, for all things have simply yielded to what is better like air—which in itself is not luminous—completely mixed with light."[64]

Maximus was not the first patristic theologian to use the term eros in a theological context. Pseudo-Dionysius the Areopagite, whom we encountered also in the previous chapter, also used eros to describe God in His attributes in his treatise on the *Divine Names*. According to John Rist, he is the first to do so in a way that satisfies the Christian demand that God loves all things, not loving aspects of his own divinity, but truly going out of Himself toward the other in love.[65] Rist states that the Areopagite uses eros and agape (love) synonymously, with eros often denoting a more intensive form of agape.[66] In this love, God's "Providential Eros" is flowing downwards; this is not a discussion of human eros as ascent to God.[67] Rist observes that Pseudo-Dionysius's emphasis on God as eros takes place primarily around the understanding of God who is beauty and who lacks for nothing in Himself, but who, as the cause of all beauty in the universe, draws all things to Himself: "God as Beauty is a unifying force in the cosmos."[68] Rist continues that for Pseudo-Dionysius, "God is Eros and the cause of Eros in all other things. This Eros in other things is the mark of their dependence on God and their need of Him. Eros is a unitive force throughout the cosmos, and that unity is God Himself."[69]

Maximus, drawing on the theology of Pseudo-Dionysius, continues very clearly in this trajectory. I will cite him at length here from his *Fifth Century of Various Texts*, to set the tone for the rest of the chapter. The following theological texts also show a similar interplay between the terms eros, desire, and love to the one we saw from the psychological side, and—intriguingly—a "love-force" of God, a "power" that perhaps retains some resonance with libido, if we appropriate it in connection with humanity.

83. . . . Observe how the divine force of love—the erotic power pre-existing in the good—has given birth to the same blessed force within us, through which we long for the beautiful and the good. . . .

84. Theologians call the divine sometimes an erotic force, sometimes love, sometimes that which is intensely longed for and loved. Consequently, as an erotic force and as love, the divine itself is subject to movement and as that which is intensely longed for and loved it moves towards itself everything that is receptive of this force and love. . . . [T]he divine itself is subject to movement since *it produces an inward state of intense longing and love in those receptive to them*; and it moves others since by nature it attracts the desire of those who are drawn towards it. In other words, it moves others and itself moves since it thirsts to be thirsted for, longs to be longed for, and loves to be loved.

85–86. The divine erotic force also produces ecstasy, compelling those who love to belong not to themselves but to those whom they love. . . . One must also in the name of truth be bold enough to affirm that the Cause of all things through the beauty, goodness, and profusion of his intense love for everything, goes out of Himself in His providential care for the whole of creation. By means of the supra-essential power of ecstasy, and spell-bound as it were by goodness, love, and longing, He relinquishes His utter transcendence in order to dwell in all things while yet remaining within Himself. Hence those skilled in divine matters call him a zealous and exemplary lover, because of the intensity of His blessed longing for all things and because *he rouses others to imitate His own intense desire*. . . .

87. God is said to be the originator and begetter of love and the erotic force. For he externalized them from within Himself, that is, He brought them forth into the world of created things. This is why Scripture says that "God is love" (1 John 4:16), and elsewhere that He is "sweetness and desire" (see Song of Songs 5:16. LXX), which signifies the erotic force. For what is worthy of love and truly desirable is God Himself. . . .

88. You should understand that God stimulates and allures in order to bring about an erotic union in the Spirit, that is to say, He is the go-between in this union, the one who brings the parties together, in

order that He may be desired and loved by His creatures. God stimulates in that He impels each being, in accordance with its own
principle, to return to Him. . . .

89. The erotic impulsion of the Good, that pre-exists in the Good, is
simple and self-moving; it proceeds from the Good, and returns
again to the Good, since it is without end or beginning. This is why
we always desire the divine and union with the divine. For loving
union with God surpasses and excels all other unions.

90. We should regard the erotic force, *whether divine, angelic, noetic,
psychic or physical, as a unifying and commingling power.* It impels
superior beings to care for those below them, beings of equal dignity
to act with reciprocity, and, finally, inferior beings to return to those
that are greater and more excellent than they.

91. Spiritual knowledge unites knower and known, while ignorance
is always a cause of change and self-division in the ignorant.[70]

We see here his powerful and lyrical language, evoking the eternal play
and motion of love and desire, life- and love-force, call and response, longing and satisfaction. We see an ontological force for unity, and knowledge
through union. We see also the implication that humans are created with
desire and born for eros, for communion with God and with each other.
Desire and eros are ontological to the human being.[71]

To look for "traces" of healing, then, we might now consider how
wounded desire manifests and heals from a very particular perspective, the
depth-psychological perspective. A wounding to our ontological core, seen
theologically, would presumably show up in psychopathology, and conversely, a healing of our psyche should be related to what is healing of our
ontological core. I believe that this is shown to be true, if we focus our
reflections on the movements of desire, on eros.

Eros Ensnared

As we saw in the previous chapter, for St. Maximus, sin leads to a fragmentation of the person. Ulanov, over a thousand years later, echoes the depth-
psychological experience of this truth. She writes: "Sin is splitting. . . .
The psychoanalyst directs us back to this central insight of Christianity:
an altogether negative splitting results from stopped-up loving, from a

consciousness too small to embrace self and other simultaneously." But what is this stopped-up loving? It implies that there is love at the core, which has been unsuccessful in finding expression, rather than the absence of love altogether. For example, Ulanov considers the theories of Harold Searles, a psychoanalyst noted for his work on schizophrenia in the twentieth century. Citing him, she relates:

> The murderous aggression so evident in a personality invaded by schizophrenic disorder turns out, upon examination, to be a massive defense against repressed loving and the need to love. The pre-schizophrenic child will even sacrifice his or her chance for sanity, the possibility of individuality, to try to rescue a fragile, anxiety-ridden mother whose own sanity hangs in precarious balance. The child assumes the mother's illness to spare her its ravaging effects and above all not to leave her alone in her suffering. "He introjects her primarily in an effort to save her by taking her difficulties, her cross, upon himself." Who would think to find this Christlike sacrifice in the depths of madness![72]

We cannot help but be struck here by the instinct of "assumption" as salvific that is also inherent to the person—that the desire for communion is so strong that we may enter into the madness, blankness, or even violence of another so as not to leave him or her alone, nor to be left alone ourselves as children without the parent. Instinctively we seek relatedness, the eros of both offering and receiving it. We, too, seem to have an instinct to assume in order to save and heal.[73] That this only leads to a psychopathology in the person at a later stage speaks not of a choice toward immorality, and certainly must not speak of a punishment of God upon them, but of a devastating reality of distorted love and a delusion so piercingly common to childhood perceiving that we can (and must) act as God.

What does it mean then, psychologically, for desire to become undistorted, turned away from that which has no being to that which has true existence? We might first look at this from the other side, which is what might it look like psychologically when our eros *is* attached to that which has no existence, when we have "fallen in love with that which does not exist," and is caught in despair?

Eros as instinct is not silenced by despair. As a God-given instinct, it continues to have being, but may also manifest in other ways. It may become rerouted toward that which cannot offer a loving response—thus, in a sense, toward nonbeing, as in Andre Green's "dead mother" theory. In such situations, the person unconsciously remains with the mother who—through her own depression or perhaps mourning—was filled with deadness though still alive, and therefore lives dead but unmourned in the psyche of the child, present only through inexplicable absence and a sense of blank meaninglessness. Eros, and indeed pleasure, are subsumed in depressive loyalty—a fusion with absence and death—and cannot be lured away to living others until the loss to the self has been made conscious and can be worked through in its devastating impact.[74] Kavaler-Adler writes about the "demon lover," a demanding, seductive, betraying and abandoning interior conglomeration of incorporated "bad objects" that lives in the blocked places of the heart's yearning for a true other, for genuine love, until it is recognized and released by a mourning process.[75] Theorists such as Fairbairn and Guntrip, whose theories I will explore in particular detail shortly, have a great deal to say about schizoid disorders and the fear of love that freezes our hearts, numbs affect, and imprisons in frigid terror the capacity for earthy living out of hearts of flesh rather than hearts of stone.

Despair is also implicitly the basis for the creation of Winnicott's pathological false self and Karen Horney's neurotic self.[76] The false self or neurotic solutions, carry in them the seeds of the desire for life, but without hope. The experience of despairing eros also creates envy. As Ulanov and Ulanov write:

> An analytical relationship must submerge both the rigid, idealized good and the persecutory bad back into the turbulent currents of the patient's hungry love . . . the analysand must again feel the hunger that envy expresses, the need for something beyond the self, the longing for contact with a good given rather than self-produced, the yearning toward a good altogether outside one's own control. Feeling these needs, desires, longings, hunger and yearnings opens a patient wide to a vulnerable state, breaking down the hard defenses that envy has given rise to and thus making reception of the good once more a possibility.[77]

Without such a process, we are stuck in our envy, which—when unconscious—

> produces a state of confusion between good and bad objects. Attacking the good . . . replaces taking it in. . . . Like Lucifer, we resent the

fact that we ourselves are not the origin of good, that we do not control and own it, and we angrily refuse it, quitting the scene to set up a realm where we can rule instead.[78]

Our eros has become attached to distortion, we experience "coercion in trying to love what cannot give fulfillment,"[79] and out of despair arises envy and narcissism. We are caught in the complexities of our inner worlds and the vicissitudes of the outer world, no longer able to experience self or other in a clear and loving way.

Narcissistic disorder (as opposed to what depth psychologists deem healthy, normal, narcissistic energy) manifests in the inability to love the other as other. The other is viewed not as existing unto themselves but as an extension of self, what theorists have termed a "self-object."[80] It is not natural narcissistic cathexis (investment of energy) in the self that is the problem, but the inability to truly differentiate between self and other, instead utilizing others as mirrors of one's self, objects that exist solely to support and uphold the sense of self.[81] This is developmentally normal to early childhood, but disorders arise when it does not undergo modification through maturation. As Fairbairn clarifies:

> The phenomenon of narcissism, which is one of the most prominent characteristics of infantile dependence, is an attitude arising out of identification with the object. Indeed, *primary narcissism* may be simply defined as just such as *a state of identification with the object, secondary narcissism* being *a state of identification with an object which is internalized.*[82]

Earlier I mentioned the concept of *philautia*, usually translated as "self-love." This, as I understand it, has little to do with a neurotic disavowal of a basic self-esteem, and certainly—in light of Maximus's emphasis on the integration of the person—is not meant to occasion a split between conscience and desire, nor to dismantle our fundamental integrity. After all, we are—in his own words—"portions of God."[83] Tellingly, Maximus defines *philautia* as "the passion of attachment to the body" and insists it is "the mother of the passions" that leaves us exposed to every other passion, against our will.[84] Elsewhere he maintains that it is "mindless" and "irrational" love of the body (which he contrasts with disciplined nourishment and care of the body, born of love and self-control, perhaps akin to "healthy narcissism").[85]

In the context of his larger theological emphasis of our having fallen in love with that which does not exist, I believe *philautia* can be understood as distorted desire and pleasure-seeking arising out of the core delusion that we are primarily material and bodily with no transcendent referent. As such, our bodily self-preservation, and our passions and emotions also without transcendent referent, become our prime focus and orientation.[86] In other words, it is a kind of self-idolatry that echoes of narcissistic disorder. Clement observes that, "Maximus the Confessor, speak[s] here of *philautia*, self-love, self-centredness, that snatches the world away from God to annex it, making neighbors into things. There is no longer the Other, nor other people, only the absolute I."[87]

From another angle, Fr. Alexios Trader, in his study of patristic theology and cognitive behavioral therapy, devotes several pages to the parsing out of similarities and differences between egocentricity and the patristic understanding of *philautia*.[88] He sees them as deeply intertwined, albeit separate conceptually and organically. Egocentricity presents as a cognitive distortion; it creates an inability to recognize the reality of one's actual relationship to the external world. It is more of a misfunction of a rational faculty than an issue of morality. *Philautia* is a misappropriation of one's self as the primary love object, the main object of concern,[89] and hence a distortion of the direction of desire. Therefore it is seen as a true spiritual malaise, as it is a choice to love in a self-idolatrous direction. We can see how, when *philautia* reigns, all other desires are subjugated under it, as all other desires must come to serve the self.

Depth psychology, as already alluded to, tends to consider the formation of cognition, the ego's sense of self, and the developmental unfolding of eros—whether it becomes narcissistic or not—as fully related. I will discuss this in detail shortly.

In addition to highlighting the roles and distortions of eros, what I have attempted to show in the clinical examples of my own experience, which I gave above, is also the sufferings endured by an inner psychic structure that prohibits love of the other. It is this excruciating suffering, deeply buried, that I will attempt to uncover in this chapter. The inability to love here meets, in the following sections, an understanding that—once again—sidesteps the ordinary leanings of morality in favor of a deeper appraisal of the communication and sufferings of the psyche. Of course, the greatest Christian commandments have to do with love, and embedded within that, the orientation of our desire; thus, it is natural that a morality of love should

arise in the course of theological reflection. Yet, here depth psychology offers a particular insight into how what appears to be the absence of love is,
in fact, the distortion of love.

Desire, Eros, and the Formation of the Inner World

Although many have disagreed with Freud since he first put forth his theories over one hundred years ago, perhaps both theologians and psychoanalysts might find agreement with what he writes in his *On Narcissism:
An Introduction*: "A strong egoism is a protection against falling ill, but in
the last resort we must begin to love in order not to fall ill, and we are
bound to fall ill if, in consequence of frustration, we are unable to love."[90]
Even though Freud's initial theories focused on libido solely as biological
and sexual instinct seeking discharge,[91] his pioneering work set the tone
for later psychoanalysts to keep investigating the deepest—and often
unconscious—motivating drives and conflicts within the person, concerning in particular the function of eros.

Building on Freud, object-relations theorists such as Donald Fairbairn
in the twentieth century expanded the understanding of the libido—the
main life-force and instinct of the person—as not primarily pleasure-
seeking and biological/instinctual, but rather object-seeking and relational.[92] Fairbairn wrote:

> The libido theory is based, of course, upon the conception of eroto-
> genic zones. It must be recognized, however, that in the first instance
> erotogenic zones are simply channels through which libido flows, and
> that a zone only becomes erotogenic when libido flows through it.
> *The ultimate goal of libido is the object.*[93]

This statement is particularly striking for the purposes of these reflections
on object-relations, if we call into view a similar turn of phrase—although
with a different referent—by St. Maximus. He wrote:

> The aim of faith is the true revelation of its object. And the true rev-
> elation of faith's object is ineffable communion, with Him, and this
> communion is the return of believers to their beginning as much as
> to their end . . . and therefore the satisfaction of desire.[94]

Interestingly, here faith is used almost synonymously with desire, a utilization also seen early on in this book by Orthodox theologian Alexander

Schmemann while discussing spiritual life and spiritual death, and the desire that seeks life, even through death, if necessary. I will return to this
theme again later. Maximus himself defines faith as "a relational power or
relationship which brings about the immediate . . . union of the believer
with the God in whom he believes."[95]

To return to depth psychology, Fairbairn and later Harry Guntrip, saw
the primary source of psychopathology as correlated to a negative experience of relationships, and the internalization of these relationships at the
earliest levels of development.[96] As Guntrip wrote:

> Since the need for an object arises from the fact that without object-
> relations no strong ego-development is possible, we must conclude
> that the satisfaction of libidinal needs is not an end in itself but is an
> experience of good-object relationships in which the infant discov-
> ers himself as a person, and his ego-development proceeds firmly and
> self-confidently.[97]

This is a complicated technical area but it is one that merits a deeper
viewing in order to understand at the most profound psychic levels the role
and importance of eros, as well as the vicissitudes of its natural function
according to certain major depth- psychological theories.

Parting company with Freud, Fairbairn refuted the notion of the formation of psychic structure being composed primarily around instinctive
impulses and their "guilty" repression of libidinal instincts—chiefly those
of sexuality and aggression—and instead saw the psyche's development as
a series of responses to relationship, internalizations of relationship, and
the attempt to manage the inevitable conflicts that these formative relationships would bring.[98] His understanding of guilt is poignant; rather than
seeing guilt as a product of repressed and unacceptable sexual or aggressive wishes, he sees it as a *defense* against an even more troubling aspect of
experience, that of the earliest childhood encounters with libidinally frustrating (or perhaps dangerous, abandoning, seducing, or depriving) objects.[99] These so called "bad objects" are deeply internalized and banished
to the unconscious, and the sense of badness is instead taken upon the child
him- or herself, in their very sense of self.[100] This occurs "on the principle
that the child finds it more tolerable to regard himself as conditionally (i.e.,
morally) bad than to regard his parents as unconditionally (i.e., libidinally)
bad."[101] In this process, hope is maintained solely through the internaliza-

tion of "good objects" as the superego (arbiter of moral values), which the child then becomes "guilty" of failing. Yet, in this way they have maintained a fragile hope of redemption as against the despair of the actual experience of powerlessness against "bad objects." In other words, they have sold out their own goodness to protect themselves from the despair of the bad environment. In turn, they internalize a moral code and moral conflicts that may keep them intensely preoccupied, though without ever getting to the internal "crypt" where the stinking corpses of the bad objects have been laid. Yet, for Fairbairn, there is no real healing at the level of morality; it is to the depths of this crypt that the patient and analyst must descend, and here that release and healing must occur.[102] It is striking, here, to note an observation by St. Maximus that has also to do with the difference between morality and true communion with the "object" of God:

> The Spirit . . . has to persuade the intellect to desist from moral philosophy in order to commune with the supra-essential Logos through direct and undivided contemplation. . . . For when the intellect has become free from its attachment to sensible objects, it should not be burdened any longer with pre-occupations about morality as with a shaggy cloak.[103]

Although Maximus's emphasis is on the passionate attachment of the intellect, through distorted desire, to the self and to the material world, his emphasis elsewhere on the distortion, caused by passions, of the interior representations of objects carries a striking, and perhaps unexpected, experiential resonance to Fairbairn's observations.[104] For both, healing lies not in morality qua morality, but communion.

Thus, rather than appealing to Freud's notion of a "death instinct" to explain seemingly innately destructive behavior (a theory to which Melanie Klein also adhered),[105] Fairbairn set a different tone in observing psychopathological development not as a result of fixation at a particular libidinal phase, but as an attempt to manage internalized bad objects, and as a defense against the failure to fully repress them (the first and simplest move to defend the ego-sense against them).[106] Their threatening to burst through to consciousness, bringing with them the stench of despair and destruction, would give rise to the four "classic psychopathological defenses"—namely, phobias, obsessions, hysteria, and paranoia.[107] And yet, the inextricable pain of the child, and later the adult, is also bound up with these bad objects in that they were also love objects, and objects needed by the child. As seen above, what he meant by internal objects were internal representations of external objects with whom the person was formatively related. He thus came to see the resistance to change experienced in any analysis of the unconscious as arising out of what he called the "positive libidinal attachment"[108] to these internalized "bad objects."[109]

In sum, as the infant comes into relationship with the world around him or her, the persons that form its external world, in particular its primary care-giver, also become "introjected" into the infant's interior world, and related to (or banished, as we saw above) within this intrapsychic space. As a source of anxiety, the infant seeks to "manage" them in order to meet her or his libidinal needs. What is to be emphasized here is that there is never a point where the child is functioning in a primarily unrelated way; *eros is always the driver*.[110]

The problem, as seen, arises when eros is frustrated—for example, through abandonment, indifference, or possessiveness and over-identification on the part of the primary caretakers. In such cases, if we consider desire as the driver of erotic libido, we can begin to see how the channels that seem available to the forming ego of the child feel limited in expression. Hence Fairbairn is able to say, for example, that "it must always be borne in mind . . . that it is not the libidinal attitude that determines the object-relationship, but the object-relationship that determines the libidinal attitude."[111] He continues:

> Frustration of his desire to be loved as a person and to have his love accepted is the greatest trauma that a child can experience and it is this trauma above all that creates fixations in the various forms of infantile sexuality to which a child is driven to resort in an attempt to compensate by substitutive satisfactions for the failure of his emotional relationships with his outer objects. Fundamentally these substitutive satisfactions . . . all represent relationships with internalized objects, to which the individual is compelled to turn in default of a satisfactory relationship with objects in the outside world.[112]

Thus we see a simple truth that erotic desire constitutes the greatest driver of libido within the person, and that wounded-ness in this area to the "libidinal attitude" represents a core wound to the faculty of desire and—as we shall see—to the utilization of libido.

Schizoid Splitting, Ego Weakness, and the Lost Heart

How then do we arrive at places, so well known to many, of deep dissociation from our hearts? After all, as Guntrip points out, these "psychopathologies" represent points along a spectrum we all participate in.[113] Thus, it is not only those who suffer from severe schizoid or depressive pathologies who are impacted by the psychic structures and formations that these theorists elucidate in various ways. And certainly Orthodox spiritual and pastoral literature speaks often of the split between mind and heart.[114]

Because of the way cognition develops along with attachment, for a child whose attachments[115] are wounded at an early enough stage of development leading to what is termed a "schizoid" development, the experience becomes an unexpected interpretation of unconsciously *believing that their love is destructive*. As Fairbairn observes: "It will be seen . . . that the great problem of the schizoid individual is how to love without destroying by love, whereas the great problem of the depressive individual is how to love without destroying by hate."[116] But he goes on further to say that:

> The conflict underlying the schizoid state is, of course, much more devastating than the conflict underlying the depressive state . . . the devastating nature of the conflict associated with the early oral phase lies in the fact that, if it seems a terrible thing for an individual to destroy his object by hate, it seems a *much more terrible thing for him to destroy his object by love*. It is the great tragedy of the schizoid individual that his love seems to destroy and it is because his love seems so destructive that he experiences such difficulty in directing libido towards objects in outer reality. He becomes afraid to love, and therefore he erects barriers between his objects and himself.[117]

To continue in this exploration of mechanics a bit further, it is important to follow Fairbairn to his conclusions concerning the manifestations of this phenomenon:

> In proportion as libido is withdrawn from outer objects it is directed towards internalized objects . . . reference has already been made to the narcissism which results from an excessive libidinization of internalized objects, and such narcissism is specially characteristic of the schizoid individual.[118]

What is striking here is that what appears to be a relating only to self, is in fact a relating to others, but those others have been internalized in an infantile developmental attempt to manage the anxiety that relating to them has brought upon the child. As Guntrip points out, identification is a substitute for a lost object-relationship.[119] It is this inner identification, however distorted, that begins to constitute the interiority of the child, even if the identification consists of fear and guilt. "Fear and guilt are both object-relations, as undoubtedly in the end human beings prefer bad relationships to none at all."[120]

The impact of such an inner state on the life of the person is devastating, though from outwards appearances it may not seem to be so. In fact, a person can have a highly "functioning" life, viable emotions, or even hysteria, and seemingly abundant relations, but with an inner sense of absence that manifests over time in various ways. Most notably:

> The vital heart of the self is lost, and an inner "deadness" is experienced. For practical purposes he is "not all there," and the living, feeling, loving heart of him seems absent; not absolutely, for it is hidden deep in the unconscious, but it can only later be drawn back into consciousness, resurrected or reborn, at the price often of the most severe mental disturbance. It is when the child feels a primitive *despair* of being able to *do* anything to cope with his environment, that drastic withdrawal is the only thing left, and *feelings of despair, loneliness, weakness, and incapacity to love always lie hidden behind the cold detached mask of the schizoid personality*, however stable he may appear to be.[121]

Obviously, such a state of futility is not easily made conscious, though it may in fact be that which drives the person to analysis. To return to the quotation I used in the introduction, as Vasileios Thermos has pointed out, such existential falsehood, covering over an ego impotence and deep sense of futility, is "difficult to diagnose and even more difficult to confess."[122]

Carrying these theories forward in his own explorations, Guntrip elsewhere states succinctly: *"Primary ego un-relatedness is the substance of ego weakness."*[123]

What constitutes this ego weakness? What does he mean by primary ego unrelatedness if we have just shown that, in fact, all of what is occurring intrapsychically is a form of relating? This, again, is complicated but necessary terrain. It has to do with the interweaving of a sense of self as contingent on the necessity of relating and being related to. The nascent ego of the child introjects the various persons, "object-relations"—good and bad—to form internalized relations from which grows a sense of self. However, in the face of severe danger or relational despair, part of the ego may retreat altogether into flight from despair and desolation, going into hiding and withdrawal. This withdrawn and hiding self constitutes the schizoid ego.

> *Severe schizoid states disclose a total fear of the entire outer world. . . . The world is a frightening emptiness when it does not respond and meet the infant's needs, and a frightening persecutor when it actively and hurtfully impinges. . . . Impingement, rejection and deprivation of needs for object-relationships must be bracketed together as defining the traumatic situation which drives the infant into a retreat within himself in search of a return to the womb.*[124]

Yet, for the overall ego, this hidden piece represents a constant threat, as this "schizoid ego" is withdrawn from the world of object-relating entirely. It is not *incapable* of relatedness, but is simply *refusing* it on the grounds that the experience of relationship has become equated with danger. Thus, the fantasy interior world of bad object-relations, discussed earlier, begins also to serve as a way of feeling alive and connected in the face of this regressive urge. The inner world of the person is driven by a need to feel alive, to have a sense of self, and yet this aliveness is always missing a central piece, the "lost heart" of the person. Therefore, it can only manifest itself in overly intellectualized connections at a conscious level, and deeply distorted apprehensions of self and other at the unconscious level, akin to Winnicott's observation that the false self derives a sense of being only through opposition.[125]

> Behind all these methods by which the schizoid person struggles to save himself from too far-reaching a withdrawal from outer reality with its consequences of loss of the ego, lies the hidden danger of a secret part of the personality which is devoted to a fixed attitude of retreat from life in the outer world. It is the part of the total self that most needs help and healing. Its two most extreme expressions are regressive breakdown and fantasies of a return to the womb or a passive wish to die. In the face of the internal threat, the business of maintaining an ego is fraught with unceasing anxiety. The schizoid problem is an "ego" problem.[126]

Guntrip, in explicating this overall problem, highlights a four-fold ego split that take place. The first level of splitting between the "hitherto unitary, pristine ego occurs, into a part dealing with the outer world . . . and a part that has withdrawn into the inner mental world."[127] Now the child has become split between inner and outer. But as the inner world must be "peopled," so to speak, with object-relations in order to uphold any nascent sense of self, the child continues to perceive the interior object-relations in similar ways to the exterior—namely, as threatening. This devolves into yet another splitting within their own interiority between an ego that seeks attachment and connection, and an ego that fears and destroys it:

> Just as the exciting object arouses libidinal needs while the rejecting object denies them, so the attachment to the exciting object results in a libidinal ego characterized by ever-active and unsatisfied desires which come to be felt in angry and sadistic ways; and the attachment to the rejecting object results in an anti-libidinal ego based on an identification which reproduces the hostility of the rejecting object to libidinal needs. Inevitably the libidinal ego is hated and persecuted by the anti-libidinal ego as well as by the rejecting object, so that the infant has now become divided against himself. This is easy to recognize in the contempt and scorn shown by many patients of their own needs to depend for help on other people or on the analyst. It is seen also in the fear and hate of weakness that is embedded in our cultural attitudes.[128]

I will look more closely at the "anti-libidinal ego" shortly, but it is important here to recall that libido for these theorists is primarily erotic, in the sense of object-seeking, while the "libidinal attitude" arises out of experiences of relating, of desire and eros, and of the subsequent satisfaction or frustration offered by the object. The antilibidinal ego, therefore, might also be said to be "anti-erotic" both in the sense of eros toward others, as well as in the sense of eros as a unifying force within the psyche.

To summarize, this world of interior fantasy—peopled by object-relations both good and bad, characterized by masochism, sadism, frustration, guilt and fear—serves a twofold purpose: Firstly, the introjected objects provide a sense of ego-relatedness, albeit to a fantasy, and so there is a defense against the ego loss that would be experienced in the absence of any object-relation at all; secondly, the interior objects also represent actual object-relations to which the infant has a *real* attachment, which means that giving up the fantasy attachment brings about a grief similar to losing an actual person—hence, the enormous resistance to change.[129] In other words, even in this nightmarish and futility-ridden world, the child is struggling to preserve their own sense of personhood and communion with others, albeit in a deeply distorted way.

Descent into Hades

I mentioned in the previous section what Guntrip calls the lost "vital heart" of the self.[130] This is the schizoid ego in its primary schizoid state—totally withdrawn and unavailable for contact. It is, in his reasoning, the piece of psyche that constitutes the most frightening threat to the rest of the person—to what he calls the "central ego"[131]—precisely because of its strongly regressive pull away from object-relating, and hence away from the possibility of being constituted fully as a self, as a full ego. It constantly poses the perceived threat of psychic death or, at least, of destabilization.

It is partly in reaction to, as a kind of compensation for, this piece of self-in-retreat that the dynamics of the libidinal and antilibidinal ego are set into play against each other. In a sense, one might say that—as compelling as these dynamics are experientially, giving rise to all kinds of self-understandings and narratives at a conscious level—they are a smokescreen for a deeper, more terrifying issue for the person: namely, the piece that has gone into hiding, which may even actively drive the person to seek death as a symbol of womb-like passivity and uninterruption of being. This severely regressed, inaccessible piece of self can only be found again at great cost to the patient in terms of energy and destabilization. It presents an unconscious source of terror for the person, and this in turn only strengthens the perceived need for the role of the antilibidinal ego:

> How can the need of the exhausted regressed ego for recuperation and rebirth from a reproduction of the womb-state be met at all, and how can it be met without the risk of undermining the central ego of everyday living? . . . [Left to his or her self, the individual] can only do what he was driven to do as a child, struggle to repress his regressive trends by developing a hard and hostile attitude to any "weakness" in himself, i.e., develop an anti-libidinal ego which is really the child's determined effort to keep himself going by being independent.[132]

I have brought us this far in technical detail in order to descend together to the core problem.[133] In the suffering and the attempt of the patient to find a solution to this suffering on his or her own, the antilibidinal ego arises, which is dynamically charged with an energy that stems from a will to live, even as in practice it manifests as destructive.[134] The patients have, unconsciously, charged a defense with the power to destroy the very thing they need to live. This defense, this antilibidinal ego, must be unearthed and dismantled in order for healing to become possible. This can constitute the greatest of challenges, as—according to Guntrip—the antilibidinal ego seeks to eradicate any traces of the very thing that could begin to reconstitute the person in an authentic way—vulnerable dependency on reliable otherness:[135]

> *The sado-masochistic deadlock between the cruel anti-libidinal ego attacking the weak and suffering libidinal ego in the deep unconscious is the hard core of the illness, against which the central ego, so far as its internal functions are concerned, is a defense.* That ego-weakness is not due to lack of energy is evident from the tremendous energy shown by the anti-libidinal ego in psychic self-attack. The libidinal ego feels weak because the focus of energy has shifted to the anti-libidinal self-persecuting function. *Ego-weakness can exist along with psychic strength.*[136]

This is an excellent image of "distortion" of innate psychic energy, caused by a splitting of the ego function, in turn caused by troubled relationships and threatening environment of the infant. One might venture to perceive the influence of "original sin" on the child's entry into the world and thence its own development as a person. And, even though—as I have said earlier in this chapter—this cluster of theories is not the sole way to understand psychopathology, this gives us a viable image of how to engage with that which is "antierotic" (the destructive antilibidinal ego) in the person, and the havoc it wreaks:

> Infantile fear, regressive flight from reality, and resulting ego-weakness in the face of the real outer world are at the bottom of all personality disorders. Our natural impulse-life is not normally anti-social but becomes such through the forced self-assertion and even violence of an anti-libidinal attempt to over-compensate weakness.[137]

The brutalized sense of self becomes weak, forced to compensate, and is consistently at odds with the social and erotic faculties of life, which desire and catalyze relatedness. Illness arises as a mark of profound suffering. Viewed through the lens of this cluster of theorists, eros and its import in the development of ego, or rather distorted eros and its devastation of the ego, lies at the basis of "psychotic, psychosomatic, and psychoneurotic tensions and illness."[138]

The inextricable link thusly shown between desire, eros, libido, and ego-sense is highlighted in the drama of the antilibidinal ego and the libidinal ego, as they fight an almost Manichean duel that covers all the while for the missing self, the lost heart of the person. The fantasies of the interior world distract our minds and distort our eros. We may be reminded as well of St. Athanasius's insistence, which we saw earlier, that we live deluded by shadowy illusion that can only be healed and dispelled by the *Person* of Christ.[139] As Guntrip says early on of the problem of schizoid phenomena: "The only real solution is the dissolving of identification and the maturing of the personality, the differentiation of ego and object, and the growth of a capacity for cooperative independence and mutuality, i.e., psychic rebirth and development of a real ego."[140] We might consider, as well, Jung's insistence that in the process of individuation, a shift occurs in which

> arises a consciousness which is no longer imprisoned in the petty, oversensitive, personal world of the ego, but participates freely in the wider world of objective interests. This . . . consciousness is no longer that touchy, egotistical bundle of personal wishes, fears, hopes and ambitions . . . instead it is a function of relationship to the world of objects, bringing the individual into absolute, binding, and indissoluble communion with the world at large.[141]

In other words, the possibility to differentiate between self and other, to relate erotically to the other, and hence the death of pathological narcissism, arises out of desire *met* in erotic fulfillment through true relatedness with the other. Maturation of the ego, as Guntrip says, requires an object in order that the interior world of infantile identification may be dissolved and the psyche experience a rebirth. It *requires* eros and it requires love so that our own love and eros may be healed. From a depth-psychological perspective, this requires the eros and love of another person. From an ontological perspective, this requires the eros and love of God. And in both cases, this requires hope.[142]

As was shown in the last chapter, an ontology of life-force in being, and of God as Person—the "object-relation," and indeed the eros of Jesus

Christ—become a necessary and absolutely pivotal counterpoint to the antilibidinal "god" who demands its pound of flesh. It is critical that a person of faith not hear pastoral language around "the death of self" through the ears of the antilibidinal ego, or it will only reinforce the masochistic flagellation of being that is already in motion. At this pivotal axis, there is also a profound poignancy of choice, because to return to being, to seek out the lost self, and to allow a "controlled regression" in therapy at best requires great humility; more often it also requires a different kind of death of self, one less easily articulated from a conscious level.

In severe cases, letting go of these ego defenses can feel like going mad, falling into nothingness.[143] In less severe cases, it is still destabilizing for the conscious ego when an unconscious piece emerges, as if a new shoot from the mud.[144] As Ulanov writes: "To heal an early agony resulting from dependency not met . . . we must depend on someone present. . . . We must remember how dependent we were and what it felt like not to be held and fall into the void."[145] We need to reexperience the experience that led to the initial despair, relinquishing our defenses—slowly, and in a place where it is safe to do so—so that this experience may be, in a way, "recapitulated" and healed by a greater sense of self, now with an other. We need rekindled hope to allow these risky experiences to bring us to new places in ourselves, places we may never have consciously experienced.

But *this* is a death of self that, like the seed husk falling away, makes room for new growth, when held by another's freely given love and presence. This is, in my understanding, the trajectory of death of self that is entailed in acceding—as St. Irenaeus admonished—that it is the nature of God *to create* and the nature of the human *to be created*, rather than create themselves.[146] This death of self is in every respect different than the self-inflicted death of self that is an attempted turn to nonbeing in the face of the painful dilemma of being. Every birthing is a death of the old, of the reality that existed before the new came into being. The "loss of identification" feels like a loss of self, a death of ego, but it is in fact a birth.

In Chapter 2, I cited St. Athanasius who insisted that God does not envy anything its existence, but desires that all should live.[147] Later in the passage, he cites Scripture from the Wisdom of Solomon, saying that it was through envy of the devil that death entered the world.[148] While it is not my intention here to dwell upon the possibility of choice and free will in an infant, or in illness, I think it worth lifting up as a kind of mirror the choice put forth in the Wisdom of Solomon, from the same section that inspired St. Athanasius. Here it is written:

> Do not invite death by the error of your life, or bring on destruction by the work of your hands; because *God did not make death, and he does not delight in the death of the living. For he created all things so that they might exist; the generative forces of the world are wholesome,* and there is no destructive poison in them, and the dominion of Hades is not on earth. For righteousness is immortal.[149]

The author then goes on to describe those who have defiantly taken a position of cynicism, disbelieving in God and seeking only the pleasures of the moment, those who say such things as:

> Let us oppress the righteous poor man; let us not spare the widow or regard the gray hair of the aged. But let our might be our law of right, for what is weak proves itself to be useless.[150]

But, the author cautions, such people have been deceived in their understanding of life:

> Thus they reasoned, but they were led astray, for their wickedness blinded them, and they did not know the secret purposes of God, nor hoped for the wages of holiness, nor discerned the prize for blameless souls; for God created us for incorruption, and made us in the image of his own eternity, but through the devil's envy death entered the world, and those who belong to his company experience it.[151]

To reiterate, it is not my intention to cast a moral judgment on those whose life circumstances—through the lens of these theories—were such from an early age that their infant self necessitated a splitting in order to survive, that their tiny volition was a movement away from relatedness. Earlier in the chapter, I discussed some of the various and debilitating struggles that a person can undergo, which lead to such despair. But I propose we can read this Wisdom literature in light of an unsentimental concept of consequence.

Life and death are, finally, choices.[152] Despair corrupts and deceives the person into choosing death. Where there is a choice for death, as I will discuss shortly, envy abounds as well. But healing from this deceit—from the vagaries of the antilibidinal ego, and the mute despair of the inaccessible, hidden self—requires not only the ever-present holding of being and the healing potentialities embedded in the psyche, as seen in the previous chapter. It also requires genuine hope in the erotic possibilities of connection with the good object-relation, the object that does not impose upon the fragility of the ego, that survives our destructive attempts,[153] and that can—as therapists can only attempt in their own way—descend into the Hades of each individual person and rescue that person from his or her own self-created hell through empathetic presence, assumption, and cobearing of pain.[154] It requires the rebirth of desire, which is midwifed by hope.

"Being With" and Healing: The Rebirth of Desire

It is possible, I hope, to sum up the preceding sections as having been a discourse on how desire becomes wounded at the deepest of levels, from a depth-psychological perspective, and how this wounded desire leads to a kind of "choice" that brings death: the ego of the person, the very sense of self, is decimated. Without desire, eros is a potential for relationship but is not necessarily realized as loving communion between self and other, for—as has now been discussed from various angles, both psychological and theological—it can become attached to that which has no being and draw the ego-sense of the person in that direction, and hence into deep existential anxiety, rather than toward participation in the love of the "other" that evokes and bestows a sense of self.[155]

Yet, Guntrip sees great hope in the natural capacity for healing and regeneration that exists in the "primary natural self," potentiated by the care and love of another:

> If the primary natural self, containing the individual's true potentialities, can be reached, protected, supported and freed from the internal persecutor, it is capable of rapid development and integration with all that is valuable and realistic in the central ego. The total psyche, having regained its proper wholeness, will be restored to full emotional capacity, spontaneity, and creativeness. Resistance to this therapeutic process is long kept up by the anti-libidinal ego which dedicates all the patient's anger, hate, and aggression to crushing his needs and fears. The anti-libidinal ego is not integrated *qua* anti-libidinal. Its aggression is taken back into the service of the libidinal ego and matured.[156]

This is also a striking parallel to Maximus's emphasis on integration and his understanding of the faculty of aggression (*thumos*), which—as was discussed earlier—is ultimately employed in the passionate seeking of the person's eros, integrated now at all levels and "wholly gathered" up, striving toward God,[157] and ultimately being met by the God who delights in seeing creatures "ever insatiably satisfied with the one who is inexhaustible."[158]

This communion, freely engaged in, is born of desire, as Loudovikos insisted earlier, and not imposed upon us as a fact of being.[159] And yet, as we have also seen in the demonstration of schizoid phenomena, the wounding of this desire and hence the refusal of erotic connection, communion, and ultimately love with an actual "object," decimates the person's sense of self. Thus, it is not surprising that at an ontological level, this refusal is also devastating. As Loudovikos writes: "For Maximus, lack of communion between entities is identified with their separation from God and turn to nothingness. Refusal of communion, then, is non-being, and communion is the only possible way in which being can be actualized."[160]

What, then, has the power to evoke the desire of a person in such a way as to rekindle the possibilities of love and the life-bringing development of a sturdy ego-sense through erotic attachment? Whose presence ignites hope in the midst of a foundational despair? If, as Metropolitan John Zizioulas writes, faith is a faith in presence even in the face of absence,[161] what can bestow presence in a place where absence has become the perception of what is ultimately real?

The problem, from a therapeutic perspective, has been one of despair that turned into isolation. The rigidity of defense must be somehow softened enough that the patient can, perhaps for the first time, begin to experience the needs of the "regressed ego." While its need for dependence is met by the therapist, the ego's growth entails not a continued collapse but "a steady recuperation from deep strain, diminishing of deep fears, revitalization of the personality, and rebirth of an active ego that is spontaneous and does not have to be forced and driven."[162]

Clinicians specializing in narcissistic disorders have highlighted the importance of the role of empathy in effecting deep transformation in clinical settings.[163] Guntrip and Winnicott also looked to what they called the "female element" of being, that ability to simply "be," rather than "do," which also entails a "being with."[164] What are the consequences of severe rupture to this way of being, or its utter devaluation? What Ulanov terms "false doing." It is a kind of doing that is split from a deep sense of being, and so constantly hovers above a sense of void, a deep despair, and indeed, existential terror:

> False-doing arises from interruption of being. Instead of possessing a continuity of being from which a vigorous and unforced doing flows naturally . . . we suffer a crumbling at the center of ourselves. Our being has been invaded, taken over by alien elements, and exists now only in fragments. . . . Instead of finding in religion affirmation for our human being in all its perplexity and possibility, moral prescriptions dictate how we should be, creating guilt in us for failing to measure up. Instead of forming a true self under the beneficent gaze of a loving other who reflects us back to ourselves, we assign ourselves, or are assigned, a role to play through the other's unconscious projections. We erect a warning system that will repel invasion and hide our vulnerable core behind an impenetrable wall. In thus protecting our dependent, unformed being, we seal its fate. It remains locked up and inaccessible behind a shell of defenses against being hurt. If we cannot be found, our reasoning goes, we cannot be hurt. . . . We soon come to fear being seen as much as not being seen . . . worst of all, *this fear of being grows into a hatred of being.*[165]

Where lies healing of such fear and hatred of being itself?

It is, perhaps, appropriate at this moment to lift up an image of the feminine so integral to Orthodoxy, that of the Virgin Mary, the Theotokos. Her freely given "yes" to God changed the course of history, and the great mystery of her receiving, bearing, and nurturing of God Himself has stood forth as an icon of the initiating of the healing transformation of the cosmos for over two thousand years. In the beloved icon of the Annunciation, shown above, we see her embodying this very holding presence that births the Other. It is beautifully recalled, as well, in the poetry and paradox of a section of this sixth-century Akathist to the Theotokos (the Virgin Mary)[166]:

> Hail Space containing the Spaceless God.
> Hail Gate of sacred mystery . . .
> Hail Reconciler of Stark Opposites . . .
> Hail Unwedded Bride
> . . .

An angel of the highest rank
was sent from heaven above
To say to the Virgin: "All Hail!"
But at his bodiless salutation, Lord,
He saw you slip into the body's form.
He stood astounded and amazed
And cried out to her saying:

Hail The Cause of radiant joy
Hail The Ending of the curse
Hail Lapsed Adam's restoration
Hail Redemption of the tears of Eve
Hail Heights Unscaleable, beyond our grasp.
Hail Depths Profound, beyond angelic sight.
Hail Imperial throne.
Hail Bearer of the One who bears all things.
Hail Star heralding the Sun
Hail Womb of God's own enfleshment.
Hail Through whom creation is renewed
Hail Through whom the Creator himself became a child

All Hail, Unwedded Bride.[167]

This glorious image of the woman, who came to bear the reconciliation of the opposites[168] of matter and spirit, depths and heights, finitude and infinity within herself in willingly and actively yielding to God's call, also stands strongly forth as the image of the strength and empathetic love—whether offered by male or female—which bears with an Other, and births an Other. The process of analysis, of uncovering the hiddenmost parts of a patient, and staying with the patient so that they may dare their own weakness, requires just such a bearing with, an intentional yielding to God's continuing creation so that the new and strong may be born. As Guntrip describes:

> One comes across states which suggest that there is a regressed ego . . . immobilized in fear, and having never emerged since the first drastic schizoid retreat in infancy. Some patients after long analysis, can find themselves suddenly totally "cut off" and living in the deepest, most hidden schizoid part of their total self *which they have at last contacted and must live in and with, till they regain emotional rapport with the outer world at that deep level.*[169]

It is, as this suggests, not always a question of what we can "do," but how to "be with," trusting in the "wholesomeness of the forces of life" (cited above from Wisdom of Solomon), which can be evoked, *but only in the presence of an Other* who loves us, with an Otherness that confers a sense of self on us rather than seeking to absorb or annihilate it for his or her own purposes. Then, at last, the psyche can begin to release and heal.

And yet, if we look closely, Orthodoxy also gives us a striking nuance to the archetypal trope, which sometimes tips into stereotype, of the "feminine" as a passive or simply receiving container limited to nurturing, gestating, indeed mothering, energy. The Orthodox tradition emphasizes Mary's free will, rather than submission, and as we have seen in St. Maximus, and in modern psychoanalytic theory, *there is no freedom of will without freedom of desire.* Thus, in Mary's very being both as a human woman and as a symbol of the feminine mode of being over centuries, *desire* is the catalyst for her response. Her will does not override her natural desire as "submission" with a masochistic trope; rather, her will and desire are in union. This is why she is free. Notably, given what we may surmise of her historical social context, she does not route her freedom through her betrothed, or through her father. She neither seeks their permission nor interpretation for what her own feminine self has been given to know and ponder. She engages directly with the God who engages directly with her. This is the radical feminine freedom that births our salvation history.

In a homily on the Annunciation, after clarifying that the name Mary means "Lady," St. Gregory Palamas wrote in the twelfth century that "she is the Lady . . . because she is free from servitude and a partaker of divine nature [and] because she is *the fount and root of the freedom of the human race,* especially after the ineffable and joyful Birth."[170] He continues to say: "She conceived the divine fire within her and was not burnt . . . and through her the bearer of the sins of the world was united with the human race. . . . The Virgin Mother, and she alone, is the frontier between created and uncreated nature."[171] Thus Mary's desire expressed in freedom lies at the heart of our salvation, giving birth to the Lord's gift of life and life in abundance.

The drive toward full-hearted communion, which is destroyed and distorted by the despair induced by the antilibidinal ego, or is drawn into illusion and eros toward that which has no existence, is recapitulated in a place of grace—between analyst and patient, between person and God.

That Orthodox Christianity proclaims the ever-presence of the Person of God—incarnating out of love and born of freedom in order to be with and for each human person—bespeaks the healing power of the personal and the erotic in ontological terms that match very closely the importance of eros in the depth-psychological healing of the person.

As Ulanov writes:"[Mary] takes what is offered and receives into her being the great house of being. . . . Receiving God's grace we join in God's life. The Trinity dwells among us. That is what happens when the fire burns in us. Think of people who have lived this love, into the world, people in whose presence, whether they are male or female, you feel the capacity to be born."[172]

Beauty and the Ascent of Hope

Desire, as we have seen, is ontological to the person. That God is seeking us, calling us, alluring us, in our innermost recesses of desiring becomes a call, in turn, to wholeness. Desire births the eros that brings union without losing differentiation. Maximus writes:

> God in His goodness made [the person] as a union of soul and body, so that the soul . . . should, on the one hand, by means of its desire and the whole power of its total love, cling closely to God through knowledge, and growing in *likeness to God*, be divinized; and, on the other hand . . . make prudent use of the body, with a view to ordering it to the mind through the virtues . . . itself mediating to the body the indwelling presence of its Creator, making God Himself—who bound together the body and the soul—the body's own unbreakable bond of immortality. The aim is that "what God is to the soul, the soul might become to the body" and that the Creator of all might be proven to be One . . . so that the many, though separate from each other in nature, might be drawn together in a unity as they converge around the one human nature.[173]

There is no place here for a "schizoid" faith,[174] which leaves out the body and its instincts and desires, proceeding only from a dissociated mind. That eros has a role in the religious life has long been known and reflected upon. What has been less reflected upon is, I believe, how it is our *ontological* capacity for eros that is capable of bringing wholeness to the embodied reality of our lives in a depth-psychological sense.

Christos Yannaras links the two eloquently in his reflections on libido and desire, where—drawing from Lacan—he writes: "In humans . . . sexuality is embodied in desire—in the primordial desire for life-as-relation."[175] It is this overall desire for "life-as-relation" that the sexual instincts participate in, but they do not constitute the whole of it.[176] At the same time, the whole of this desire cannot be lived out without inclusion of body-based libido and instinct. As Loudovikos points out, for Maximus, even though the ultimate goal is "eternal well-being," this by definition includes "being" and "well-being" as givens within itself.[177] In other words, all that belongs to being belongs also to eternal well-being, and the body and soul—both together—belong to being.

It is the call and response of divine eros to our own capacity for erotic desire that initiates our desire, and hence our movement toward God. As we saw earlier, God's desire rouses us to desire, and God's erotic love induces us to respond reciprocally. Desire moves us forward, in what Loudovikos has termed an "eschatological ontology of dialogical reciprocity . . . an inexhaustible erotic surprise."[178]

Yannaras speaks of beauty as that which invites and evokes desire, as "invitation-to-relation." As he writes:

> Beauty *charms* . . . it attracts, it stimulates the desire for relation, for participation, for communion, for intercourse . . . the beauty of nature offers indications of real—not illusory—grounds for a possible realization of relation between humanity and a personal causal principle of existence: between humanity and a rational God, a God-Logos.[179]

The crisp sweet crunch of a fresh apple off the tree, the heady perfumed seduction of night-blooming tuberose, the tangy salt spray of sea water, the first purple crocus breaking through the snow—are these not invitations to relation with the beauty of the created world? As Pseudo-Dionysius wrote:

> For anyone who reflects, the appearances of beauty become the themes of an invisible harmony. Perfumes as they strike our sense represent spiritual illumination. Material lights point to that immaterial light of which they are the images.[180]

The world is displayed in its beauty, alluring us through wonder to the beginnings of opening to the divine. Maximus, reflecting on a phrase by

St. Gregory of Nazianzus, "the sublime Word plays," cites Pseudo-Dionysius on the God who through "overflow of His intense love for all things, goes out of Himself in His providences for all beings . . . spellbound by goodness, love, and longing, and is led down from His position above all . . . to be in all."[181] He then goes on to paint a delightful picture of how parents will frequently "condescend" to the level of their children, "indulgently" taking part in "childish games," or "showing them many colored flowers and colorfully dyed clothing to beguile their senses, thereby attracting their attention and filling them with amazement."[182] But eventually, too, these children are sent onwards to school, after which the parents can begin to converse with them in a "more mature manner." So too, he reasons, perhaps God,

> by leading us through the nature of visible creations . . . seeks to amaze or attract our attention by the sight and knowledge of these things . . . after which He directs us to the contemplation of the more spiritual principles . . . and finally leads us by way of theology up to the more mystical knowledge of Himself.[183]

As also cited earlier, for Maximus, spiritual knowledge unites the knower and the known, and leads to integration rather than inner division.[184] We see this beautifully meditated upon in his *The Church's Mystagogy*, a reflection on the Divine Liturgy and the *mysterion* of the Eucharist. Here, he engages with the transforming grace of the Holy Spirit, which "remolds" each person "in proportion to what is more divine" in them and "*leads [them] to what is revealed*" through the *mysteria* being celebrated.[185]

Poignantly, for the hidden self, the schizoid self, the lost heart of the person, St. Maximus writes that this is happening "even if he does not himself feel this . . . unable [yet] to see either into the depths of the reality of the grace operating in it, which is revealed through each of the divine symbols of salvation being accomplished."[186] The symbols are the erotic language spoken by God to the soul of the salvific reality of our *tropoi* (ways of being) being reconciled with the ontological *logoi* (seeds of being) with which we have been gifted in having been given existence, bringing ultimately full reconciliation with the Logos, author of all being.

Eros: Healing Fire

It is through the relationship of beings to the Creator that they also find unity with each other, though without the dissolution of identity or uniqueness.[187]

Maximus writes: "It is through [the Church] that absolutely no one at all is in himself separated from the community since everyone converges with all the rest and joins together with them by the one, simple, and indivisible grace and power of faith."[188] This is a simple and elegant summation of how the relationship that is faith also becomes communion with others.

The personal and relational is foundational to the spiritual life. One sees this, in the sacrament of confession, for example as discussed by Aristotle Papanikolaou. Here, desire undergoes a healing and transformation through truth-telling and the symbolic mediation of God's eros in the person who witnesses the confession.[189] It is also found in the relationship of the person and their spiritual mother or father, one who prays for them, and guides them in the Christian life. When we frequent the church, Maximus proclaims, the angels themselves are present and supplicating for us,[190] reminding us that in Orthodox thought, communion between beings is not bound by space or time. A radiant example is given by theologian John McGuckin:

> [St. Symeon] tells us of a vision of lights one evening as he was saying his night prayers in his chambers: a radiance that filled the room, taking away his sense of space and time, and eventually resolving as one powerful light in the presence of another even brighter radiance. He interpreted the event as his consciousness of his spiritual father interceding for him before Christ . . . [this] . . . notion of mediation . . . how the saints can carry others into the presence of God . . . comes out in a variety of images, such as the notion of the Church as a golden chain, whose links are the saints in each generation, those spirit-bearers (*pneumatophoroi*) who pass on the kerygma of salvation to each generation, not merely as a preached message, but as the only form in which God transmits charism from one soul to another, that is as the lived experience of love, and the "sensible" awareness of the presence of the Holy Spirit.[191]

Aristotle Papanikolaou underscores what we saw earlier, that for Maximus, love of God leads to love of others.[192] Psychologically, we might also say that what we despairingly withhold of ourselves from others, we also withhold from God.

The Orthodox *mysteria* are a counter to this despair. In their material reality, hope breaks into material reality as well. God's erotic igniting of our desire kindles and fans the flames of hope. "Hope," Ulanov writes, "means we dare to yearn, desire, expect, dream of, hunger for."[193] The sacraments, in their various forms, offer an indestructible personal presence to the person, again and again, week after week. This is a subtle undermining and, eventually perhaps, a full overthrowing of the antilibidinal ego, because it undermines the schizoid fear of their love as destructive, and hence the frozen despair of relationship. God's energies flow into us, touching our eros, evoking a response. God's divine eros brings light, fire, illuminating our desire, freeing it from narcissistic ensnarements of our own and others' creation, moving us in love toward the Existing One—hence, to all that has being, to actual others.[194]

Loudovikos, meditating on the works of St. Maximus and his emphasis on communion between creature and God as the locus of healing and "becoming," writes:

> Desire is the only means we human beings have to consubstantiality. Desire is the only vehicle of the Whole . . . which makes possible the existential realization of the Eucharistic-ontology-of-becoming-in-communion in which divine grace cooperates with human free intention. *It is impossible to build a Christian anthropology without an ontology of desire.*[195]

Thus it is a work of faith to find our desire, and open up to its healing. *It is a work of faith to open to eros.* Then something kindles what seemed like dead coals. Eros, as Ulanov writes, "is like a huge spark that ignites our passion and then confronts us with the question of how we will live this fire in ordinary space and time."[196]

In daring, willing, desiring to approach every sacrament, in the fear of God and with faith and with love, we engage this hope in our bodies, in matter. And we are met. Loudovikos comments: "Grace reshapes [each person] . . . existentially and ontologically, not in an imaginary way or according to the aesthetic fancies of some supposed 'religious feeling.'"[197]

The sacraments, combined with our willingness to turn to God, condition and reeducate our desire and our freedom.[198] We may also understand this process as possible in light of the *logoi* of beings, the "fire in the essence of things," which confer faculties of virtue on our souls that can be activated and grow when the will of the person turns toward God's grace, and is met in the sacramental life. Virtue is acquired through erotic attachment. Maximus throws open the door for God's fire to ignite our desire at the deepest levels of our being, such that its warmth radiates up through all our levels of being, recalling, reconfiguring, remembering our energies, emotions, and eros, turning them toward the Existing One, and hence toward life and away from death.

For Maximus, ontology precedes morality. Being precedes the *manner* of being.[199] Virtue arises out of being, not being out of virtue. He writes "The cup is placed before the baptism, because virtue exists for the sake of truth, not truth for the sake of virtue."[200] For him, truth, divine knowledge, communion, experience of the God "who in His totality as wholly filled [us] and left nothing in [us] empty of His presence"[201] is the goal of the struggle, "while virtue means the struggles which those who desire the truth undertake for its sake."[202] And so Loudovikos comments: "What stands out prominently here is the primacy of ontology in relation to ethics (*askesis*), and above all the eucharistic ontological foundations of the latter."[203] It is communion, relationship, which becomes the basis for transformation. This is echoed elsewhere by Ulanov, who writes of the God experienced in the Eucharist:

> This God lets himself be eaten like a good mother, receiving our hungry attacks and voracious appetites. We consume this God, who nevertheless survives and remains faithful to us. This perception relocates ethics as the doing that follows being . . . Being precedes the doing that overflows from being.[204]

Our anxieties about our destruction of the "good-object" are allayed. God's presence, from a depth-psychological perspective, and actual grace-filled energies, from a theological perspective, combine to fill us with an abundant assurance of being, which leads to joy and gratitude. Rather than the antilibidinal ego—akin to Freud's sadistic superego—that informs our morality, our morality arises out of being, desire, and communion.

In the Eucharist, we receive into ourselves the God who is the eternal and indestructible Good that is "given rather than self-produced . . . the good altogether outside one's own control." Despair, and so envy, the demonic refusal to embrace a good not of our own making, begins to heal.[205] Hope, as Ulanov writes, "is not a bleak hanging on but juiced with desire for a fuller life, a life of gladness, gaiety, meaning and contributing to others. . . . Hope . . . ushers in the world . . . it is relational. What we hope for extends to others too."[206] This hope, as we have seen, must touch the foundation of despair in us, touch our wounded desire and instincts, such that it calls *all* of us forth from the tomb, not just a dissociated part. Such hope unleashes our eros from the chains of despair, allowing its generativity, creativity, opening new doors, unlike in illness that is always getting what we expect.[207]

We are met in our darkest places, and where there was death and refusal of life, there is now repentance, healing, and growth. As God's purifying fire works within us, it illuminates the darkness, surfacing the dragons in the heart, allowing for their healing and transformation. Perhaps what gets purified in God's refining erotic fire is not our human desiring, our vulnerability, or our dependence—as our ego ideals or antilibidinal ego might push to be so—but rather our idolatries, our turning to nonbeing, our refusals of life.

In that the sacraments require the presence of our whole bodies, we also bring what Horney calls "the actual self,"[208] to the meeting with God, not just our ideal selves. This means God meets us as we truly are, embodied, not as we may wish to preserve ourselves in dis-embodied fantasies. In time, we may experientially begin to trust our actual self is being held, not just the self we created out of a need to "self-hold." We are reconciled in small bites, week after week, month after month, like small children being fed, showing us the way back to Paradise, back to our true selves. We don't need to try to be God, but rather receive God's healing.

Thus Loudovikos is able to highlight in Maximus not a moralistic or legalistic reconciliation between the person and God, but experiential, a "*tropos* . . . of achieving unity between the 'meanest' and 'most honorable' things in ontological and not merely moral terms."[209] This echoes what St. Maximus teaches us about divine eros as an energy of integration, overcoming opposites. Eros unites, without confusion or loss of particularity, all the fragmentations and divisions in the cosmos, from male and female, the material and the immaterial, to heaven and earth.[210] The person becomes the mediator of this mystery.[211]

In the *mysteria*, we are brought into encounter with God, whose Spirit works within us in mysterious ways, and slowly the passions within us begin to be re-ordered, un-distorted. Desire, through confession, through communion, comes to be for the Existing One, the indestructible one who meets us at every Divine Liturgy, surviving our own destructiveness and sinful refusals of life.[212] What is required is our free will, our desiring volition, our choice to strive toward and to receive. As our desire comes to be for the Existing One, so too is it reconditioned, given a taste for, all else that truly has existence. Eros ignites.

Conclusion

This work has been a journey of exploration, an attempt to track energies, follow experiences, find traces and paw-prints, of the primal healing energies of life. It has gone down deep into swirling mixtures of images, of life most mysteriously proffered, of salvation and healing, of desire liberated and love unleashed, and also chaotic pain and suffering. It has encountered signs of the wondrous workings of teleotic healing, of potential embedded in creation, as though gazing down into an abyss of starry sky, pulsing with mysterious aliveness, generating unexpected life, opening into eternity. And it has peered gently into the frightened, hidden realm of the lost heart, and received the hope of the possibility of its healing and restoration to communion, and thence even growth into a full-blooded heart capable of passionate, desiring, daring, erotic attachment to God, to others, and to life itself. It has seen the strong, unquenchable fire of love offered in the most humble of ways.

More conceptually, this exploration has shown that there is a strong overlap between certain schools of depth psychology and Orthodox theology in the emphasis placed on the goodness of being and all creation; the possibility (and unfortunate rampant truth) of severe distortion of this goodness, in particular through a distortion of perception through fantasy; the correlation between well-being and the capacity for eros, love and communion; the importance of free will and its fundamental connection to the faculty of desire. In all these places, that which Orthodoxy declares as ontological, inherent to the structures of our being, shows up as integral to healing from a depth-psychological perspective.

It also remains true that there are significant places of nonmeeting (of those explored, as certainly there are many ways of putting these two fields together that would yield other results as well). These occur namely around understandings of sexuality and around the articulated centrality of Jesus Christ as Lord, and the corresponding intentional life of faith, prayer, and participation in the official *mysteria* of the Church. This does not always imply a necessary conflict, since much depends on the particularities of the situation, but they are areas where neither Orthodox theology nor depth psychology find particular need of the other, and given their disagreements, may not be inclined to further discourse.

The question that remains for this conclusion is whether or not this exploration makes any difference. Can this work be applied to clinical situations? Pastoral situations? The life of faith?

From a clinical perspective, whether that of medical/psychiatric chaplaincy or in the analytic treatment room, it would seem that the implications of this exploration—and hopefully those that will follow on it—may allow for a honing in on a metaphysical and anthropological intersection that could well impact the starting position of the clinician, as well as what they are open to as the work unfolds. If it is indeed the case that there is an implicit metaphysic that depth psychology has long participated in even without articulating it, then perhaps it is also the case that by beginning to name it, further exploration can be done in this realm that can yield new clinical possibilities. Of utmost importance is the emphasis the Incarnation places on the value of our frail, fleshy, human lives in all their quirks and foibles—God present to us here, not elsewhere, even in suffering and loss. And while I have not focused overly much on the Christian importance of Christ's death and Resurrection, I would argue these initial encouraging findings certainly open out into territory remaining to be explored. While psychoanalytic thought has traditionally asked for a relinquishing of wishful thinking in the face of the realities of life, Christianity in light of the Resurrection offers a wildly different hope whose manifestations we may rightly wonder about in the clinical setting. As Orthodox theologian David Bentley Hart movingly writes:

> The doctrine of the resurrection . . . requires of faith something even
> more terrible than submission before the violence of being and ac-
> ceptance of fate . . . ; it places all hope and all consolation that what
> is lost will be given back, not as heroic wisdom . . . but as the gift it

always was. The finality of Christ's death on the cross . . . has been unceremoniously undone and we are suddenly denied the consolations of pity and reverence, resignation and recognition, and are thrown out upon the turbid seas of boundless hope and boundless hunger.[1]

As clinicians we must ask ourselves the hard questions: What are our limits of hope for our patients in terms of healing? How open are we to their overwhelming grief and mourning of loss as true loss? With what courage do we accompany their inevitable descents into their own Hades? And, for some of us a harder question still: What grief and hope and hunger do we still hold open for ourselves?

The implicit ramifications of an exploration such as this one lead us in these directions clinically.

Pastorally, we have seen that not only are there traces, even foundations, of Orthodox ontology in depth psychology, but that the fullness of the psyche, even in its spontaneous, seemingly irrational, and even destructive outbursts of imagery or symptom, participates in the life of God and remains teleotic. As such, pastoral caregivers may find a wider range of colors from which to inform their own palette of spiritual perceiving and receiving of the suffering the person is trying to communicate; something that has become intractable to communication in any other form. This does not, and should not, put the pastoral caregiver in the role of the analyst. But having a sense of how the unconscious works allows for a different kind of "holding" on the part of the pastor or chaplain, one that receives both conscious and unconscious, and helps the person to feel more fully known. This can be the beginning of real and previously unknown hope.

The last question, as to whether this study impacts the life of faith is, in a sense, the starting point of a different exploration. But I believe it hinges a great deal on that sense of being known that I just alluded to. One does not have to be suffering from psychopathology to know a sense of alienation of oneself from one's God. In particular, this can be a common feeling when faith is circumscribed by a conscious piety—as I noted early on—while disavowing large parts of the psyche proscribed usually mainly by one's own ego ideal, although perhaps deeply informed by religion. Then one lives constantly at odds with one's God.

But when the psyche, with "all its feelers and feathers"[2] as Ulanov writes, is brought in, then what happens? When we engage with our own personal journey, our own images, our own graspings and stumblings for God, faith comes alive in a new way. Ulanov writes:

> [Our images of God] always confer upon us an enlarged sense of self, a more lively sense of self. In this space our capacity to have faith is born—faith as a lavish, going out of self in trust of the other, faith as the capacity to love straight out, with all one's heart, mind, and strength and body, out of a self that is alive and real, moving toward an other that we believe in utterly.[3]

But as we have seen, this faith is in turn also *met* by the God who is not just of our own imaginings, and not just a metaphysic of being, but is *Person*, personal, present, and whose ontological energies are mediated sacramentally, catalyzing and transfiguring our innermost structures.

Here, I find Ulanov's phrase about "becoming provident" to be an intriguing one. Becoming provident, Ulanov writes, is when the ego becomes attuned to what Jung called the "Self," the totality of the person, conscious, unconscious, and even, as Ulanov postulates, that within us that knows about God and opens out into the transcendent.[4] It means "looking all the time to house the Self . . . [which] conveys a sense of the enlargement of the spirit, of the autonomous Other, of the bigger center that exists both within and beyond us."[5] There is a sense of being connected, from the core of oneself, to that which knows us and yet is beyond us. Here, the ego is able to receive the communications of the Self, to come to know the Self through its "promptings, its chastenings, its hints of direction . . . and above all, its being, its being right there."[6] And here, an astonishing sense can arise, which is that the ego also "senses that the Self is mirroring *it*. We know that we are *known*. An Other exists in us, right at the center of us, making a center out of us . . . [it] does not so much discover as uncover us. . . . Could the Self then act in us like a bridge to . . . God?"[7]

Jung claimed that an experience of the Self could not be distinguished from an experience of God. Ulanov, as we have seen, is careful to differentiate God from the Self, saying elsewhere that the Self is not God but that in us that knows about God.[8] I agree with Ulanov in this parsing, and, as emphasized earlier, Jung himself never claimed to be talking about metaphysics qua metaphysics but rather our psychic experience of metaphysical claims. That there is that within us that lives at a deeper level of knowing and communion than our own ego-awareness does not make it God (though when we stumble up against it, or find ourselves blocked by it, it may feel like an act of God). But its presence does open out into the possibility of living a life filled with a sense of rooted, and connected, open and receiving, destiny, rather than—as Bollas contrasted—a life of shunted, forced, and confined fatedness.[9]

It is this entirety of being that is brought into communion with the ontological energies of God, where—as cited from McGuckin earlier—the disciple comes into "ontological harmony" with the One Who Is, and so also comes into life.[10] And this is a life, finally, that sings with aliveness because it knows no core and lasting opposition within itself, only the constant unfurling and unfolding to become, house, and offer more. This does not eliminate struggle, but it holds our struggles in a greater meaning, one in which we can rest secure, knowing we have planted our own true roots in it, and learning, with astonishment, that all the while we were looking for it, it already knew and was arranging us. In awe, we meet Providence.[11]

Healing takes courage. It is painful. Pride suffers greatly. It can be terrifying to let go of our constructs, our defenses, our personas, and turn instead to the living God who calls us into being, who knows us already in our entirety, and who we, in turn, struggle and pray to come to be able to know more fully.[12] For, as St. Maximus reminds us, spiritual knowledge unites the knower and the known.[13] But we have great hope in the images of salvation that Orthodoxy offers us.

That which is not assumed is not healed. But the psyche, in all of its mysterious complexity, in its ontological foundations of being, its telos toward healing and wholeness, and its primary instincts of desire and eros, is assumed. Where death seemed to reign, there is indestructible life. Our work is to go out in faith and love to meet it, receive it into the very depths of our psyches, and offer it back to God. Joy beckons.

Christ is Risen from the dead, trampling down death by death, and upon those in the tombs bestowing life.[14]

ACKNOWLEDGMENTS

I am very grateful to the editorial team at Fordham University Press, Orthodox Christianity and Contemporary Thought series. In particular the encouragement and support of Dr. Aristotle Papanikolaou, professor of theology and Archbishop Demetrios Chair in Orthodox Theology and Culture, and the hard work and facilitation of William Cerbone, editor, rights and permissions manager, made this publication possible. My thanks as well to Edward W. Batchelder for his meticulous and thoughtful copyediting and his patience with my insisted-upon idiosyncrasies of rhetoric.

My gratitude to Union Theological Seminary, New York, where I did the research that formed the basis of this book. I will always remember with admiration several inspiring classes with Dr. Christopher Morse, Dietrich Bonhoeffer Professor Emeritus of Theology and Ethics, who taught an entire group of astonished and newly hopeful seminarians that "we were loved by a love that will never let us go." I also wish to thank the Very Rev. Dr. Maxym Lysack, of Christ the Saviour Orthodox Church in Ottawa, Canada, whose wisdom steadied and supported this work in its early stages, and who introduced me to St. Maximus the Confessor in so many ways.

My heartfelt gratitude to Margaret Klenck, M. Div., Jungian analyst, for her clinical clear sightedness, broad theoretical knowledge, abundant wisdom and full-hearted devotion to healing processes of the deepest order. *Sine qua non.*

I wish to especially acknowledge my formative academic mentors, particularly in having been supported in such a new interdisciplinary endeavor that has required an openness to the new—most generously given—on all their parts. My great gratitude to the Very Rev. Dr. John Behr, George Florovsky Distinguished Professor of Patristics at St. Vladimir's Orthodox Theological Seminary, for having shown interest in my nascent explorations of patristic theology and psychoanalytic theory long before I ever imagined I would become Orthodox, and for having been unremittingly kind and helpful since our first meeting. I also offer deeply appreciative thanks to Dr. Harry Wells Fogarty, Adjunct Professor of Psychiatry & Religion, Union Theological Seminary, New York, for many years of learning from his deep grasp of healing. His support has been invaluable and taught me a deeper meaning of the word "hospitality" than I had ever previously understood.

It is difficult to adequately thank the Very Rev. Dr. John Anthony McGuckin, Anne Marie and Bent Emil Nielsen Professor Emeritus of Late Antiquity and Byzantine Christian History at Union Theological Seminary, New York, and Dr. Ann Belford Ulanov, Christiane Brooks Johnson Memorial Professor Emerita of Psychiatry & Religion, Union Theological Seminary, New York. Each, in their own way, has stood as a beacon of hope that we are truly met by "the Existing One" in both the heights and the depths. To my thanks to Dr. McGuckin I also add gratitude to Mat. Eileen McGuckin, for many cups of tea and much laughter and support. To both of them, I am grateful for not only introducing me to Orthodoxy, but bringing the joy and beauty of it to life in so many ways. Finally, my deep thanks to Dr. Ulanov, whose wisdom, teaching and mentorship changed my life. I carry forward deepest gratitude to her for pointing to "the real" in her own work so that others might find courage to risk it, for welcoming tigers (and elephants), and for seeing what needed to be seen.

Lastly, I wish to thank my family. My love and gratitude to my brother Ashok, and to my mother, Karin, for their unremitting encouragement. And, to my late father Praveen, for teaching me to always try to face into the truth. Late in his life he wrote that ultimately scientific exploration and the search for spiritual truth naturally come together, as do "doing" and "being." I hope he might have seen his influence in this book, and I hope that he and the Church Fathers are having wonderful conversations.

NOTES

Introduction

1. By depth psychology, I mean the broad field that encompasses the various schools of psychoanalysis (Freudian, object-relations, etc.) as well as analytical psychology (Jungian). My primary interest in these fields is their investigation of what has come to be known as the contents and workings of the "unconscious," as opposed to simply conscious narratives and self-understandings.

2. See A. B. Ulanov, *The Feminine in Jungian Psychology and Christian Theology* (Evanston, Ill.: Northwestern University Press, 1971); A. B. Ulanov, *Receiving Woman: Studies in the Psychology and Theology of the Feminine* (Philadelphia: The Westminster Press, 1981); A. B. Ulanov, *The Unshuttered Heart: Opening to Aliveness/Deadness in the Self* (Nashville: Abingdon Press, 2007). I am introducing here an enormous topic, which will not itself be covered in depth so much as used to frame the focus of my discourse—the possible meeting spaces between Orthodox Christianity and depth psychology. Of particular note is also her discussion of the traditional acceptance of there being a "feminine mode of being" and then the more recent disavowal of such a mode because it became stiflingly "prescriptive" for women. She diagnoses the situation accordingly: "The problem is not . . . conceiving a mode of being human as feminine. Problems arise when the gap between the symbolic and concrete levels of existence collapses. Awareness of these images as symbols for ways of being in relation to reality rescues all of us by reinstating the symbolic as a viable order of being, not allowing to be taken literally and applied like a tourniquet to women and men" (Ulanov, *The Unshuttered Heart*, 94).

3. Ulanov, *The Feminine*, 142.

4. Ulanov, *The Feminine*, 168

5. Ulanov, *The Unshuttered Heart*.

6. Jung, however controversially, early on attributed the clarity and reasoning attributes of logos thought to masculine consciousness, and eros and the feeling and relational functions to feminine consciousness. See C. G. Jung, "The Syzygy: Anima and Animus," in *Aion: Researches into the Phenomenology of the Self*, ed. and trans. Gerhardt Adler and R. F. C. Hull, vol. 9 of *Collected Works* (Princeton: Princeton University Press, 1969).

7. Ulanov, *Receiving Woman*, 166–68.

8. "The feminine mode of being is not all cozy and cheery. It is a fierce force, a primordial one . . . [the feminine mode] had, for centuries and countless people, been projected upon the figure of Mary and contained there. In our century, many . . . have withdrawn this projection . . . Where has all this energy gone? . . . Mary is not just meek and mild, but vigorous, daring, aggressive, the mother of the great revolution, for it is she who bears into the world the One who ends all religions . . . where has all this feminine energy gone? . . . It has gone into the depths, I think, creating the new discipline of depth psychology. Women have had everything to do with this new discipline. They have been its materia prima. . . . An equally important fact about depth psychology is the enormous amount of energy devoted in it to feminine modes of being." A. B. Ulanov, *The Wisdom of the Psyche* (Cambridge, Mass.: Cowley Publications, 1988), 75–77.

9. See, e.g., St. Athanasius, *On the Incarnation*, ed. and trans. John Behr (Crestwood, N.Y.: St. Vladimir's Seminary Press, Popular Patristics Series, 2011), 4.

10. See also the Holy Anaphora of the Divine Liturgy of St. John Chrysostom:

> It is meet and right to sing of Thee, to bless Thee, to praise Thee, to give thanks to Thee and to worship Thee in every place of Thy dominion. For Thou art God ineffable, inconceivable, invisible, incomprehensible, ever-existing and eternally the same, Thou and Thine only-begotten Son and Thy Holy Spirit. *Thou it was who brought us from non-existence into being, and when we had fallen away, didst raise us up again, and didst not cease to do all things until Thou hadst brought us up to heaven* and hadst endowed us with "Thy Kingdom which is to come. For all these things we give thanks to Thee, and to Thine only-begotten Son and to Thy Holy Spirit; for all things of which we know and of which we know not, whether manifest or unseen; and we thank Thee for this liturgy which Thou hast found worthy to accept at our hands, though there stand by Thee thousands of archangels and hosts of angels, the Cherubim and the Seraphim, six-winged, many eyed, who soar aloft." (https://oca.org/orthodoxy/the

-orthodox-faith/worship/the-divine-liturgy/eucharistic-canon-anaphora; emphasis mine)

11. Romans 6:23, *The New Oxford Annotated Bible: New Revised Standard Version with the Apocrypha* (Oxford: Oxford University Press, 2007). Unless otherwise noted, all biblical citations are from this edition.

12. See Ulanov, *The Unshuttered Heart*. See also Christopher Bollas, *Forces of Destiny: Psychoanalysis and the Human Idiom* (London: Free Association Books, 1996).

13. Jung, *Aion*, par. 18; Donald W. Winnicott, "Ego Distortion in Terms of True and False Self," in *The Maturational Processes and the Facilitating Environment: Studies in the Theory of Emotional Development* (London: Karnac, 2007); Karen Horney, *Neurosis and Human Growth: The Struggle toward Self-Realization* (New York: W.W. Norton & Co., 1991).

14. I use the term "livingness" here as used by Ann Belford Ulanov: "Livingness is living in the reality of what is beyond the psyche, beyond social or physical conditions and constructions, beyond theories and religions. It is living in that reality which somehow, inexplicably, bestows itself upon us. . . . We feel glad, happy, fully alive. We touch the spirit by which we live. . . . If analysis works, it delivers us into this livingness. Symbolic discourse is not the goal. Reality is. After analysis, what? Livingness." Ann B. Ulanov, *Attacked by Poison Ivy: A Psychological Understanding* (Lake Worth, Fla.: Nicolas Hays Press, 2001), 161–63.

15. See, e.g., St. Athanasius, *On the Incarnation*, 4, and Ulanov, *Attacked by Poison Ivy*, 161–63.

16. John A. McGuckin, *The Orthodox Church: An Introduction to Its History, Doctrine, and Spiritual Culture* (West Sussex: Wiley-Blackwell, 2011), 277–79.

17. Ecumenical Patriarch Bartholomew, "The World As Sacrament—The Theological and Spiritual Vision of Creation: His All Holiness Ecumenical Patriarch Bartholomew," https://mospat.ru/en/2010/05/26/news19252/. I will discuss this at greater length in the next chapter.

18. This is not to confuse God's energies in creation with a pantheistic view of God as fully knowable in creation. The latter is not an Orthodox tenet. See, e.g., McGuckin, "The Doctrine of the Orthodox Church II: The Economy of Salvation," in *The Orthodox Church*, 182–276.

19. C. G. Jung, *Alchemical Studies*, ed. and trans. Gerhardt Adler and R. F. C. Hull, vol. 13 of *Collected Works* (Princeton: Princeton University Press, 1967), par. 75.

20. Alexander Schmemann, *Of Water and the Spirit: A Liturgical Study of Baptism* (Crestwood, N.Y.: St. Vladimir's Seminary Press, 1974), 61.

21. The Paschal Troparion: http://oca.org/orthodoxy/prayers/selected-liturgical-hymns.

22. Schmemann, *Of Water and the Spirit*, 62.

23. Schmemann, *Of Water and the Spirit*, 62.

24. Schmemann, *Of Water and the Spirit*, 62–63.

25. Schmemann, *Of Water and the Spirit*, 63.

26. Schmemann, *Of Water and the Spirit*, 62.

27. "Symbolic" here is used in Jolande Jacobi's description of C. G. Jung's use of the term, as presenting "an objective, visible meaning behind which an invisible, profounder meaning is hidden." The invisible meaning is also factual, but exists beyond our capacity for fully descriptive representation or apprehensions. See J. Jacobi, *Complex/Archetype/Symbol in the Psychology of C. G. Jung*, Bollingen Series (Princeton: Princeton University Press, 1959), 77.

28. Jacobi, *Complex/Archetype/Symbol*, 64.

29. It is also interesting to note here two very different examples of the interplay between fear of death and psychological well-being, which relate, in a way, respectively to the two main areas I will cover later, that of "being" and that of "eros": The first is that of Carl Jung who, in a videoed interview, proffered that when people live in shrinking fear of approaching death, their psychological well-being is diminished. In his study of the unconscious, he noted nothing in patients who were near death that spoke of an awareness of coming "death," as in termination of existence, but that rather the unconscious seemed to "disregard" impending death and to continue on in its unfolding life. He therefore suggested that a person live forward, in the face of death, because this was in keeping with what the natural deep psyche was suggesting. *BBC "Face to Face" Interview*, https://www.youtube.com/watch?v=FPGMWF7kU_8.

The second example, from the fourth century, is that of St. Gregory of Nyssa's recounting of his own violent grief in the face of the recent loss of his brother St. Basil, and the impending death of his beloved sister, St. Macrina, his "Teacher." He brings his grief to his sister, who at first accepts it and then begins to correct him. She queries the source of his grief, and comes to scold him for succumbing to despair about the immortality of the soul (a despair that he defends in wonderfully understandable terms, begging not to be forced to simply acquiesce to dogmatic teaching in the face of such experience of loss and abhorrence of death). Eventually she lengthily and skillfully guides him back to the hope embedded in Christian theology. See Gregory of Nyssa, *On the Soul and Resurrection*, trans. Catharine P. Roth (Crestwood, N.Y.: St. Vladimir's Seminary Press, 2002).

In light of a discussion of this text by J. Warren Smith, it is interesting to note that this hope entails the possibility of "recovering" the lost "object" (to use the psychological term)—his brother (and soon, his sister)—and hence death here is also interpreted as an "interruption" of eros, the desire for his beloved family, which gives rise to a kind of "relational" or "erotic" despair, and hence grief and suffering, until overcome by hope of reunion gained through correct theological understanding. See J. Warren Smith, *Passion and Paradise: Human and Divine Emotion in the Thought of Gregory of Nyssa* (New York: The Crossroad Publishing Company, 2004).

30. Origen, *Dialogue with Heraclides*, (SC 67. 70, II:17–19); St. Gregory of Nazianzus, *The First Letter to Cledonius the Presbyter, Epistle 101*, in *On God and Christ: Five Theological Orations and Two Letters to Cledonius*, trans. Lionel Wickham (Crestwood, N.Y.: St. Vladimir's Seminary Press, Popular Patristics Series, 2002), par. 5.

31. In Orthodoxy the preferred word for sacrament is *mysterion*. See, e.g., McGuckin, *The Orthodox Church*, 277–379.

32. E.g., Holy Anaphora in the Divine Liturgy of St. Basil; see http://oca.org /reflections/fr.-steven-kostoff/on-the-liturgy-of-saint-basil-the-great.

33. For an enlightening discussion of theological method, see the preface to John Behr, *The Mystery of Christ: Life in Death* (Crestwood, N.Y.: St. Vladimir's Seminary Press, 2006).

34. I owe the original seed of inspiration for this method to Fr. John Behr, who suggested running an Orthodox ontological claim against clinical case-studies to see if there was a correlation to be found (personal conversation in spring of 2013).

35. See, e.g., Christos Yannaras, *Relational Ontology*, trans. Norman Russell (Brookline, Mass.: Holy Cross Orthodox Press, 2011). I will discuss this again later.

36. See discussion of this topic in David Bentley Hart, *The Beauty of the Infinite: The Aesthetics of Christian Truth* (Grand Rapids, Mich.: William B. Eerdmans, 2003).

37. See 1 Corinthian 9:19–23.

38. See, e.g., discussion of St. Gregory of Palamas in Vasileios Thermos, *In Search of the Person: "True" and "False Self" According to Donald Winnicott and St. Gregory Palamas*, trans. Constantine Kokenes (Montreal: Alexander Press, 2002), 21–30.

39. I will discuss this again later in Chapter 3. See *Merriam-Webster Dictionary* http://www.merriam-webster.com/dictionary/ontology, accessed on March 30, 2015; see also G. C. Tympas, *Carl Jung and Maximus the Confessor on Psychic Development: The Dynamics between the "Psychological" and the "Spiritual"* (New York: Routledge, 2014).

40. Wilfred Bion, *Attention and Interpretation* (London: Karnac Books 1984); Winnicott, "Ego Distortion"; C. G. Jung, *Two Essays on Analytical Psychology*, ed. and trans. Gerhardt Adler and R. F. C. Hull, vol. 7 of *Collected Works*, par. 258.

41. See Maximos the Confessor, *Ambiguum 7*, and *Ambiguum 10*, in *On Difficulties in the Church Fathers: The Ambigua*, vol. 1, ed. and trans. Nicholas Constas (Cambridge, Mass.: Harvard University Press, 2014).

42. See, e.g., D. W. Winnicott, "Nothing at the Centre," "Fear of Breakdown," and "The Importance of the Setting in Meeting Regression in Psycho-Analysis," in *Psycho-Analytic Explorations*, ed. C. Winnicott, R. Shepherd, and M. Davis (Cambridge, Mass.: Harvard University Press, 1989); Ann Belford Ulanov, "Body" and "Aggression and Destructiveness," in *Finding Space: Winnicott, God, and Psychic Reality* (Louisville, Ky.: Westminster John Knox Press, 2005); McGuckin, *The Orthodox Church*, xi.

43. See Yannaras, *Relational Ontology*. Consider also John Zizioulas:

> By being person man recognizes being as a "presence" in an event of communion in which things are "present" in their catholicity and integrity as beings. Knowing emerges in this way only out of loving: love and truth become identical. But this can be possible only if nature and person are not in a relation of opposition . . . but the fallen state of creation with its implications of individuality inevitably results in a distance of contrast between beings . . . which makes knowing receive temporal priority over loving . . . knowing, therefore, begins, inevitably in this situation with a process of *gathering information* about the other being . . . and since this can only happen by way of relating all this to what I already know through a rational process, my first step towards communion with the other being takes place in my *rational* capacity. One can only love what one knows, since love comes from knowledge, we are told by Thomas Aquinas—except that this is our fallen situation and should not become part of our metaphysical anthropology, still less of our approach to Trinitarian theology . . . once the possibility of knowledge arises as independent of and prior to the act of communion (love) with the other being, it becomes possible for man to dissociate his thought from his act and thus falsify the event of truth. (John D. Zizioulas, *Communion and Otherness: Further Studies in Personhood and the Church*, ed. Paul McPartlan [London: T&T Clark, 2006], 230–31)

44. See, e.g., St. Athanasius, *On the Incarnation*, 8.

45. Zizioulas, *Communion and Otherness*, 57: "Unless we understand the world as a product of our consciousness, psychology and ontology must remain clearly distinct, and ontology must be given priority and ultimacy in our theological considerations."

46. I am partially indebted for this line of thinking to various reflections by Frederick Turner, *Rebirth of Value: Meditations on Beauty, Ecology, Religion and Education* (Albany: State University of New York Press, 1991).

47. See Sigmund Freud, *Totem and Taboo: Some Points of Agreement between the Mental Lives of Savages and Neurotics* (New York: W.W. Norton & Co., 1952).

48. Although I will explore this in later chapters, for example, looking at the work of Fr. John Behr on asceticism in St. Irenaeus, as well as the thought of St. Maximus the Confessor, I wish also at this point to express my gratitude for the ongoing sermons and lectures of Fr. Maxym Lysack, who has greatly helped clarify my thinking in this area. See, for example, his sermons *On the Disintegration of Life Through Sin* https://soundcloud.com/christthesaviouroc/2014-07-06-on -the-disintegration-of-life-through-sin; *The Rich Young Ruler Who Knew Too Much* https://soundcloud.com/christthesaviouroc/2014-12-14-the-rich-young-ruler -who-knew-too-much; *The Healed Leper Who Gave Thanks* https://soundcloud .com/christthesaviouroc/2014-12-21-the-healed-leper-who-gave-thanks.

49. See again Maximus, *Ambiguum 7* and *Ambiguum 10*.

50. See Maximus, *Ambiguum 7* and *Ambiguum 10*; Athanasius, *On the Incarnation*, 8; McGuckin, *The Orthodox Church* 187–91.

51. See forward by Bishop Kallistos Ware, in Matthew C. Steenberg, *Of God and Man: Theology as Anthropology from Irenaeus to Athanasius* (London: T&T Clark, 2009), vii.

52. For a quick and helpful overview, see John McGuckin, sections on "Atonement" and "Original Sin," in McGuckin, *Westminster Handbook to Patristic Theology* (Louisville, Ky.: Westminster John Knox Press, 2004).

53. For discussion of medical models and engagement with religious thought, see Gary B. Ferngren, *Medicine and Religion: A Historical Introduction* (Baltimore: Johns Hopkins University Press, 2014).

54. A heartening of example of this problem being recognized in a *New York Times* Op-Ed appeared as I was writing this: T. M. Luhrmann "Redefining Mental Illness": http://www.nytimes.com/2015/01/18/opinion/sunday/t-m-luhrmann -redefining-mental-illness.html.

55. See, e.g., psychoanalyst and author Michael Robbins's Letter to Editor, *New York Times*, August 13, 2014:

> The wisdom that, whatever the organic contribution, schizophrenia represents an unusual configuration of personality that arises from pathogenic childhood experiences and, at least in some instances, can be basically modified by an intensive psychoanalytically informed relationship has all but been lost. In the past, some psychiatric hospitals supported such treatment, but now that medicine and psychiatry have been co-opted by the pharmaceutical industry, the treatment standard is symptom suppression and superficial social readjustment. In the process, an important aspect of our humanism has been lost as well. (http://www.nytimes.com/2014/08/22 /opinion/two-psychiatrists-on-treating-schizophrenia.html)

56. Such a medical approach stands in sharp contrast to, for example, Carl Jung: "The art of letting things happen, action through non-action, letting go of

oneself as taught by Meister Eckhart, became for me the key that opens the door to the way. *We must be able to let things happen in the psyche.* For us, this is an art of which most people know nothing. Consciousness is forever interfering, helping, correcting, and negating, never leaving the psychic processes to grow in peace. It would be simple enough, if only simplicity were not the most difficult of all things." Jung, *Alchemical Studies*, par. 20; emphasis mine. It is also perhaps worth another paper to consider how this understanding of psychological process, what one might also call a kind of *kenosis*, might relate to the correlation between the Orthodox understanding of the Logos and the Taoist understanding of "the Way," as discussed in the work by Hieromonk Damascene, *Christ, the Eternal Tao* (Platina, Calif.: Valaam Books, 2012).

57. Ann Belford Ulanov, personal communication, 5/14/18.

58. I will discuss this again at greater length in Chapter 3.

59. Jean Claude Larchet, *Mental Disorders and Spiritual Healing: Teachings from the Early Christian East* (Hillsdale, N.Y.: Sophia Perennis, 2005); Jean Claude Larchet, *The Theology of Illness* (Crestwood, N.Y.: St. Vladimir's Seminary Press, 2002); Jean Claude Larchet, *Therapy of Spiritual Illness: An Introduction to the Ascetic Life of the Orthodox Church* (Montreal: Alexander Press, 2012).

60. Hierotheos Vlachos, *Orthodox Psychotherapy: The Science of the Fathers*, trans. Esther Williams (Levadhia, Greece: Birth of the Theotokos Monastery, 1994); Archbishop Chrysostomos *A Guide to Orthodox Psychotherapy: The Science, Theology, and Spiritual Practice behind It and Its Clinical Applications* (Lanham: University Press of America, 2007).

61. Alexis Trader, *Ancient Christian Wisdom and Aaron Beck's Cognitive Therapy: A Meeting of Minds* (New York: Peter Lang, 2011).

62. Stephen Muse, ed., *Raising Lazarus: Integral Healing in Orthodox Christianity* (Brookline, Mass.: Holy Cross Orthodox Press, 2004).

63. John Chirban, ed., *Personhood: Orthodox Christianity and the Connection between Body, Mind, and Soul* (Westport, Conn.: Bergin & Garvey, 1996); John Chirban, editor, *Sickness or Sin? Spiritual Discernment and Differential Diagnosis* (Brookline, Mass.: Holy Cross Orthodox Press, 2001).

64. G. C. Tympas, *Carl Jung and Maximus the Confessor*.

65. Thermos, *In Search of the Person*; Vasileios Thermos, *Thirst for Love and Truth: Encounters of Orthodox Theology and Psychological Science* (Montreal: Alexander Press, 2010).

66. Vladeta Jerotic, *Individuacija I (ili) Obozenje* (Belgrade: Ars Libri, 2010).

67. Pseudo-Macarius, *Fifty Spiritual Homilies and the Great Letter*, trans. and ed. George Maloney (Mahwah, N.J.: Paulist Press, 1992), 43:7:

> There is the example of the eye, little in comparison to all the members of the body and the pupil itself is small, yet it is a great vessel. For it sees in

one flash the sky, stars, sun, moon, cities, and other creatures. Likewise, these things are seen in one flash, they are formed and imaged in the small pupil of the eye. So it is with the mind toward the heart. And the heart itself is but a small vessel, yet there also are dragons and there are lions; there are poisonous beasts and all the treasures of evil. And there are rough and uneven roads; there are precipices. But there is also God, also the angels, the life and the kingdom, the light and the Apostles, the treasures of grace; there are all things. Just as a fog hangs over the whole earth, so that one does not see his fellow man, so is the darkness of this world covering all creation and humanity. Humans, obscured by the darkness, are in the night and spend their life in fearful places. Like a thick smoke in a one-room house, so is sin with its filthy thoughts. It settles down and creeps over the thoughts of the heart along with an infinite number of demons.

1. Psyche and Creation: Initial Reflections on Orthodox Theology and Depth Psychology

1. The Nicene-Constantinople Creed of 381.
2. Trisagion Prayer (often said as part of daily prayers):

O Heavenly King, the Paraclete, the Spirit of Truth, who are present everywhere, filling all things, Treasury of Good and Giver of Life, come and dwell in us, cleanse us of every stain, and save our souls, O Good One.
    Holy God, Holy Mighty, Holy Immortal—Have Mercy on Us (x 3)
    Glory to the Father and to the Son and to the Holy Spirit, Now and Ever, unto the Ages of Ages. Amen.
    All Holy Trinity, have mercy on us. Lord, forgive us our sins. Master, pardon our transgressions. Holy One, visit and heal our infirmities for your name's sake.
    Lord Have Mercy (x3)
    Glory to the Father and to the Son and to the Holy Spirit, now and ever, and to the ages of ages. Amen.
    Our Father in heaven, hallowed be your name. Your kingdom come. Your will be done, on earth as it is in heaven. Give us this day our daily bread, and forgive us our trespasses as we forgive those who trespass against us, and do not lead us into temptation, but deliver us from the evil one. (For Yours is the kingdom and the power and the glory, of the Father, and of the Son, and of the Holy Spirit, now and ever and to the ages of ages.) Amen.
    Lord have mercy. (x6)
    Glory to the Father, and to the Son, and to the Holy Spirit, now and ever, and to the ages of ages. Amen. (John A. McGuckin, trans. and ed.,

Prayer Book of the Early Christians [Brewster, Mass.: Paraclete Press, 2011], 8–9)

3. Holy Anaphora of the Divine Liturgy of St. Basil; see http://oca.org /reflections/fr.-steven-kostoff/on-the-liturgy-of-saint-basil-the-great.

4. St. Athanasius, *On the Incarnation*, ed. and trans. John Behr (Crestwood, N.Y.: St. Vladimir's Seminary Press, Popular Patristics Series, 2011), 4.

5. See the chapter on *Mysteria* in John A. McGuckin, *The Orthodox Church: An Introduction to Its History, Doctrine, and Spiritual Culture* (West Sussex: Wiley-Blackwell, 2011).

6. Patriarch Bartholomew, "The World As Sacrament—The Theological and Spiritual Vision of Creation: His All Holiness Ecumenical Patriarch Bartholomew" https://mospat.ru/en/2010/05/26/news19252/.

7. McGuckin, *The Orthodox Church*, 190.

8. See Maximos, *Ambiguum 7* and *Ambiguum 10* in *On Difficulties in the Church Fathers: The Ambigua*, vol. 1, ed. and trans. Nicholas Constas (Cambridge, Mass.: Harvard University Press, 2014).

9. Elizabeth Theokritoff, *Living in God's Creation: Orthodox Perspectives on Ecology* (Crestwood, N.Y.; St. Vladimir's Seminary Press, 2009), 54.

10. Theokritoff, *Living in God's Creation*.

11. See John A. McGuckin, "The Eros of Divine Beauty in St. Maximus the Confessor," in *The Concept of Beauty in Patristic and Byzantine Tradition*, ed. John A. McGuckin (New York: Scholars Press, 2015), 192. I will return to this as well in the section on St. Maximus in Chapter 2, and again at the end of Chapter 4.

12. St. Athanasius, *On the Incarnation*, 8.

13. St. Athanasius, *On the Incarnation*, 7.

14. St. Athanasius, *On the Incarnation*, 7 and 8.

15. Olivier Clement, *The Roots of Christian Mysticism* (Hyde Park, N.Y.: New City Press, 1993), 96.

16. This use of the term "true self" in Orthodox reflection should not be confused with the term as used by D. W. Winnicott, though there may be some overlap in manifestation. For more on personhood see, e.g., J. Chirban, ed., *Personhood: Orthodox Christianity and the Connection between Body, Mind, and Soul* (Westport, Conn.: Bergin & Garvey, 1996).

17. Ann Ulanov and Barry Ulanov, *Religion and the Unconscious* (Philadelphia: Westminster Press, 1975), 21–22.

18. See, e.g., Nikolai Velimirovich, *The Universe as Symbols and Signs: An Essay on Mysticism in the Eastern Church* (South Canaan, Pa.: St. Tikhon's Seminary Press, 2010).

19. McGuckin, *The Orthodox Church*, xi.

20. McGuckin, *The Orthodox Church*, 198.

21. Ulanov and Ulanov, *Religion and the Unconscious*, 22.

22. McGuckin, *The Orthodox Church*, 191.

23. See, e.g., Kallistos Ware, "'In the Image and Likeness': The Uniqueness of the Human Person," in Chirban, *Personhood*, 1–13.

24. McGuckin, *The Orthodox Church*, 190.

25. For an interesting modern pastoral meditation on this topic, particularly as it juxtaposes to Western Christian traditions, see Stephen Freeman, *Everywhere Present: Life in a One-Storey Universe* (Chesterton, Ind.: Conciliar Press, 2011).

26. C. G. Jung, cited in Ann Ulanov, *The Feminine in Christian Theology and Jungian Psychology* (Evanston, Ill.: Northwestern University Press, 1971), 7. A German wordplay, meaning "if it works, it is real."

27. For an important essay on morality as an internal process evolving out of relationship and environmental provision, rather than external imposition— religious or otherwise—see Donald W. Winnicott, "Morals and Education," in *The Maturational Processes and the Facilitating Environment* (London; Karnac, 2007). As he poignantly sums up: "This is the first principle of moral education, that *moral education is no substitute for love*" (97). And elsewhere: "There is more to be gained from love than from education [when] love means the totality of [care], that which facilitates maturational processes. It includes hate. Education means sanctions and the implantation of parental or social values *apart from* the child's inner growth or maturation . . . moral education follows naturally on the arrival of morality in the child by the natural developmental processes that good care facilitates" (100). This links well to what will be touched on in Chapter 4, whereby virtue, ontologically speaking, is acquired through participation in the *substance* of God and arises out of being and erotic attachment to the Good.

28. See, e.g., the chapters on "Salvation and the Call to Ascent," in McGuckin, *The Orthodox Church*.

29. Maximus, *Ambiguum 7*, 114–15 emphasis mine.

30. See, e.g., Ann B. Ulanov, "The Perverse and the Transcendent," in *The Functioning Transcendent: A Study in Analytical Psychology* (Wilmette, Ill.: Chiron Publications, 1996).

31. All figures and information concerning this case taken from Medard Boss, *Psychoanalysis and Daseinanalysis* (New York: Da Capo Press, 1982), 5–27.

32. Jung wrote about the importance of the truth and reliability of the "objective image" produced by the psyche, which gives face and context to psychic upheaval, and which may allow the person and the analyst to intentionally engage with the contents of the psyche as they seek to communicate themselves, and thereby avoid being overwhelmed by them. See C. G. Jung, *Memories, Dreams, Reflections*, ed. Aniela Jaffe, trans. Richard and Clara Winston (New York: Vintage

Books, 1989), 177. We will see this method of working with images again in Chapter 3 in a case study discussed by Ulanov.

33. Donald W. Winnicott, "Ego Distortion in Terms of True and False Self," in *The Maturational Processes and the Facilitating Environment: Studies in the Theory of Emotional Development* (London: Karnac, 2007).

34. Ann Belford Ulanov, personal communication, March, 2015.

35. Ulanov, personal communication, March, 2015.

36. "The 13th fairy I take to represent on a personal level an abyss of hurt of feelings for not being loved. But that experience of loss is itself lost, buried under fury and revenge. This makes for a knot not yet untied." Ann B. Ulanov, "The 13th Fairy," in *Knots and Their Untying: Essays on Psychological Dilemmas* (New Orleans: SpringJournal Inc., 2014), 10–11.

37. John Zizioulas, *Communion and Otherness: Further Studies in Personhood and the Church*, ed. Paul McPartlan (London: T&T Clark, 2006), 32–36.

38. Examples are Sigmund Freud, C. G. Jung, Donald W. Winnicott, Ann B. Ulanov, Anne-Marie Rizzuto, Neville Symington, and Vladeta Jerotic.

39. See discussion in Hierotheos Vlachos, *Orthodox Psychotherapy: The Science of the Fathers*, trans. Esther Williams (Levadhia, Greece: Birth of the Theotokos Monastery, 1994).

40. It is fair to say that for some depth psychologists, the two remain related. Jung, for example, wrote: "Many hundreds of patients have passed through my hands . . . among all my patients in the second half of life—that is to say, over thirty-five—there has not been one whose problem in the last resort was not that of finding a religious outlook on life. It is safe to say that every one of them fell ill because he had lost what the living religions of every age have given to their followers, and none of them has been really healed who did not regain his religious outlook." See C. G. Jung, "Psychotherapists or the Clergy," in *Psychology and Religion: West and East*, ed. and trans. Gerhardt Adler and R. F. C. Hull, vol. 11 of *Collected Works* (Princeton: Princeton University Press, 1969), par. 509.

41. *Consensum patrum* is a term used often to describe the collected teachings, witness, and agreements of the Church over the centuries.

42. See St. Maximus the Confessor, *Ad Thalassium 1*, and *Ad Thalassium 21*, in *On the Cosmic Mystery of Jesus Christ: Selected Writings from St. Maximus the Confessor*, trans. P. Blowers and R. L. Wilken (Crestwood, N.Y.: St. Vladimir's Seminary Press, 2003). See also Maximos, *Ambiguum 10* in *On Difficulties in the Church Fathers*.

43. For further discussion about the moral neutrality of the "appetites" and the importance of the mind that directs them, see John Behr, Chapter 5, "Glorify God in Your Body," in *The Mystery of Christ: Life in Death* (Crestwood, N.Y.: St. Vladimir's Seminary Press, 2006), 141–71.

44. Christos Yannaras, "Psychoanalysis and Orthodox Anthropology," in Chirban, *Personhood*, 88.

45. This brings up Maximus's concept of the natural will, *thelema*, and deliberative will, *gnome*. I will trace the outlines of his thought in this area in greater detail in Chapter 4.

46. For a pastoral discussion of this, see Fr. Maxym Lysack podcast "Seeing Our Sins in Humility," http://www.ancientfaith.com/video/lawofthespirit.

47. "This is how God does things. For his custom is to persuade, not to manhandle mortal men. What's forced has no reward, it seems to me. And in fact, when someone comes to the rescue against passions, he does not attack them always with painful things alone, but gives one cure for desire, another for misery, looking in kindness to save the one who struggles, concocting better remedies by the pleasant counsels of art." Gregory of Nazianzus, "On the Two Covenants and the Appearing of Christ," in *On God and Man: The Theological Poetry of St. Gregory of Nazianzus*, trans. Peter Gilbert (Crestwood, N.Y.: St. Vladimir's Seminary Press, 2001), 45–50.

48. See Sigmund Freud, *Beyond the Pleasure Principle*, trans. James Strachey (New York: W.W. Norton & Co, 1990); Melanie Klein, *Envy and Gratitude and Other Works 1946–1963* (New York: The Free Press, 1975); Winnicott, "Ego Distortion"; W. R. D. Fairbairn, *Psychoanalytic Studies of the Personality* (London: Routledge, 1992); Harry Guntrip, *Schizoid Phenomena, Object Relations, and the Self* (London: Karnac, 2001).

49. This will be discussed in detail in Chapter 4.

50. See, e.g., interview with Bishop Kallistos Ware on women's ordination and same-sex unions: http://www.ancientfaith.com/podcasts/illuminedheart /metropolitan_kallistos_ware_on_gender.

51. See, e.g., Ann B. Ulanov "Two Sexes," in Philip Turner, ed., *Men and Women: Sexual Ethics in Turbulent Times* (Cambridge, Mass.: Cowley Publications, 1989).

52. John Behr, "A Note on the Ontology of Gender," *St. Vladimir's Theological Quarterly* 42, no. 3–4 (1998), 363–67.

53. This trend, culturally, extends beyond biological sexual differentiation to encompass "modalities of being" as correlated to masculine and feminine as well. As mentioned in the preface, there is an interesting perspective on this from Ulanov:

> A . . . temptation . . . is to throw out both the masculine and feminine modalities of being and knowing in favor of a unisexual androgyne. This alternative represents the danger of regression to a pre-sexual, disembodied, ethereal identity, where the whole issue of sexual differentiation has not yet emerged into awareness and is not allowed to do so. Instead of integrating

two modalities of being into a fresh and unique personality of man or woman, we lose the clear definition of either to a blurry indefiniteness that masquerades as man-woman. That sort of identity differs significantly from the strong male who possesses large feminine sensibilities, or the vibrant female who manifests vigorous masculine qualities. The men and women who possess their contrasexual sides confidently and clearly stand out from the shapeless unisexual as flexible and open, large in their identities as men or women. In contrast, the androgyne exudes an indefiniteness that on closer inspection often turns out to be an as yet uprooted identity that cannot endure the stresses of sexual commitment. In psychological terms we are talking about the difference between a pre-Oedipal and a post-Oedipal personality. (Ann B. Ulanov, *Receiving Woman: Studies in the Psychology and the Theology of the Feminine* [Philadelphia: The Westminster Press, 1981], 166–67)

There is a difference between transcending sexual differentiation and abolishing it out of fear of all it entails.

54. My personal stance, borne only out of my own experience, is that there is significance and there is a real difference, and that this difference and the sparks that jump across the "otherness" of it are life-giving. There are risks in affirming such difference, but there are also risks in diminishing it. See Ulanov, who writes: "A woman . . . from the time of childhood and all through her education, has had to develop both masculinity and femininity. This has been one of the opportunities our Western culture offers the female, but not without serious complications, for in her conscious development according to patriarchal values there has also been in her a self-estrangement from her instinctive femininity . . . The self for the woman is, of course, feminine." Ulanov, *The Feminine*, 269.

55. Behr, "A Note," 364–65.

56. Behr, "A Note," 365.

57. Valerie Karras, cited in Behr, "A Note," 369.

58. My own critique of some of the work of Evdokimov, which in large parts is also very beautiful, is not the allocation of semiontological basis to sexual differentiation, but that his description of the feminine is at times so close in reading to Jung's notion of the "anima" of the masculine as to make one uncertain as to whether his feminine has a rooted life of her own, or exists mainly as a projection of the masculine. See Paul Evdokimov, *Woman and the Salvation of the World: A Christian Anthropology on the Charisms of Women*, trans. Anthony P. Gythiel (Crestwood, N.Y.: St. Vladimir's Seminary Press, 1994); Paul Evdokimov, *The Sacrament of Love: The Nuptial Mystery in the Light of the Orthodox Tradition*, trans. Anthony P. Gythiel and Victoria Steadman (Crestwood, N.Y.: St. Vladimir's Sem-

inary Press, 1985). While such projections may elicit an indignant disavowal of the masculine, or else an identification with it in order not to be subsumed into inequality, the territory I believe to be in greater need of exploration is that of the feminine qua feminine. I am reminded of Ulanov citing Rilke: "Some day there will be girls and women whose name will no longer signify merely an opposite of the masculine, but something in itself, something that makes one think, not of any complement and limit, but only of life and existence: the feminine human being" (Ulanov, *The Feminine*, 137). Ulanov cites Castillejo in affirming that a woman's spirit is clearly feminine, not masculine (*The Feminine*, 336). There is a spiritual life of the feminine. And this is true, even as it is also true that "*nevertheless in the Lord woman is not independent of man nor man of woman.*" (I Cor 11:11, cited in Ulanov, *The Feminine*, 287). The ideal in marriage, then, becomes not a polarization of masculine and feminine, or a reduction into approved "roles," but a *polarity* of masculine and feminine that is person to person, within which life is lived "from the inside out," not in terms of abstract expectations but of inner relatedness to the other: "One is simply oneself alone in polarization; in polarity one cannot be oneself, except in and out of the love one shares" (Ulanov, *The Feminine*, 302).

59. Behr, "A Note," 369.

60. Behr, "A Note," 370.

61. Behr, "A Note," 370.

62. Behr, "A Note," 371.

63. See, e.g., St. Gregory of Nazianzus, *Theological Oration 37*, discussed by McGuckin: "Why, he asks, does Roman law punish the female adulteress with severe penalties, but a man who commits adultery has no penalty under the law? The answer is that the law was obviously made by men. 'I do not accept this law. I cannot approve this custom,' Gregory says. It is a legislation that is unjustly hard on women and children, who suffer from it while men are related with impunity. Such a law cannot reflect the God who is equitably even-handed to all." John A. McGuckin, *Saint Gregory of Nazianzus: An Intellectual Biography* (Crestwood, N.Y.: St. Vladimir's Seminary Press, 2001), 333–34. See further Gregory of Nazianzus, *Theological Oration 37, VI:* "There is one maker of man and woman . . ." http://www.newadvent.org/fathers/310237.htm.

64. See, e.g., Maximus, *Ambiguum 7*; *Ambiguum 10*; *Opuscule 3*, in Andrew Louth, *Maximus the Confessor* (London: Routledge, 1996).

2. "That Which Is Not Assumed Is Not Healed"

1. John Behr, *The Way to Nicaea: The Formation of Christian Theology*, vol. 1 (Crestwood, N.Y.: St. Vladimir's Seminary Press, 2001), 73.

2. Behr, *The Way to Nicaea*, 73–75.

3. Behr, *The Way to Nicaea*, 75; emphasis mine.

4. Origen, *Dialogue with Heraclides* (SC 67. 70, II:17–19); St. Gregory of Nazianzus, *The First Letter to Cledonius the Presbyter, Epistle 101*, in *On God and Christ: Five Theological Orations and Two Letters to Cledonius*, trans. Lionel Wickham (Crestwood, N.Y.: St. Vladimir's Seminary Press, Popular Patristics Series, 2002), par. 5; emphasis mine.

5. St. Gregory, *Epistle 101*, par. 5. A broader excerpt:

> Whoever has set his hope on a human being without mind is actually mindless himself and unworthy of being saved in his entirety. The unassumed is the unhealed, but what is united with God is also being saved. Had half of Adam fallen, what was assumed and is being saved would have been half too; but if the whole fell he is united to the whole of what was born and is being saved wholly. They are not, then, to begrudge us our entire salvation or to fit out a Savior with only bones and sinews and the picture of a human being. If the human being is without a soul—why, that is what the Arians say too, intending to apply the suffering to the Godhead, the mover of the body also being the sufferer! If he has a soul, but if he has no mental consciousness, can he be human?

6. See also St. Gregory, "Against Apollinarius," Poem 1.1.10 "De Incarnatione, adversus Apollinarium," in *On God and Man: The Theological Poetry of St. Gregory of Nazianzus*, trans. Peter Gilbert (Crestwood, N.Y.: St. Vladimir's Seminary Press, Popular Patristics Series, 2001), (PG 37, 464–70), par. 468.

7. St. Gregory, *Epistle 101*, par. 5, and also St. Gregory, "Against Apollinarius."

8. See, e.g., St. Irenaeus, *Against Heresies*, in Alexander Roberts and James Donaldson, eds., *The Writings of Irenaeus: Against Heresies and Fragments* (Berkeley: Apocrophile Press, 2007), 3.19; St. Athanasius, *On the Incarnation*, ed. and trans. John Behr (Crestwood, N.Y.: St. Vladimir's Seminary Press, Popular Patristics Series, 2011), 54

9. See, e.g., Maximus, *Ambiguum 7* in *On Difficulties in the Church Fathers: The Ambigua*, vol. 1, ed. and trans. Nicholas Constas (Cambridge, Mass.: Harvard University Press, 2014); McGuckin, *The Orthodox Church: An Introduction to Its History, Doctrine, and Spiritual Culture* (West Sussex: Wiley-Blackwell, 2011), 189; Behr, *The Way to Nicaea*, 199.

10. St. Gregory, *Epistle 101*.

11. McGuckin, "Irenaeus," in *Westminster Handbook to Patristic Theology* (Louisville, Ky.: Westminster John Knox Press, 2004), 185.

12. For an overview of Irenaeus's use of this concept, see John Behr, *Irenaeus of Lyons: Identifying Christianity* (Oxford: Oxford University Press, 2013). In some ways, this is an interesting theological parallel to the use of empathy as outlined

by Heinz Kohut, in the healing of narcissism. See Heinz Kohut, *The Analysis of the Self: A Systematic Approach to the Psychoanalytic Treatment of Narcissistic Personality Disorders* (Chicago: University of Chicago Press, 1971).

13. Irenaeus, *Against Heresies*, 3.18.17, cited in Behr, *Irenaeus*, 280.

14. D. V. Twomey and D. Krausmuller, eds., *Salvation According to the Fathers of the Church: The Proceedings of the Sixth International Patristic Conference* (Maynooth/Belfast: Four Courts Press, 2010), 28.

15. McGuckin, "Irenaeus," in *Westminster Handbook*, 185.

16. Twomey and Krausmuller, *Salvation*, 28.

17. Hans Urs von Balthasar, *The Glory of the Lord: A Theological Aesthetics*, vol. 2 (San Francisco: Ignatius Press, 2004), 68; emphasis mine.

18. Von Balthasar, cited in Twomey and Krausmuller, *Salvation*, 27.

19. Behr, *Irenaeus*, 273.

20. Von Balthasar, cited in Twomey and Krausmuller, *Salvation*, 27.

21. Basil Studer, *Trinity and Incarnation: The Faith of the Early Church*, Trans. Matthias Westerhoff, ed. Andrew Louth (London: T&T Clark, 1993), 55.

22. Behr, *The Way to Nicaea*, 22. For those familiar with the works of Carl Jung and his in-depth study of Gnosticism, it may be helpful to note here that early Gnosticism may well have described and intuited movements of the psyche, and projected that interiority onto the cosmos. As a phenomenological and symbolic description of a psychological system, it can be put in interesting conversation with Orthodox theology. As a competing theological and metaphysical system, it is incompatible and—I would argue—does not offer much hope for psychology either as the psyche belongs to the creation from which liberation, not transfiguration, is ultimately sought.

23. Twomey and Krausmuller, *Salvation*, 27.

24. Twomey and Krausmuller, *Salvation*, 27; emphasis mine.

25. Studer, *Trinity and Incarnation*, 57.

26. See Behr, *Irenaeus*, e.g., 245–57.

27. Behr, *Irenaeus*, 252.

28. Irenaeus, *Against Heresies*, 5.6.1., cited in Behr, *Irenaeus*, 258.

29. Behr, *Irenaeus*, 255.

30. Irenaeus, *Against Heresies*, 4.20.7, cited in Behr, *Irenaeus*, 257.

31. Gustaf Aulen, *Christus Victor: An Historical Study of the Three Main Types of the Idea of the Atonement* (Eugene, Ore.: Wipf & Stock, 2003), 25.

32. Aulen, *Christus Victor*, 31–33.

33. Aulen, *Christus Victor*, see 31–33.

34. Aulen, *Christus Victor*, 55; emphasis mine.

35. St. Irenaeus, *Against Heresies*, 5.

36. John A. McGuckin, ed., *The Westminster Handbook to Origen* (Louisville, Ky.: Westminster John Knox Press, 2004), ix; see "Origenist Crises."

37. McGuckin, *The Westminster Handbook to Origen*; see "Disciples of Origen."

38. McGuckin, *The Westminster Handbook to Origen*, ix.

39. Studer, *Trinity and Incarnation*, 78.

40. Behr, *The Way to Nicaea*, 175.

41. McGuckin, *The Westminster Handbook to Patristic Theology*, 208.

42. McGuckin, *The Westminster Handbook to Patristic Theology*, 207.

43. Studer, *Trinity and Incarnation*, 81.

44. C. Kannengiesser, "Christology," in McGuckin, *The Westminster Handbook to Origen*, 74. See also J. O'Keefe, "Allegory," in McGuckin, *The Westminster Handbook to Origen*, 49–50.

45. Kannengiesser, "Christology," in McGuckin, *The Westminster Handbook to Origen*, 82.

46. Kannengiesser, "Christology," in McGuckin, *The Westminster Handbook to Origen*, 76.

47. Studer, *Trinity and Incarnation*, 82; emphasis mine.

48. Studer, *Trinity and Incarnation*, 85–86.

49. For further discussion of the immense importance of free will in Origen, see J. O'Leary, "Grace," in McGuckin, *The Westminster Handbook to Origen*, 114–17.

50. Kannengiesser, "Christology," in McGuckin, *The Westminster Handbook to Origen*, 77.

51. Kannengiesser, "Christology," in McGuckin, *The Westminster Handbook to Origen*, 77.

52. Kannengiesser, "Christology," in McGuckin, *The Westminster Handbook to Origen*, 77.

53. Origen, *HomJer* 9.1, cited in Behr, *The Way to Nicaea*, 176.

54. Behr, *The Way to Nicaea*, 176.

55. Nathan Kwok-kit Ng, *The Spirituality of Athanasius: A Key for Proper Understanding of This Important Church Father* (Bern: Peter Lang, 2001), 52.

56. Ng, *The Spirituality of Athanasius*, 52

57. Khaled Anatolios, *Athanasius* (London: Routledge, 2004), 42.

58. Anatolios, *Athanasius* (London: Routledge, 2004), 42.

59. See Behr, *Irenaeus*, 307.

60. Anatolios, *Athanasius*, 40.

61. St. Athanasius, *On the Incarnation*.

62. Athanasius, *On the Incarnation*, 1.

63. McGuckin, in Twomey and Krausmuller, *Salvation*, 38; emphasis mine.

64. Athanasius, *On the Incarnation*, 3; emphasis mine.

65. Athanasius, *On the Incarnation*, 4.

66. Athanasius, *On the Incarnation*, 5.

67. Athanasius, *On the Incarnation*, 3.

68. Athanasius, *On the Incarnation*, 7.

69. Athanasius, *On the Incarnation*, 9.

70. McGuckin in Twomey and Krausmuller, *Salvation*, 38; emphasis mine.

71. Athanasius, *On the Incarnation*, 21.

72. Athanasius, *On the Incarnation*, 12.

73. Athanasius, *On the Incarnation*, 12.

74. John Behr, *The Nicene Faith: Part One True God of True God* (Crestwood, N.Y.: St. Vladimir's Seminary Press, 2004), 73.

75. Athanasius, *On the Incarnation*, 13.

76. Athanasius, *On the Incarnation*, 13.

77. Athanasius, *On the Incarnation*, 20, citing Hebrews 2:14.

78. See Athanasius, *On the Incarnation*, 27.

79. Athanasius, *On the Incarnation*, 25.

80. Athanasius, *On the Incarnation*, 25.

81. Athanasius, *On the Incarnation*, 14. This is reminiscent of St. Irenaeus, who says also:

> Or what medical man, anxious to heal a sick person, would prescribe in accordance with the patient's whims, and not according to the requisite medicine? But that the Lord came as the physician of the sick, He does Himself declare, saying, "They that are whole need not a physician, but they that are sick; I came not to call the righteous but sinners to repentance." How then shall the sick be strengthened, or how shall sinners come to repentance? Is it by persevering in the very same courses? Or, on the contrary, is it by undergoing a great change and reversal of their former mode of living, by which they have brought upon themselves no slight amount of sickness, and many sins? But ignorance, the mother of all these, is driven out by knowledge. Wherefore the Lord used to impart knowledge to His disciples, by which also it was His practice to heal those who were suffering, and to keep back sinners from sin. (Irenaeus, *Against Heresies*, 3.5.2)

82. Vladimir Kharlamov, "Rhetorical Application of Theosis," in *Partakers of Divine Nature: The History and Development of Deification in the Christian Traditions*, ed. Michael J. Christensen and Jeffrey A. Wittung (Grand Rapids, Mich.: Baker Academic, 2007), 122.

83. Kharlamov, "Rhetorical Application," 122.

84. Norman Russell, *The Doctrine of Deification in the Greek Patristic Tradition* (New York: Oxford University Press, 2004), 172.

85. Athanasius, *On the Incarnation*, 30.

86. Behr, *The Way to Nicaea*, 199.

87. Athanasius, *On the Incarnation*, 54.

88. McGuckin, "Gregory of Nazianzus," in McGuckin, *The Westminster Handbook to Patristic Theology*, 151.

89. McGuckin, "Gregory of Nazianzus," 152.

90. John McGuckin, *St. Gregory of Nazianzus: An Intellectual Biography* (Crestwood, N.Y.: St. Vladimir's Seminary Press, 2001), 390.

91. McGuckin, *St. Gregory of Nazianzus*, 390.

92. McGuckin, *St. Gregory of Nazianzus*, 390.

93. McGuckin, *St. Gregory of Nazianzus*, 391.

94. McGuckin, *St. Gregory of Nazianzus*, 391.

95. McGuckin, *St. Gregory of Nazianzus*, 391.

96. McGuckin, *St. Gregory of Nazianzus*, 391.

97. St. Gregory, *Epistle 101*, 9.

98. St. Gregory, *Epistle 101*, 9.

99. McGuckin, *St. Gregory of Nazianzus*, 393.

100. St. Gregory of Nazianzus, *Theological Oration 37, I. and II.* Translation taken from: http://www.newadvent.org/fathers/310237.htm.

101. McGuckin, *St. Gregory of Nazianzus*, 390.

102. McGuckin, *St. Gregory of Nazianzus*, 393.

103. McGuckin, *St. Gregory of Nazianzus*, 393.

104. Andrew Louth, *Maximus the Confessor*, 3.

105. John McGuckin, "The Eros of Divine Beauty in St. Maximus the Confessor," in *The Concept of Beauty in Patristic and Byzantine Tradition*, ed. John A. McGuckin (New York: Scholars Press, 2015).

106. See Maximos the Confessor, *Ambiguum 41*, in *On Difficulties in the Church Fathers: The Ambigua*, vol. 2, ed. and trans. Nicholas Constas (Cambridge, Mass.: Harvard University Press, 2014); Lars Thunberg, *Microcosm and Mediator: The Theological Anthropology of Maximus the Confessor* (Chicago: Open Court Publishing, 1995).

107. Louth, *Maximus the Confessor*, 72.

108. Cited in Louth, *Maximus the Confessor*, 49.

109. See Maximus, *Ambiguum 41*.

110. See, e.g., Maximus the Confessor, *The First Century on Various Texts*, par. 35, in *The Philokalia: The Complete Text*, compiled by St. Nikodimos of the Holy Mountain and St. Makarios of Corinth, vol. 2, trans. and ed. G. E. H. Palmer, Philip Sherrard, and Kallistos Ware (London: Faber and Faber, 1981), 172.

111. The seventh-century controversy over whether Christ had one will or two wills. For a brief and helpful synopsis, see Louth, *Maximus the Confessor*, 12–18.

112. See Maximus, *Opuscule 3*, in Louth, *Maximus the Confessor* (London: Routledge, 1996),

113. McGuckin, "The Eros of Divine Beauty," 191.

114. McGuckin, "The Eros of Divine Beauty," 191.

115. McGuckin, "The Eros of Divine Beauty," 191–92.

116. Maximus, *Five Centuries on Various Texts*, in *Philokalia*, 91.

117. Louth, *Maximus the Confessor*, 18.

118. Louth, *Maximus the Confessor*, 18.

119. McGuckin, "The Eros of Divine Beauty," 174.

120. See the blog of Fr. Stephen Freeman: Glory to God for All Things, http://blogs.ancientfaith.com/glory2godforallthings/.

121. McGuckin, "Atonement," in McGuckin, *The Westminster Handbook to Patristic Theology*, 38.

122. See Rita Nakashima Brock and Rebecca Ann Parker, *Proverbs of Ashes: Violence, Redemptive Suffering, and the Search for What Saves Us* (Boston: Beacon Press, 2002).

123. Twomey and Krausmuller, *Salvation*, 17.

124. Anaphora of the Divine Liturgy of St. John Chrysostom. This paradox of this phrase was first brought to my attention by Fr. John Behr, in person class communication, spring 2013.

125. Athanasius, *On the Incarnation*, 24.

126. Studer, *Trinity and Incarnation*, 49.

127. Athanasius, *On the Incarnation*, 27.

128. See Aulen, *Christus Victor*.

129. It is also interesting to consider, from a Jungian perspective, both the mandala aspect and the quaternity aspect of its formation. The centrality of this theology even at a social level can perhaps also be gleaned from the Byzantine coins, possibly from the eleventh century, pictured below (Figure 8; http://www.anythinganywhere.com/commerce/coins/coinpics/byz-sb1825-1.jpg).

130. See Charles E. Brown, "The Atonement: Healing in Postmodern Society," *Interpretation* 53, no. 1 (Jan. 1999), 34–43.

131. There have been a number of recent studies on the topic of deification. Two classic studies are those of Norman Russell, *The Doctrine of Deification in the Greek Patristic Tradition* (Oxford: Oxford University Press, 2004) and Jules Gross, *The Divinization of the Christian According to the Church Fathers*, trans. Paul A. Onica (Anaheim: A & C Press, 2002). More recently, and not limited to patristic or Orthodox perspectives, see Michael Christensen and Jeffery Wittung, eds., *Partakers of the Divine Nature: The History and Development of Deification in Christian Traditions* (Grand Rapids, Mich.: Baker Academic, 2007), and Veli Matti-Karkainnen, *One with God: Salvation as Deification and Justification* (Liturgical Press, 2004).

132. See Gross, *The Divinization of the Christian* and Russell, *The Doctrine of Deification*.

Figure 8. Byzantine coins.

133. Dionysius the Areopagite, *EH 1.3*, cited in Russell, *The Doctrine of Deification*, 1.

134. Russell, *The Doctrine of Deification*, 1.

135. Russell, *The Doctrine of Deification*, 1.

136. Russell, *The Doctrine of Deification*, 2.

137. Russell, *The Doctrine of Deification*, 3.

138. Russell, *The Doctrine of Deification*, 163.

139. Although I have used a different translation throughout this work, in this instance I use an older version as this particular rendering may be more immediately familiar to those who have only come across St. Athanasius in English. Taken from *On the Incarnation*, Ch. 8, par. 54/93.

140. St. Athanasius, *On the Incarnation*, Ch. 8, par. 54/93.

141. See T. F. Torrance, "Karl Barth and the Latin Heresy," *Scottish Journal of Theology* 39 (1986): 461–82.

142. Gross, *The Divinization of the Christian*, 224.

143. Russell, *The Doctrine of Deification*, 15.

144. Christensen, "The Problem, Promise and Process of Theosis," in Christensen and Wittung, *Partakers of the Divine Nature*.

145. Christensen, "The Problem," 24.

146. Christensen, "The Problem," 25.

147. Christensen, "The Problem," 25

148. Christensen, "The Problem," 25

149. Christensen, "The Problem," 26.

150. Christensen, "The Problem," 26.

151. Christensen, "The Problem," 27.

152. Christensen, "The Problem," 27.

153. Vladimir Lossky, *The Mystical Theology of the Eastern Church* (London: James Clarke & Co., 1957), 198.

154. Lossky, *The Mystical Theology*, 204–5.

155. Lossky, *The Mystical Theology*, 204.

156. Lossky, *The Mystical Theology*, 207.

157. Andrew Louth, "The Place of Theosis in Orthodox Theology," in Christensen and Wittung, *Partakers of the Divine Nature*, 39.

158. Louth, "The Place of Theosis," 39; emphasis mine. It is also interesting to consider in what sense the psychoanalytic "adventure" involves an "ascetic" struggle in the discipline of tolerating uncomfortable feelings and changes, opening to new growth, to otherness, to repentance and confession, although in a very different setting. There is a discipline involved in being willing to be transformed there, as well. I touch on this again in Chapter 3.

159. Louth, "The Place of Theosis," 38.

160. Louth, "The Place of Theosis," 37.

161. Lossky, *Mystical Theology*, 200–1.

162. See, e.g., Myk Habets, "Reforming Theosis," in Stephen Finlan and Vladimir Kharlamov, eds., *Theosis: Deification in Christian Theology* (Eugene, Ore.: Wipf & Stock, 2006).

163. Russell, *The Doctrine of Deification*, 312

164. Russell, *The Doctrine of Deification*, 318.

165. Russell, *The Doctrine of Deification*, 318.

166. Russell, *The Doctrine of Deification*, 318.

167. Russell, *The Doctrine of Deification*, 319.

168. Russell, *The Doctrine of Deification*, 319; emphasis mine.

169. Yannaras, "Psychoanalysis and Orthodox Anthropology," in *Personhood: Orthodox Christianity and the Connection between Body, Mind, and Soul*, ed. John Chirban (Westport, Conn.: Bergin & Garvey, 1996), 85.

170. Yannaras, "Psychoanalysis," 85.

171. Yannaras, "Psychoanalysis," 85.

172. Yannaras, "Psychoanalysis," 85.

3. An Ontology of Healing?

1. See Merriam-Webster Dictionary http://www.merriam-webster.com /dictionary/ontology, accessed on March 30, 2015; see also G. C. Tympas, *Carl Jung and Maximus the Confessor on Psychic Development: The Dynamics between the "Psychological" and the "Spiritual"* (New York: Routledge, 2014), 5.

2. Tympas, *Carl Jung and Maximus the Confessor*, 5.

3. Tympas, *Carl Jung and Maximus the Confessor*, 5.

4. Tympas, *Carl Jung and Maximus the Confessor*, 5, and Nikolaos Loudovikos, *A Eucharistic Ontology: Maximus the Confessor's Eschatological Ontology of Being as Dialogical Reciprocity*, trans. Elizabeth Theokritoff (Brookline, Mass.: Holy Cross Orthodox Press, 2010), 2–4.

5. Loudovikos, *A Eucharistic Ontology*, 2–10. This unity without loss of distinction is a theme that runs throughout the work of St. Maximus himself; see *Ambiguum 7*, in *On Difficulties in the Church Fathers: The Ambigua*, vol. 1, ed. and trans. Nicholas Constas (Cambridge: Harvard University Press, 2014), and *Ambiguum 41*, in *On Difficulties in the Church Fathers: The Ambigua*, vol. 2.

6. Vasileios Thermos, "I Forgive Therefore I Am: Forgiveness as Fullness of Life," in *Thirst for Love and Truth: Encounters of Orthodox Theology and Psychological Science* (Montreal: Alexander Press, 2010).

7. McGuckin, *The Orthodox Church*, 189.

8. McGuckin, *The Orthodox Church*, 189.

9. McGuckin, *The Orthodox Church*, 189.

10. See Maximus, *Ambiguum 10*, on "being," "well-being," "eternal well-being." See also Maximus, *Opuscule 3*, in Andrew Louth, *Maximus the Confessor* (London: Routledge, 1996).

11. See, e.g., M.C. Steenberg, *Of God and Man: Theology as Anthropology from Irenaeus to Athanasius* (London: T&T Clark, 2009), 38.

12. Maximus the Confessor, *Ad Thalassium*, in *On the Cosmic Mystery of Jesus Christ: Selected Writings from St. Maximus the Confessor*, trans. P. Blowers and R. L. Wilken (Crestwood, N.Y.: St. Vladimir's Seminary Press, 2003), 2.

13. See again Maximus, *Ambiguum 7*.

14. Elizabeth Theokritoff, *Living in God's Creation: Orthodox Perspectives on Ecology* (Crestwood, N.Y.; St. Vladimir's Seminary Press, 2009), 54.

15. See Irenaeus, *Against Heresies*, Book 4.37–39, with my gratitude to Fr. John Behr for first drawing my attention to these important passages.

16. See, e.g., Maximus, *Opuscule 3*, 192–98.

17. Christos Yannaras, "Psychoanalysis and Orthodox Anthropology," in John Chirban, *Personhood: Orthodox Christianity and the Connection Between Mind, Body, and Soul* (Westport, Conn.: Bergin & Garvey, 1996), 88.

18. See Ann Belford Ulanov, "The Perils of Individuation," in *Knots and Their Untying: Essays on Psychological Dilemmas* (New Orleans: SpringJournal Inc., 2014).

19. Ulanov, "The Perils."

20. See, e.g., Anne McGuire, *Skin Disease: A Message from the Soul* (London: Free Association Books, 2004); Joyce McDougall *Theaters of the Body: A Psychoanalytic Approach to Psychosomatic Illness* (New York: W.W. Norton & Co., 1989); Ulanov, *Attacked by Poison Ivy: A Psychological Understanding* (Lake Worth, Fla.: Nicolas Hays Press, 2001).

21. This connection, by the way, was not lost on the ancients. St. Maximus also noted a correlation between the interior state, in his case observing the soul, and dreams: "Once the soul starts to feel its own good health, the images in its dreams are also calm and free from passion" (Maximus the Confessor, *The First Century on Love*, in *The Philokalia: The Complete Text*, compiled by St. Nikodimos of the Holy Mountain and St. Makarios of Corinth, vol. 2, trans. and ed. G. E. H. Palmer, Philip Sherrard, and Kallistos Ware [London: Faber and Faber, 1981], 89).

22. Ulanov writes:

> In order to survive we build up those self-states uninfected by the hurt and dissociate the traumatized self-state. We can use a false forgiveness to wall off the traumatized state. . . . If we hop over the hate that marks something terrible that happened, we treat the part of ourselves to which it happened as the Disappeared, a part that vanishes from view and cannot be found. . . . The person who cannot forgive . . . weighed down by hate of what was done to them, witnesses to what is truly, really happening. . . . Such rage makes the Disappeared appear again. (Ulanov, "What Do We Do If We Cannot Forgive?" in *Knots*, 193–94)

23. See Vasileios Thermos's discussion of Winnicott, and the "trace" of ontological truth in the necessity of forgiveness in order to live out of the fullness of being in communion, rather than as a moral or psychological "imperative" in Thermos, "I Forgive Therefore I Am," in *Thirst for Love and Truth*.

24. See, e.g., Melanie Klein, *Envy and Gratitude and Other Works 1946–1963* (New York: The Free Press, 1975).

25. See Harry Guntrip, *Schizoid Phenomena, Object Relations, and the Self* (London: Karnac Books, 2001), 90–97. I will explore the theories of Guntrip in much greater detail in the next chapter.

26. Ann B. Ulanov, "The Psychological Reality of the Demonic," in *Picturing God* (Einsiedeln: Daimon Verlag, 2002), 27.

27. See, e.g., Ann Ulanov, "Unseen Boundaries, Dangerous Crossings," in *Spiritual Aspects of Clinical Work* (Einsiedeln: Daimon Verlag, 2004).

28. See Ulanov, "The Psychological Reality of the Demonic," in *Picturing God*.

29. We may live out of a persona of "spiritual love," as Tympas writes, while psychic energy is entrapped in unconscious "unresolved tensions between archetypal libidinal eros and acutely fixated complexes. In analogous cases, the possibly dreadful implications of a controversial 'detachment' from objects (renunciation) become apparent—a 'detachment' which ultimately blocks vital processes of psychic maturation through the confrontation with complexes, images, and the object-as-other at early stages of psychic life, generating precariously unsettled attitudes." Tympas, *Carl Jung and Maximus the Confessor*, 173.

30. Irenaeus, *Against Heresies*, 4.39.2.

31. Ulanov, *Knots*, 61.

32. Ann Belford Ulanov, personal communication, March 2015.

33. Ulanov, personal communication, March 2015.

34. I use wholeness to describe the growth and ever-increasing inclusion of parts of ourselves to be lived. It is never "achieved" in a once-for-all way, but is a participation in constant process. Its opposite would be phenomena such as splitting, fragmentation, repression, and disintegration.

35. C. G. Jung, "Phenomena Resulting from the Assimilation of the Unconscious," in *Two Essays on Analytical Psychology*, ed. and trans. Gerhardt Adler and R. F. C. Hull, vol. 7 of *Collected Works* (Princeton: Princeton University Press, 1977), par. 223.

36. Ulanov, *Knots*, 61.

37. Olivier Clement, *The Roots of Christian Mysticism* (Hyde Park, N.Y.: New City Press, 1993), 176.

38. Pseudo-Dionysius Areopagite, *Divine Names, IV.20*, in *Pseudo-Dionysius: The Complete Works*, trans. Paul Rorem (Mahwah, N.J.: Paulist Press, 1988).

39. Donald W. Winnicott, "The Antisocial Tendency," in Clare Winnicott, Ray Shepard, and Madeleine Davis, eds., *Deprivation and Delinquency* (London: Routledge, 1984).

40. Donald W. Winnicott, "Fear of Breakdown," in *Psycho-Analytic Explorations*, Clare Winnicott, Ray Shepherd, Madeleine Davis, eds. (Cambridge, Mass.: Harvard University Press, 1989).

41. See again Winnicott, "Ego Distortion in Terms of True and False Self," in *The Maturational Processes and the Facilitating Environment: Studies in the Theory of Emotional Development* (London: Karnac, 2007).

42. Sue Grand, *The Reproduction of Evil* (New York: Routledge, 2002), 4.

43. Grand, *The Reproduction*, 5.

44. It is also important to mark again, at this point, that such empathetic involvement with the behavior of another does *not* constitute a condoning of such behavior. In her work, Sue Grand found that the healing process for people who had hurt or killed others *also entailed them taking responsibility* for their actions. See, e.g., *The Reproduction*, 67.

45. John McGuckin, "Nature," in McGuckin, *The Westminster Handbook to Patristic Theology* (Louisville, Ky.: Westminster John Knox Press, 2004), 234.

46. Maximos the Confessor, *Ambiguum 7*, in *On Difficulties in the Church Fathers: The Ambigua*, vol. 1, trans. and ed. Nicholas Constas (Cambridge, Mass.: Harvard University Press, 2014), par. 15–16; first emphasis mine.

47. Torstein T. Tollefsen, *The Christocentric Cosmology of St. Maximus the Confessor* (Oxford: Oxford University Press, 2008), 65.

48. Tollefsen, *The Christocentric Cosmology*, 68.

49. Tollefsen, *The Christocentric Cosmology*, 68.

50. Maximus, *Ambiguum 7*, par. 6.

51. Maximus, *Ambiguum 7*, par. 7.

52. Maximus, *Ambiguum 7*, par. 10.

53. Maximus, *Ambiguum 10*, in *On Difficulties in the Church Fathers: The Ambigua*, vol. 1, ed. and trans. Nicholas Constas (Cambridge: Harvard University Press, 2014), par. 12.

54. See, e.g., Melchisedec Toronen, *Union and Distinction in the Thought of St. Maximus the Confessor* (Oxford: Oxford University Press, 2007), 26.

55. Toronen, *Union*, 27.

56. Toronen, *Union*, 178.

57. Toronen, *Union*, 178. It can become tempting, here, to perceive St. Maximus as unfriendly to the created world because of his understanding of the fall as connected to the turning of the natural faculty of desire for God toward the sensible world, in pursuit of pleasure (see Maximus, *Ad Thalassium*, 61). However, this, in my view, does not fit in with the larger themes of his theology as one of transfiguration and unification of creation, not its disavowal. More concretely, it does not seem to me to be "world-hating" to hold that, without a central connection to that which transcends and authors the created world, the sensible/sensuous aspects of life can quickly become idols.

58. I will discuss St. Maximus's understanding of the composition of the soul in greater detail in Chapter 4.

59. Toronen, *Union and Distinction*, 179.

60. See again Maximus, *Ambiguum 10*.

61. See Toronen, *Union and Distinction*, 26–28.

62. A well-known aspect of Maximus's theology, which I will not explore here but which is nonetheless highly important to a more contextualized understanding of his cosmology and soteriology, is that of the human as "microcosm" of the "macrocosm" and one who serves as the "mediator" between all creation and the Creator through fulfilling their unifying potential. (Tollefson, *Christocentric Cosmology*, 102). See Maximus, *Ambiguum 41*. See also Lars Thunberg, *Microcosm and Mediator: The Theological Anthropology of Maximus the Confessor* (Chicago: Open Court Publishing, 1995). His emphasis on integration of opposites may lead one to immediately think of similarities in the theories of C. G. Jung, for which the reader is referred to the study by Tympas, *Carl Jung and Maximus the Confessor*.

63. Maximus, *Ambiguum 7*, par. 21.

64. Maximus, *Ambiguum 7*, par. 21.

65. Maximus, *Ambiguum 7*, par. 21. See also *Maximus the Confessor: Selected Writings*, trans. George C. Berthold (Mahwah, N.J.: Paulist Press, 1985), 94–95n141.

66. In an era of rampant individualism, it is highly worth noting that for Jung, individuation and individualism were not the same thing. He wrote: "Individuation . . . is a process by which a man becomes the definite, unique being he in fact is. In so doing he does not become 'selfish' in the ordinary sense of the word, but is merely fulfilling the peculiarity of his nature, and this, as we have said, is vastly different from egotism or individualism." C. G. Jung, "The Relations between the Ego and the Unconscious," in *Two Essays on Analytical Psychology*, ed. and trans. Gerhardt Adler and R. F. C. Hull, vol. 7 of *Collected Works* (Princeton: Princeton University Press, 1977), par. 267.

67. See, e.g., C. G. Jung, *The Red Book: Liber Novus*, ed. Sonu Shamdasani (New York: W.W. Norton & Co., 2009); C. G. Jung, *Aion: Researches into the Phenomenology of the Self*, ed. and trans. Gerhardt Adler and R. F. C. Hull, vol. 9 of *Collected Works* (Princeton: Princeton University Press, 1969); and Jung, *Two Essays on Analytical Psychology*.

68. C. G. Jung, *Memories, Dreams, Reflections*, ed. Aniela Jaffe and trans. Richard and Clara Winston (New York: Vintage Books, 1989), 177.

69. See C. G. Jung, "The Concept of Libido," in *Symbols of Transformation*, ed. and trans. Gerhardt Adler and R. F. C. Hull, vol. 5. of *Collected Works* (Princeton: Princeton University Press, 1990).

70. Jung, "The Personal and the Collective Unconscious," in *Two Essays on Analytical Psychology*, par. 220.

71. Jung, "The Archetypes of the Collective Unconscious," in *Two Essays on Analytical Psychology*, par. 186.

72. See Jung on individuation:

> The transcendent function does not proceed without aim and purpose, but leads to the revelation of the essential man. It is in the first place a purely natural process, which may in some cases pursue its course without the knowledge or assistance of the individual . . . the meaning and purpose of the process is the realization, in all its aspects, of the personality originally hidden away in the embryonic germ-plasm; the production and unfolding of the original potential wholeness. The symbols used by the unconscious to this end are the same as those which mankind has always used to express wholeness, completeness, and perfection: symbols, as a rule, of the quaternity and the circle. For these reasons I have termed this the individuation process. (C. G. Jung, "The Archetypes of the Collective Unconscious," in *Two Essays on Analytical Psychology*, par. 186)

It is interesting, in light of this, to consider what Jung might have made of the symbol given in Chapter 2 of IC/XC/NI/KA, always shown as a quaternity. It is also interesting to hearken back to St. Irenaeus who wrote, concerning the number four:

It is not possible that the Gospels can be either more or fewer in number than they are. For, since there are four zones of the world in which we live, and four principle winds . . . it is fitting that [the Church] should have four pillars, breathing out immortality on every side, and vivifying men afresh. . . . For the cherubim too were four-faced, and their faces were images of the dispensation of the Son of God. . . . For living creatures are quadriform, and the Gospel is quadriform, as is also the course followed by the Lord. For this reason were four principal . . . covenants given to the human race: one prior to the deluge, under Adam; the second, that after the deluge, under Noah; the third, the giving of the law, under Moses; the fourth, that which renovates man, and sums up all things in itself by means of the Gospel, raising and bearing men upon its wings into the heavenly kingdom. (Irenaeus, *Against Heresies*, in *The Writings of Irenaeus: Against Heresies and Fragments*, ed. Alexander Roberts and James Donaldson [Berkeley: Apocrophile Press, 2007], 3.11.8)

73. Jung, "The Archetypes," par. 187.

74. Jung, "The Personal," par. 210.

75. The following is a pivotal dream in this case as recounted by Jung: "Her father (who in reality was quite small of stature) was standing with her on a hill that was covered with wheat fields. She was quite tiny beside him, and he seemed to her like a giant. He lifted her up from the ground and held her in his arms like a little child. The wind swept over the wheat-fields, and as the wheat swayed in the wind, he rocked her in his arms." Jung, "The Personal," par. 211.

76. Jung, "The Personal," par. 214.

77. Jung, "The Personal," par. 214. He continues: "The energy of the transference is so strong that it gives one the impression of a vital instinct."

78. Jung, "The Personal," par. 215.

79. Jung, "The Personal," par. 217.

80. Jung, "The Personal," par. 217.

81. C. G. Jung, "Commentary on *The Secret of the Golden Flower*," in *Psychology and the East*, trans. R. F. C. Hull (Princeton: Princeton University Press, 1978), par. 77; emphasis mine.

82. Jung, "The Personal," par. 217.

83. See C. G. Jung, "Christ, a Symbol of the Self," in *Aion*, par. 73.

84. For a detailed discussion of similarities and differences between St. Maximus's logoi of beings and Jung's archetypes, see Tympas, *Carl Jung and Maximus the Confessor*. Tympas is sensitive to areas of overlap, mutual enhancement, as well as significant differences.

85. Jung, *Two Essays in Analytical Psychology*, par. 248.

86. Christopher Bollas, "The Transformational Object," in *The Shadow of the Object* (New York: Columbia University Press, 1987).

87. Christopher Bollas, "The Destiny Drive," in *Forces of Destiny: Psychoanalysis and the Human Idiom* (London: Free Association Books, 1989).

88. Karen Horney, *Neurosis and Human Growth: The Struggle towards Self-Realization* (New York: W.W. Norton & Co., 1991). See Symeon Kragiopoulos, *Do You Know Yourself*, trans. Monk Kosmas and Peter Xides (Manton, Calif.: Divine Ascent Press, 2010) for an Orthodox monastic utilization of Horney's approach to the types of neurotic solutions people employ and how those may manifest in the spiritual life.

89. Clement, *The Roots*, 177.

90. Pseudo-Dionysius Areopagite, *Divine Names*, in *Pseudo-Dionysius: The Complete Works*, trans. Paul Rorem (Mahwah, N.J.: Paulist Press, 1988), 4:20.

91. See also Ulanov, *Attacked by Poison Ivy*, 161–63. I allow myself here to use the phrase "life in abundance" in order to suggest that there may be an experiential and psychological analogue in this work to the "life in abundance" of John 10:10. At the same time I also wish to be clear that psychological well-being is not the same as life in Christ. However, because Orthodox theology does postulate the presence of the *imago dei*, and because this book is an exploration of how such claims may manifest psychologically, I allow myself the poetic usage of the term as those who experience through a deep analysis the "livingness" that Ulanov describes in the above reference may well feel, as she writes, that they "touch the spirit by which they live."

92. C. G. Jung, "The Transcendent Function," in *Structure and Dynamics of the Psyche*, ed. and trans. Gerhardt Adler and R. F. C. Hull, vol. 8 of *Collected Works* (Bollingen: Pantheon Books, 1960), par. 184.

93. Ann Belford Ulanov, seminar discussion in "Spiritual Aspects of Clinical Work," Union Theological Seminary, Fall 2011.

94. See, e.g., Pia Chaudhari, "Freedom for Relationship: An Initial Exploration of the Theology of Zizioulas and the Psychoanalytic Insights of Winnicott in Dialogue" *Pastoral Psychology* 62, no. 4 (Aug. 2013), 451–60.

95. I think here, for example, of the dragon Smaug in J. R. R. Tolkien's *Lord of the Rings*, and also the dragon inhabiting the island in C. S. Lewis's *Voyage of the Dawn Treader*.

96. See, e.g., Ann B. Ulanov, *The Unshuttered Heart: Opening to Aliveness/Deadness in the Self.* (Nashville: Abingdon Press, 2007), 21. See also Ann B. Ulanov, "Transference, The Transcendent Function, and Transcendence," in *Spiritual Aspects of Clinical Work* (Einsieldeln: Daimon Verlag, 2004), 327.

97. Ulanov, *The Unshuttered Heart*, 21.

98. Ulanov, *The Unshuttered Heart*, 21.

99. Ulanov, *The Unshuttered Heart*, 22.

100. Ulanov, *The Unshuttered Heart*, 22.

101. Ulanov, *The Unshuttered Heart*, 22.

102. Ulanov, *The Unshuttered Heart*, 22. I will discuss the importance of desire in the next chapter. For now, the importance lies observing the interplay of image and symptom, as symbolic communication and displaying purpose, respectively, from a level below conscious willing.

103. Ulanov, *The Unshuttered Heart*, 23.

104. Ulanov, *The Unshuttered Heart*, 46.

105. Ann Belford Ulanov, class lecture, "Depth Psychology and Theology" (310), Union Theological Seminary, Spring 2009.

106. Ann B. Ulanov, *Finding Space: Winnicott, God and Psychic Reality* (Louisville, Ky.: Westminster John Knox Press, 2005), 74.

107. Ulanov, *Finding Space*, 144.

108. Ulanov, *Finding Space*, 144.

109. Ulanov, *Finding Space*, 144.

110. Ulanov, *Finding Space*, 143–44.

111. See Ulanov:

> False-doing arises from interruption of being. Instead of possessing a continuity of being from which a vigorous and unforced doing flows naturally, nurtured by mothers or lovers or God, we suffer a crumbling at the center of ourselves. Our being has been invaded, taken over by alien elements, and exists now only in fragments. Instead of finding our face reflected in the loving gaze of our mother, we see her preoccupied with her own problems and using us for their solution. The child is unnaturally forced to mother the mother. Instead of finding in religion affirmation for our human being in all its perplexity and possibility, moral prescriptions dictate how we should be, creating guilt in us for failing to measure up. Instead of forming a true self under the beneficent gaze of a loving other who reflects us back to ourselves, we assign ourselves, or are assigned, a role to play through the other's unconscious projections. We erect a warning system that will repel invasion and hide our vulnerable core behind an impenetrable wall. In thus protecting our dependent, unformed being, we seal its fate. It remains locked up and inaccessible behind a shell of defenses against being hurt. If we cannot be found, our reasoning goes, we cannot be hurt . . . We soon come to fear being seen as much as not being seen . . . worst of all, this fear of being grows into a hatred of being. (Ann B. Ulanov, *Receiving Woman: Studies in the Psychology and the Theology of the Feminine* [Philadelphia: The Westminster Press, 1981])

In the Orthodox tradition, where asceticism plays such an important, therapeutic role, it is important to be able to discern between ascetic impulses that arise out of a negation of being, or are co-opted by a deep hatred of being (and desire), versus asceticism that comes out of being and desire itself, as a desire for even more of God. I will return to this again in Chapter 4, but for now I just wish to highlight that depth psychology can offer a deep, compassionate insight into a possible psychological origin of the shell that manifests as empty, prideful living. It is a deeply unconscious "hatred of being."

112. St. Irenaeus, *Against Heresies*, 4.39.2.

113. John Behr, *Asceticism and Anthropology in Irenaeus and Clement* (Oxford: Oxford University Press, 2000), 117.

114. Behr, *Irenaeus*, 307.

4. Eros: Healing Fire

1. See John McGuckin, *The Orthodox Church: An Introduction to Its History, Doctrine, and Spiritual Culture* (West Sussex: Wiley-Blackwell, 2011), 300–306; Margaret Klenck, "The Psychological and Spiritual Efficacy of Confession," *Journal of Religion and Health* 43, no. 2 (June 2004), 139–50.

2. Ann B. Ulanov, *Knots and Their Untying: Essays on Psychological Dilemmas* (New Orleans: SpringJournal Inc., 2014), 106.

3. See, e.g., Maximus, *Letter 2: On Love*, in Andrew Louth, *Maximus the Confessor* (London: Routledge, 1996), 84–93.

4. W. R. D. Fairbairn, *Psychoanalytic Studies of the Personality* (London: Routledge, 1992), xii.

5. Harry Guntrip, *Schizoid Phenomena, Object Relations, and the Self* (London: Karnac, 2001), 11.

6. Ulanov, *Knots*, 107; emphasis mine.

7. Ulanov, *Knots*, 107.

8. Ulanov, *Knots*, 108.

9. Ulanov, *Knots*, 106.

10. C. G. Jung, "The Concept of Libido," in *Symbols of Transformation*, ed. and trans. Gerhardt Adler and R. F. C. Hull, vol. 5 of *Collected Works* (Princeton: Princeton University Press, 1990), par. 194.

11. Jung, introduction to "The Concept of Libido," par. 185–89.

12. C. G. Jung, "The Syzygy: Anima and Animus," in *Aion: Researches into the Phenomenology of the Self*, ed. and trans. Gerhardt Adler and R. F. C. Hull, vol. 9 of *Collected Works* (Princeton; Princeton University Press, 1969), par. 29.

13. Jung, "The Concept of Libido," par. 194.

14. Jung, "The Concept of Libido," par. 197.

15. Ulanov, *Knots*, 107.

16. Guntrip, *Schizoid Phenomena*, 91–92; emphasis mine.

17. See Heinz Kohut, *The Analysis of the Self: A Systematic Approach to the Psychoanalytic Treatment of Narcissistic Personality Disorders* (Chicago: University of Chicago Press, 1971), 106.

18. Edward F. Edinger, *Anatomy of the Psyche: Alchemical Symbolism in Psychotherapy* (LaSalle: Open Court, 1988), 54–55.

19. G. C. Tympas, *Carl Jung and Maximus Confessor on Psychic Development: The Dynamics between the "Psychological" and the "Spiritual"* (New York: Routledge, 2014), 172.

20. See Maximos the Confessor, *Ambiguum 42*, in *On Difficulties in the Church Fathers: The Ambigua*, vol. 2, ed. and trans. Nicholas Constas (Cambridge: Harvard University Press, 2014). Although here Maximus is discussing love, and not eros as desirous longing, the relational and connective function of love links it back to eros as function of relationship.

21. See discussion in Nikolaos Loudovikos, "The Communion of Entities through Their *Logoi*" and "The Becoming of Entities through Their *Logoi*," in *A Eucharistic Ontology: Maximus the Confessor's Eschatological Ontology of Being as Dialogical Reciprocity*, trans. Elizabeth Theokritoff (Brookline, Mass.: Holy Cross Orthodox Press, 2010).

22. Maximos the Confessor, *Ambiguum 7*, in *On Difficulties in the Church Fathers: The Ambigua*, vol. 1, trans. and ed. Nicholas Constas (Cambridge, Mass.: Harvard University Press, 2014), 123; emphasis mine.

23. E.g., Maximos the Confessor, *The Third Century on Love*, par. 64, in *The Philokalia: The Complete Text*, compiled by St. Nikodimos of the Holy Mountain and St Makarios of Corinth, vol. 2, trans. and ed. G. E. H. Palmer, Philip Sherrard, and Kallistos Ware (London: Faber and Faber, 1981), 93.

24. Olivier Clement, *The Roots of Christian Mysticism* (Hyde Park, N.Y.: New City Press, 1993), 268.

25. Rev. Dr. Maxym Lysack, personal correspondence.

26. Ann B. Ulanov, *Picturing God*, *Picturing God* (Einsiedeln: Daimon Verlag, 2002), 180; emphasis mine.

27. This is, of course, bound up in St. Maximus's involvement with the Monothelitic controversy. I have touched on this issue in Chapter 2, in the section on St. Maximus the Confessor. In this chapter the focus will be on the depth-psychological, rather than the Christological, implications of *thelema*.

28. Maximus, *Ambiguum 7*.

29. Lars Thunberg, *Microcosm and Mediator: The Theological Anthropology of Maximus the Confessor* (Chicago: Open Court Publishing, 1995), 169.

30. Thunberg, *Microcosm and Mediator*, 171.

31. Thunberg, *Microcosm and Mediator*, 171.

32. Thunberg, *Microcosm and Mediator*, 171.

33. Louth, *Maximus the Confessor*, 60.

34. Maximus, *Opuscule 3*, in Louth, *Maximus the Confessor*, 193.

35. Louth, *Maximus the Confessor*, 193; emphasis mine.

36. Paul M. Blowers, "The Dialectics and Therapeutics of Desire in St. Maximus the Confessor," *Vigiliae Christianae* 65, no. 4 (2011), 428.

37. Louth, *Maximus the Confessor*, 61.

38. Louth, *Maximus the Confessor*, 61.

39. Louth, *Maximus the Confessor*, 62.

40. Maximus, *Ambiguum 7*, 91; emphasis mine. It is interesting to consider whether, *experientially*, we might be reminded of Jung's observations that "the superego is a necessary and unavoidable substitute for the experience of the self." C. G. Jung, *Psychology and Religion: West and East*, ed. and trans. Gerhardt Adler and R. F. C. Hull, vol. 11 of *Collected Works* (Princeton: Princeton University Press, 1969), par. 394.

41. Nikolaos Loudovikos, *A Eucharistic Ontology: Maximus the Confessor's Eschatological Ontology of Being as Dialogical Reciprocity*, trans. Elizabeth Theokritoff (Brookline, Mass.: Holy Cross Orthodox Press, 2010), 214.

42. See John D. Zizioulas, *Being as Communion: Studies in Personhood and the Church* (London: Darton Longman & Todd, 2004) and *Communion and Otherness: Further Studies in Personhood and the Church*, ed. Paul McPartlan (London: T&T Clark, 2006).

43. Loudovikos, *A Eucharistic Ontology*, 237.

44. Thunberg, *Microcosm and Mediator*, 174–75.

45. Maximus, *Ambiguum 10*, 3.9, 163.

46. Maximus, *Ambiguum 10*, 3.9, 163.

47. Maximus, *Ambiguum 10*, 3.9, 163–64.

48. Maximus cites this kind of appetitive desire as a passion given in contingency of the fall, which when transformed, can serve the person in the spiritual life. Maximus the Confessor, *Ad Thalassium 1*, in *On the Cosmic Mystery of Jesus Christ: Selected Writings from St. Maximus the Confessor*, trans. P. Blowers and R. L. Wilken (Crestwood, N.Y.: St. Vladimir's Seminary Press, 2003). See Paul M. Blowers, "Gentiles of the Soul: Maximus the Confessor on the Substructure and Transformation of Human Passions," *Journal of Early Christian Studies* 4, no. 1 (Spring 1996), 57–85.

49. See Blowers, "The Dialectics and Therapeutics of Desire."

50. In his meditation *On the Lord's Prayer*, St. Maximus discusses the saying of St. Paul that in Christ there is "neither male nor female" (Gal 3:28). He takes male and female, here, to signify anger and desire, respectively. I will touch on his use of allegory to discuss gender again later, but what is intriguing here is that he seems to see the humility of the person seeking to live in the likeness of Christ as dissolving the antipathy and distortion of the faculties of aggression and de-

sire. As we see from the above, it is not that he sees these faculties as fundamentally flawed, so his intimation of their union rather than opposition and reutilization in the authentic humility of the person becomes an interesting point of comparison to Winnicott's discussion of the necessary re-fusion of split eros and aggression in order to live from an authentic (and even humble) "true self" experience, rather than the prideful construct of the "false self." Maximus the Confessor, *On the Lord's Prayer*, in *The Philokalia*, 293. See Donald W. Winnicott, "Ego Distortion in Terms of True and False Self," in *The Maturational Processes and the Facilitating Environment: Studies in the Theory of Emotional Development* (London: Karnac, 2007); Vasileios Thermos, *In Search of the Person: "True" and "False Self" According to Donald Winnicott and St. Gregory Palamas*, trans. Constantine Kokenes (Montreal: Alexander Press, 2002).

51. Maximus, *The Second Century on Love*, par. 48, in *The Philokalia*, 73.

52. See Maximus, *Ad Thalassium 1, Ad Thalassium 21*, and *Ad Thalassium 61* in *On the Cosmic Mystery of Jesus Christ: Selected Writings from St. Maximus the Confessor*, trans. P. Blowers and R. L. Wilken (Crestwood, N.Y.: St. Vladimir's Seminary Press, 2003). See again Blowers, "Gentiles of the Soul" for reflections on the transformation and healing of the passions.

53. Blowers, "The Dialectics and Therapeutics of Desire," 438–39.

54. Louth, *Maximus the Confessor*, 31.

55. Maximus, *The Second Century on Love*, par. 41, in *The Philokalia*, 72.

56. Maximus, *The Second Century on Love*, par. 17, in *The Philokalia*, 67–68. It is interesting here that he notes that a man who seeks out a woman solely for sensual pleasure "misuses" her. One could read this as a reprimand not only of pleasure seeking but of using women as "objects."

57. See Maximus the Confessor, *Ad Thalassium 61*, in *On the Cosmic Mystery of Jesus Christ*; Maximos, *Ambiguum 8*, in *On Difficulties in the Church Fathers*, 143, and *Ambiguum 7*, in *On Difficulties in the Church Fathers*, 121. Challengingly, in *Ambiguum 7*, Maximus describes Adam's transgression as resulting in a choice for "union with a prostitute" rather than union with the Spirit of God. This is, of course, an alarming phrase concerning Eve. I think, however, we need to be careful to understand that in this particular text, Maximus is addressing the question of how it is that we are allowed to suffer such misery in the created world, subject to impermanence, decay, heartbreak, and death, as he continues on to bewail the fact that we have fallen in love with that which has no existence (122). He is, I believe, showing how Adam's "eros" moved toward the impermanent and the deceitful. I have not done a study on St. Maximus and women, nor on his use of allegory, but I find it telling that elsewhere he refers to "woman" as symbolic of divine virtue, acting in an erotic way, to allure us away from deceit (in reference to the phrase "Women are extremely strong but truth conquers all" 1 Esdras 3:12) saying that here women means "the divinizing virtues which give

rise to the love . . . that wrests the soul away from all that is subject to generation and decay . . . it intermingles the soul with God Himself in a kind of erotic union. . . . Women signify the supreme realization of the virtues, which is love." Maximus, *The Third Century of Various Texts*, 30–31 in *Philokalia*, 216–17. If we hold these two very different texts together, I wonder if we might not see women here used as allegory for eros itself, in its destructive form and its salvific form respectively. Though of course women can not be reduced to allegory, in this allegorical understanding of the "feminine" he would be reminiscent, in a way, of Jung who loosely correlated "eros" to woman's primary mode of consciousness and "logos" to that of the man. C. G. Jung, "The Syzygy," par. 29. For further discussion, see Ann B. Ulanov and Barry Ulanov, *Transforming Sexuality: The Archetypal World of Anima and Animus* (Boston: Shambhala Press, 1994).

58. See, e.g., Adam G. Cooper, *The Body in St. Maximus the Confessor: Holy Flesh, Wholly Deified* (Oxford: Oxford University Press, 2005), 215.

59. Cooper, *The Body in St. Maximus*, 215. For further discussion about the moral neutrality of the "appetites" and the importance of the mind that directs them, see John Behr, "Glorify God in Your Body," in *The Mystery of Christ: Life in Death* (Crestwood, N.Y.: St. Vladimir's Seminary Press, 2006), 141–71.

60. Maximus, *The Four Hundred Chapters on Love*, 3.4, in *Maximus Confessor: Selected Writings*, trans. George C. Berthold (Mahwah, N.J.: Paulist Press, 1985), 62.

61. Cooper, *The Body in St. Maximus*, 215.

62. Maximus, *Ambiguum 10*, 161.

63. Maximus, *Ambiguum 7*, 91–93.

64. Maximus, *Ambiguum 10*, 213.

65. John M. Rist, "A Note on Eros and Agape in Pseudo-Dionysius" *Vigiliae Christianae* 20, no. 4 (Dec. 1966), 235–43.

66. Rist, "A Note," 237.

67. Rist, "A Note," 238.

68. Rist, "A Note," 242.

69. Rist, "A Note," 243.

70. Maximus, *Fifth Century on Various Texts 83–91*, 280–82 emphases mine.

71. See also discussion in Blowers, "The Dialectics and Therapeutics of Desire in Maximus."

72. Ulanov, *Receiving Woman*, 46–47.

73. I think here of Winnicott's example of the daughter who suffered a breakdown in place of the mother. See D. W. Winnicott, "Psycho-Somatic Disorder," in *Psycho-Analytic Explorations*, ed. C. Winnicott, R. Shepherd, and M. Davis (Cambridge: Harvard University Press, 1989), 103–14.

74. Andre Green, "The Dead Mother," in *On Private Madness* (London: Karnac, 1996).

75. Susan Kavaler-Adler, "A New Metapsychology for Clinical Phenomenology and Psychic Health," in *Mourning, Spirituality, and Psychic Change: A New Object Relations View of Psychoanalysis* (New York: Bruuner-Routledge, 2003), 4–7.

76. Winnicott, "Ego Distortion"; Karen Horney, *Neurosis and Human Growth: The Struggle toward Self-Realization* (New York: W.W. Norton & Co., 1991).

77. Ann Ulanov and Barry Ulanov, *Cinderella and Her Sisters: The Envied and the Envying* (Philadephia: The Westminster Press, 1983), 75.

78. Ulanov and Ulanov, *Cinderella*, 33.

79. Louth, *Maximus the Confessor*, 59.

80. See Heinz Kohut, *The Analysis of the Self: A Systematic Approach to the Psychoanalytic Treatment of Narcissistic Personality Disorders* (Chicago: University of Chicago Press, 1971).

81. Kohut, *The Analysis*; see the preface and "Introductory Considerations."

82. W. R. D. Fairbairn, *Psychoanalytic Studies*, 48.

83. Maximus, *Ambiguum 7*, 97.

84. Maximus, *The Second Century on Love*, par. 8, in *The Philokalia*, 66.

85. Maximus, *The Second Century on Love*, par. 59, in *The Philokalia*, 75; Maximus, *The Third Century on Love*, par. 8–9, in *The Philokalia*, 84.

86. See John A. McGuckin, "Classical and Byzantine Christian Notions of the Self, and Their Significance Today," Lecture given at the "Andrei Saguna" Faculty of Theology at the "Lucian Blaga" University of Sibiu, Romania, Nov. 13, 2014, 10–11.

87. Clement, *The Roots*, 134–35.

88. Alexis Trader, *Ancient Christian Wisdom and Aaron Beck's Cognitive Therapy: A Meeting of Minds* (New York: Peter Lang, 2011), 90–99.

89. Trader, *Ancient Christian Wisdom*, 90–99.

90. Sigmund Freud, *On Narcissism: An Introduction*, in J. Sandler, E. Person, and P. Fonagy, eds. *Freud's "On Narcissism: An Introduction,"* (London: Karnac, 2012), 85.

91. See Sigmund Freud, "Part III. A General Theory of the Neuroses," in *Introductory Lectures to Psychoanalysis*, trans. James Strachey (New York: W.W. Norton & Co., 1966).

92. Fairbairn, *Psychoanalytic Studies*, 155.

93. Fairbairn, *Psychoanalytic Studies*, 31.

94. Maximus, *Ad Thalassium* 59 (PG 90, 202), cited in Clement, *The Roots*, 266. See Pia Chaudhari, "Uncovering Desire: Explorations in Eros, Aggression, and *Theosis* in Marriage," in *Love, Marriage, and Family in the Eastern Orthodox Tradition*, ed. T. Dedon and S. Trostyanskiy (New York: Theotokos Press, 2013), 107–18.

95. Maximus, *Second Century of Various Texts*, par. 8, in *The Philokalia*, 189.

96. W. R. D. Fairbairn, "A Revised Psychopathology of the Psychoses and the Psychoneuroses," in *Psychoanalytic Studies*; Guntrip, *Schizoid Phenomena*.

97. Guntrip, *Schizoid Phenomena*, 67.

98. Fairbairn, *Psychoanalytic Studies*, 155 and 31.

99. Fairbairn, *Psychoanalytic Studies*, 93.

100. Fairbairn, *Psychoanalytic Studies*, 65–70.

101. Fairbairn, *Psychoanalytic Studies*, 93.

102. Fairbairn, *Psychoanalytic Studies*, 70.

103. Maximus, *On the Lord's Prayer*, 293.

104. See, e.g., Maximus, *The Second Century on Love*, 73, 74, 84, and *The Third Century on Love*, par. 95 and 97, in *The Philokalia*, 77–79, 98.

105. Fairbairn, *Psychoanalytic Studies*, 154.

106. Fairbairn, *Psychoanalytic Studies*, 65–66.

107. Fairbairn, *Psychoanalytic Studies*, 65–66

108. Fairbairn, *Psychoanalytic Studies*, 157.

109. Fairbairn, *Psychoanalytic Studies*, 155.

110. I wish to remind the reader, at this point, that the cluster of theories I will explore, in detail, in this and the next few sections is meant to represent a solid area of conjecture about psychological suffering; it is not meant to be exhaustive. It may be used as a symbol, in the meaning of the word that is a binding of two realities together, that of language and that of experience. It is also only possible to conjecture what an infant is experiencing, and hence this section is not meant to concretize infantile development as the source of all ills, in a reductionist sense, by allocating all splitting solely to their nascent egos rather than psychological development proceeding along complex and varied lines. But these words have purchase because they describe experiences of real suffering and experiences of real healing, and get a depth-psychological handle on the mechanisms that drive both. It is in that spirit that I offer them.

111. Fairbairn, *Psychoanalytic Studies*, 34. Further, he states: "Autoerotism is essentially a technique hereby the individual seeks not only to provide for himself what he cannot obtain from the object, but to provide for himself an object which he cannot obtain."

112. Fairbairn, *Psychoanalytic Studies*, 40.

113. See, e.g., Guntrip, *Schizoid Phenomena*, 41–48.

114. See, e.g., discussion of the heart in Hierotheos Vlachos, *Orthodox Psychotherapy: The Science of the Fathers*, trans. Esther Williams (Levadhia, Greece: Birth of the Theotokos Monastery, 1994).

115. Lest all fall on the "mother," or "mothering one," we should note Guntrip: "In his quest for a libidinally good object the child will turn from the mother to the father and go back and forth between them many times." Guntrip, *Schizoid Phenomena*, 45.

116. Guntrip, *Schizoid Phenomena*, 49.

117. Fairbairn, *Psychoanalytic Studies*, 50; emphasis mine.

118. Fairbairn, *Psychoanalytic Studies*, 50.

119. Guntrip, *Schizoid Phenomena*, 202.

120. Guntrip, *Schizoid Phenomena*, 202.

121. Guntrip, *Schizoid Phenomena*, 97.

122. Thermos, *In Search of the Person*, 7–8.

123. Guntrip, *Schizoid Phenomena*, 223.

124. Guntrip, *Schizoid Phenomena*, 68–70, emphasis in original.

125. See Guntrip, *Schizoid Phenomena*, 97; Winnicott, "Ego Distortion."

126. Guntrip, *Schizoid Phenomena*, 65–66; see also 64–65 for descriptions of schizoid mental/intellectualist solutions.

127. Guntrip, *Schizoid Phenomena*, 71.

128. Guntrip, *Schizoid Phenomena*, 71–72.

129. Guntrip, *Schizoid Phenomena*, 72–73.

130. Guntrip, *Schizoid Phenomena*, 97.

131. See Guntrip, *Schizoid Phenomena*, 76.

132. Guntrip, *Schizoid Phenomena*, 78.

133. Again, this is a particular way of conceptualizing and articulating something that various depth-psychological schools—as in the story of the blind men touching the elephant and emphasizing different aspects of the same creature—have observed and discussed.

134. Here again we have a return to Pseudo-Dionysus's observations about all things participating in the "good," as outlined in Chapter 3.

135. See Winnicott, "Ego Distortion"; Ulanov, *Finding Space: Winnicott, God, and Psychic Reality* (Louisville, Ky.: Westminster John Knox Press, 2005), 59–62.

136. Guntrip, *Schizoid Phenomena*, 191, emphasis in original.

137. Guntrip, *Schizoid Phenomena*, 85.

138. Guntrip, *Schizoid Phenomena*, 177.

139. St. Athanasius, *On the Incarnation*, ed. and trans. John Behr (Crestwood, N.Y.: St. Vladimir's Seminary Press, Popular Patristics Series, 2011), 12. See again John Behr, *The Nicene Faith: Part One True God of True God* (Crestwood, N.Y.: St. Vladimir's Seminary Press, 2004), 73.

140. Guntrip, *Schizoid Phenomena*, 48.

141. Jung, *Two Essays on Analytical Psychology*, ed. and trans. Gerhardt Adler and R. F. C. Hull, vol. 7 of *Collected Works* (Princeton: Princeton University Press, 1977), par. 275. See Trader: "When all the soul's faculties function naturally, a person is then able to see and interpret reality as it truly is." *Ancient Christian Wisdom*, 94.

142. See Maximus, *Second Century of Various Texts*, 73–74 in *Philokalia*, 202–3.

143. See, e.g., A. B. Ulanov, "Beyond the Self: No-Thing, Abyss, and Beginnings," in *The Unshuttered Heart: Opening Aliveness/Deadness in the Self* (Nashville: Abingdon Press, 2007).

144. Ulanov, "Beyond the Self."

145. Ulanov, *Finding Space*, 60.

146. See again Irenaeus, *Against Heresies*, in Alexander Roberts and James Donaldson, eds., *The Writings of Irenaeus: Against Heresies and Fragments* (Berkeley: Apocrophile Press, 2007), 39.4.2; and John Behr, *Asceticism and Anthropology in Irenaeus and Clement* (Oxford: Oxford University Press, 2000), 117.

147. Athanasius, *On the Incarnation*, 3.

148. Athanasius, *On the Incarnation*, 5.

149. Wisdom of Solomon 1:12–15, *The New Oxford Annotated Bible: New Revised Standard Version with the Apocrypha* (Oxford: Oxford University Press, 2007); emphasis mine.

150. Wisdom of Solomon 2:9–11. One might be reminded here of Horney's discussion of "shallow living" as a solution to intolerable anxiety and aspect of neurotic self (Horney, *Neurosis and Human Growth*, 289), and also of Guntrip's insight into the schizoid disavowal of weakness (Guntrip, *Schizoid Phenomena*, see chapter on "Resistance.")

151. Wisdom of Solomon 2:21–24, *New Oxford Annotated Bible*.

152. See Symington on the development of narcissism and the rejection of the "life-giver." Neville Symington, *Narcissism: A New Theory* (London: Karnac Books, 1993), 35–37.

153. For his seminal exploration of the use of aggression and destructiveness in establishing the empirical reliability of the "object" for "object-usage," see Donald W. Winnicott, "On the Use of an Object," in *Psycho-Analytic Explorations*, specifically 217–27.

154. It is also interesting to note here the emphasis laid by Heinz Kohut on the importance of empathy in reaching through the defenses of narcissism so that the "other" becomes a viable relation. Such empathy seems to mirror, in a way, the recapitulation discussed by St. Irenaeus (discussed in Chapter 2) as well as the "assuming" being discussed in the soteriology in general. See again Heinz Kohut, *The Analysis of the Self*, and also Heinz Kohut, *The Restoration of the Self* (Chicago: University of Chicago Press, 1977).

155. See John D. Zizioulas, *Communion and Otherness: Further Studies in Personhood and the Church* (New York: T&T Clark, 2006), 55.

156. Guntrip, *Schizoid Phenomena*, 195–96.

157. See Maximus, *Second Century of Various Texts*, par. 74, in *The Philokalia* and *Ambiguum 7*; Maximus in *Ambiguum 10*, in *On Difficulties in the Church Fathers*.

158. Maximus, *The Four Hundred Chapters on Love*, 3.46 in *Maximus Confessor: Selected Writings*, 67.

159. See earlier discussion on desire in Loudovikos in this chapter.

160. Loudovikos, *A Eucharistic Ontology*, 142.

161. Loudovikos, *A Eucharistic Ontology*, 226.

162. Guntrip, *Schizoid Phenomena*, 86.

163. See again Kohut, *Analysis of the Self*; and Kohut, *Restoration of the Self.*

164. See discussion in Guntrip, *Schizoid Phenomena*, 252–71; Ulanov, *Finding Space*, 67–89.

165. A. B. Ulanov, *Receiving Woman: Studies in the Psychology and the Theology of the Feminine* (Philadelphia: The Westminster Press, 1981), 88.

166. An Akathist is a lengthy hymn that praises a particular saint, often repeating aspects of their lives and expressing the theological importance of their offering to humanity.

167. John A. McGuckin, trans. and ed., "Akathist to the Most Holy Mother of God," in *Two Akathists* (New York: Theotokos Press, 2011), 44 Oikos VIII. This Akathist was dedicated to the Virgin Mary as Protectress of the City of Constantinople. Here she is hailed as the "Unconquered champion." As McGuckin writes: "Here, in the early Greek Christian mind, she is a Warrior Queen, vigorous in her defense of her troubled children" (7). It was composed, approximately, in the sixth century.

168. Of course one thinks here of Jung and his transcendent function arising out of holding the tension of opposites, a function that—while not "transcendent" in religious sense—often has the feeling of arriving as a solution from God to intractable conflicts. See Ann B. Ulanov, "Transference, The Transcendent Function and Transcendence," in *Spiritual Aspects of Clinical Work* (Einsieldeln: Daimon Verlag, 2004).

169. Guntrip, *Schizoid Phenomena*, 80; emphasis mine.

170. St. Gregory Palamas, "On the Annunciation," in *Mary the Mother of God: Sermons by Saint Gregory Palamas*, ed. Christopher Veniamin (South Canaan, Pa.: Mount Thabor Publishing, 2005), 54–55 emphasis mine.

171. Palamas, "On the Annunciation," 58.

172. Ulanov, *The Wisdom of the Psyche*, 99

173. Maximus, *Ambiguum 7*, 121. See Melchisedic Toronen, *Unity and Distinction in the Thought of St. Maximus the Confessor* (Oxford: Oxford University Press, 2007).

174. Ulanov, *Picturing God*, 168.

175. Christos Yannaras, *Relational Ontology*, trans. Norman Russell (Brookline, Mass.: Holy Cross Orthodox Press, 2011), 24.

176. Yannaras, *Relational Ontology*, 24.

177. Loudovikos, *A Eucharistic Ontology*, 47n19.

178. Loudovikos, *A Eucharistic Ontology*, 241.

179. Yannaras, *Relational Ontology*, 71.

180. Pseudo-Dionysus, *Celestial Hierarchy I, 3*, cited in Clement, *The Roots*, 221. It is, in fact, not uncommon to hear Orthodox also tell of experiences of the presence

of an unusual fragrance, usually the scent of roses or an incense-tinged rose scent, appearing out of nowhere. Many say this is a sign of the presence and grace of the Theotokos. Relics, too, are also known to emit a celestial fragrance to some.

181. Maximus, *Ambiguum 71*, in *On the Difficulties in the Church Fathers: The Ambigua*, vol. 2, 323.

182. Maximus, *Ambiguum 71*, 323–25.

183. Maximus, *Ambiguum 71*, 323–25.

184. See again Maximus, *Letter 2: On Love.*

185. Maximus, *The Church's Mystagogy*, in *Maximus Confessor: Selected Writings*, 206; emphasis mine.

186. Maximus, *The Church's Mystagogy*, 206–7.

187. Maximus, *The Church's Mystagogy*, 186.

188. Maximus, *The Church's Mystagogy*, 187.

189. Aristotle Papanikolaou, "Liberating Eros: Confession and Desire," *Journal of the Society of Christian Ethics* 26, no. 1 (Spring/Summer, 2006): 155–36.

190. Maximus, *The Church's Mystagogy*, 206.

191. John A. McGuckin, "Symeon the New Theologian's Hymns of Divine Eros: A Neglected Masterpiece of the Christian Tradition," *Spiritus: A Journal of Christian Spirituality* 5, no. 2, (Fall 2005), 182–202.

192. Maximus, *Centuries on Love*, 1.13, cited in Papanikolaou, "Liberating Eros," 130.

193. Ulanov, *Knots*, 135.

194. Loudovikos, *A Eucharistic Ontology*, 202, see also 173.

195. Loudovikos, *A Eucharistic Ontology*, 238; emphasis mine.

196. Ulanov, *Knots*, 107.

197. Loudovikos, *A Eucharistic Ontology*, 15.

198. See, e.g., Papanikolaou, "Liberating Eros."

199. Maximus, *Ambiguum 1*, in *On the Difficulties in the Church Fathers.*

200. Maximus, cited in Loudovikos, *A Eucharistic Ontology*, 29.

201. Maximus, cited in Loudovikos, *A Eucharistic Ontology*, 29.

202. Maximus, cited in Loudovikos, *A Eucharistic Ontology*, 29.

203. Maximus, cited in Loudovikos, *A Eucharistic Ontology*, 29.

204. Ulanov, *Finding Space*, 58.

205. See again Ulanov and Ulanov, *Cinderella and Her Sisters*, 75 and 33.

206. Ulanov, *Knots*, 61.

207. Ulanov, *The Unshuttered Heart*, 215.

208. Horney, *Neurosis and Human Growth*, 111.

209. Loudovikos, *A Eucharistic Ontology*, 136.

210. Maximus, *Ambiguum 41*.

211. See Maximus, *Ambiguum 41*; Thunberg, *Microcosm and Mediator*.

212. See again Winnicott, "On the Use of an Object."

Conclusion

1. David Bentley Hart, *The Beauty of the Infinite: The Aesthetics of Christian Truth* (Grand Rapids, Mich.: William B. Eerdmans), 392

2. See again Ann B. Ulanov, *Knots and Their Untying: Essays on Psychological Dilemmas* (New Orleans: SpringJournal Inc., 2014), 61.

3. Ann B. Ulanov, *Picturing God* (Einsiedeln: Daimon Verlag, 2002), 177.

4. Jung, "The Self," in *Aion: Researches into the Phenomenology of the Self*, ed. and trans. Gerhardt Adler and R. F. C. Hull, vol. 9 of *Collected Works* (Princeton: Princeton University Press, 1969); Ann B. Ulanov, "Spiritual Aspects of Clinical Work," in *The Functioning Transcendent: A Study in Analytical Psychology* (Wilmette, Ill.: Chiron Publications, 1996), 26.

5. Ulanov, "Spiritual Aspects," 24.

6. Ulanov, "Spiritual Aspects," 26.

7. Ulanov, "Spiritual Aspects," 26.

8. Ann Belford Ulanov and Alvin Dueck, *The Living God and Our Living Psyche: What Christians Can Learn from Carl Jung* (Grand Rapids, Mich.: W.B. Eerdmans Publishing Co., 2008), 32–35.

9. See Bollas, *Forces of Destiny: Psychoanalysis and the Human Idiom* (Free Association Books, 1996).

10. McGuckin, *The Orthodox Church: An Introduction to Its History, Doctrine, and Spiritual Culture* (West Sussex: Wiley-Blackwell, 2011), 198.

11. See again Ulanov, "Spiritual Aspects," 26.

12. 1 Corinthians 13:12.

13. Maximus, *Fifth Century on Various Texts*, in *The Philokalia: The Complete Text*, compiled by St. Nikodimos of the Holy Mountain and St. Makarios of Corinth, vol. 2, trans. and ed. G. E. H. Palmer, Philip Sherrard, and Kallistos Ware (London: Faber and Faber, 1981).

14. Paschal Troparion.

BIBLIOGRAPHY

Anatolios, Khaled. *Athanasius*. London: Routledge, 2004.

Athanasius. *On the Incarnation*. Edited and translated by John Behr. Popular Patristics Series. Crestwood, N.Y.: St. Vladimir's Seminary Press, 2011.

Aulen, Gustaf. *Christus Victor: An Historical Study of the Three Main Types of the Idea of the Atonement*. Eugene, Ore.: Wipf & Stock, 2003.

Balthasar. *The Glory of the Lord: A Theological Aesthetics*. Vol. 2. San Francisco: Ignatius Press, 2004.

Ecumenical Patriarch Bartholomew. "The World As Sacrament—The Theological and Spiritual Vision of Creation." The Russian Orthodox Church, Department for External Church Relations. https://mospat.ru/en/2010/05/26/news19252/.

Behr, John. *Asceticism and Anthropology in Irenaeus and Clement*. Oxford: Oxford University Press, 2000.

———. *Irenaeus of Lyons: Identifying Christianity*. Oxford: Oxford University Press, 2013.

———. *The Mystery of Christ: Life in Death*. Crestwood, N.Y.: St. Vladimir's Seminary Press, 2006.

———. *The Nicene Faith: Part One—True God of True God*. Vol. 2. Crestwood, N.Y.: St. Vladimir's Seminary Press, 2004.

———. "A Note on the Ontology of Gender." *St. Vladimir's Theological Quarterly* 42, no. 3–4 (1998).

———. *The Way to Nicaea: The Formation of Christian Theology*. Vol. 1. Crestwood, N.Y.: St. Vladimir's Seminary Press, 2001.

Bentley Hart, David. *The Beauty of the Infinite: The Aesthetics of Christian Truth*. Grand Rapids, Mich.: William B. Eerdmans Publishing Company, 2003.

Bion, Wilfred. *Attention and Interpretation*. London: Karnac Books 1984.

Blowers, Paul M. "The Dialectics and Therapeutics of Desire in Maximus the Confessor." *Vigiliae Christianae* 65, no. 4 (2011).

———. "Gentiles of the Soul: Maximus the Confessor on the Substructure and Transformation of Human Passions." *Journal of Early Christian Studies* 4, no. 1 (Spring 1996).

Bollas, Christopher. *Forces of Destiny: Psychoanalysis and the Human Idiom*. London: Free Association Books, 1996.

———. *The Shadow of the Object*. New York: Columbia University Press, 1987.

Boss, Medard. *Psychoanalysis and Daseinanalysis*. New York: Da Capo Press, 1982.

Brock, Rita Nakashima, and Rebecca Ann Parker. *Proverbs of Ashes: Violence, Redemptive Suffering, and the Search for What Saves Us*. Boston: Beacon Press, 2002.

Brown, Charles E. "The Atonement: Healing in Postmodern Society." *Interpretation* 53, no. 1 (January 1999).

Chaudhari, Pia. "Freedom for Relationship: An Initial Exploration of the Theology of Zizioulas and the Psychoanalytic Insights of Winnicott in Dialogue." *Pastoral Psychology* 62, no. 4 (August 2013).

———. "Uncovering Desire: Explorations in Eros, Aggression, and *Theosis* in Marriage." In *Love, Marriage and Family in the Eastern Orthodox Tradition*, edited by T. Dedon and S. Trostyanskiy. New York: Theotokos Press, 2013.

Chirban, John T., ed. *Personhood: Orthodox Christianity and the Connection between Body, Mind, and Soul*. Westport, Conn.: Bergin & Garvey, 1996.

———, ed. *Sickness or Sin? Spiritual Discernment and Differential Diagnosis*. Brookline, Mass.: Holy Cross Orthodox Press, 2001.

Christensen, Michael J., and Jeffery A. Wittung, eds. *Partakers of Divine Nature: The History and Development of Deification in the Christian Traditions*. Grand Rapids, Mich.: Baker Academic, 2007.

Chrysostomos. *A Guide to Orthodox Psychotherapy: The Science, Theology, and Spiritual Practice behind It and Its Clinical Applications*. Lanham: University Press of America, 2007.

Chryssavgis, John, and Bruce V. Foltz, eds. *Toward an Ecology of Transfiguration: Orthodox Christian Perspectives on Environment, Nature, and Creation*. New York: Fordham University Press, 2013.

Clement, Olivier. *On Human Being: A Spiritual Anthropology*. Hyde Park, N.Y.: New City Press, 2000.

———. *The Roots of Christian Mysticism*. Hyde Park, N.Y.: New City Press, 1993.

Cooper, Adam G. *The Body in St. Maximus the Confessor: Holy Flesh, Wholly Deified.* Oxford: Oxford University Press, 2005.

Damascene, Hieromonk. *Christ, the Eternal Tao.* Platina, Calif.: Valaam Books, 2012.

Edinger, Edward F. *Anatomy of the Psyche: Alchemical Symbolism in Psychotherapy.* LaSalle, Ill.: Open Court, 1988.

Evdokimov, Paul. *The Sacrament of Love: The Nuptial Mystery in the Light of the Orthodox Tradition.* Translated by Anthony P. Gythiel and Victoria Steadman. Crestwood, N.Y.: St. Vladimir's Seminary Press, 1985.

———. *Woman and the Salvation of the World: A Christian Anthropology on the Charisms of Women,* trans. Anthony P. Gythiel (Crestwood, N.Y.: St. Vladimir's Seminary Press, 1994).

Fairbairn, W. R. D. *Psychoanalytic Studies of the Personality.* London: Routledge, 1992.

Ferngren, Gary B. *Medicine and Religion: A Historical Introduction.* Baltimore: Johns Hopkins University Press, 2014.

Finlan, Stephen, and Vladimir Kharlamov, eds. *Theosis: Deification in Christian Theology.* Eugene, Ore.: Wipf & Stock, 2006.

Freeman, Stephen. *Everywhere Present: Life in a One-Storey Universe.* Chesterton, Ind.: Conciliar Press, 2011.

———. *Glory to God for All Things.* http://blogs.ancientfaith.com/glory2god forallthings.

Freud, Sigmund. *Beyond the Pleasure Principle.* Translated by James Strachey. New York: W.W. Norton & Co, 1990.

———. *Introductory Lectures to Psychoanalysis.* Translated by James Strachey. New York: W.W. Norton & Co., 1966.

———. *On Narcissism: An Introduction.* In *Freud's "On Narcissism: An Introduction."* Edited by J. Sandler, E. Person, and P. Fonagy. London: Karnac, 2012.

———. *Totem and Taboo: Some Points of Agreement between the Mental Lives of Savages and Neurotics.* New York: W.W. Norton & Co., 1952.

Grand, Sue. *The Reproduction of Evil.* New York: Routledge, 2002.

Green, Andre. "The Dead Mother." In *On Private Madness.* London: Karnac, 1996.

Gregory of Nazianzus. *On God and Christ: Five Theological Orations and Two Letters to Cledonius.* Translated by Lionel Wickham. Crestwood, N.Y.: St. Vladimir's Seminary Press, Popular Patristics Series, 2002.

———. *On God and Man: The Theological Poetry of St. Gregory of Nazianzus.* Translated by Peter Gilbert. Crestwood, N.Y.: St. Vladimir's Seminary Press, 2001.

————. *On the Two Covenants, and the Appearing of Christ.* In *On God and Man: The Theological Poetry of St. Gregory of Nazianzus.* Translated by Peter Gilbert. Crestwood, N.Y.: St. Vladimir's Seminary Press, 2001.

————. "Theological Oration 37, I. and II." *New Advent.* http://www.newadvent.org/fathers/310237.htm.

Gregory of Nyssa. *On the Soul and Resurrection.* Translated by Catharine P. Roth. Crestwood, N.Y.: St. Vladimir's Seminary Press, 2002.

Gross, Jules. *The Divinization of the Christian According to the Church Fathers.* Translated by Paul A. Onica. Anaheim: A & C Press, 2002.

Guntrip, Harry. *Schizoid Phenomena, Object Relations, and the Self.* London: Karnac, 2001.

Habets, Myk. "Reforming Theosis." In *Theosis: Deification in Christian Theology,* edited by Stephen Finlan and Vladimir Kharlamov. Eugene, Ore.: Wipf & Stock, 2006.

Hart, David Bentley. *The Beauty of the Infinite: The Aesthetics of Christian Truth.* Grand Rapids, Mich.: William B. Eerdmans, 2003.

Horney, Karen. *Neurosis and Human Growth: The Struggle towards Self-Realization.* New York: W.W. Norton & Co., 1991.

Irenaeus. *The Writings of Irenaeus: Against Heresies and Fragments.* Edited by Alexander Robert and James Donaldson. Berkeley: Apocrophile Press, 2007.

Jacobi, J., *Complex Archetype Symbol in the Psychology of C. G. Jung.* Bollingen Series 57. Princeton: Princeton University Press, 1959.

Jerotic, Vladeta. *Individuacija I (ili) Obozenje.* Belgrade: Ars Libri, 2010.

Jung, C. G. *Aion: Researches into the Phenomenology of the Self.* Vol. 9 of *Collected Works,* edited and translated by Gerhardt Adler and R. F. C. Hull. Princeton: Princeton University Press, 1969.

————. *Alchemical Studies.* Vol. 13 of *Collected Works,* edited and translated by Gerhardt Adler and R. F. C. Hull. Princeton: Princeton University Press, 1967.

————. *Memories, Dreams, Reflections.* Edited by Aniela Jaffe and translated by Richard and Clara Winston. New York: Vintage Books, 1989.

————. *Psychology and the East.* Translated by R. F. C. Hull. Princeton: Princeton University Press, 1978.

————. *Psychology and Religion: West and East.* Vol. 11 of *Collected Works,* edited and translated by Gerhardt Adler and R. F. C. Hull. Princeton: Princeton University Press, 1969.

————. *The Red Book: Liber Novus.* Edited by Sonu Shamdasani. New York: W.W. Norton & Co., 2009.

————. *Structure and Dynamics of the Psyche.* Vol. 8 of *Collected Works,* edited and translated by Gerhardt Adler and R. F. C. Hull. New York: Pantheon Books, 1960.

————. *Symbols of Transformation.* Vol. 5 of *Collected Works*, edited and translated by Gerhardt Adler and R. F. C. Hull. Princeton: Princeton University Press, 1990.

————. *Two Essays on Analytical Psychology.* Vol. 7 of *Collected Works*, edited and translated by Gerhardt Adler and R. F. C. Hull. Princeton: Princeton University Press, 1977.

Kannengiesser, C. "Christology." In *The Westminster Handbook to Origen*, edited by John McGuckin. Louisville, Ky.: Westminster John Knox Press, 2004.

Kavaler-Adler, Susan. *Mourning, Spirituality, and Psychic Change: A New Object Relations View of Psychoanalysis.* New York: Bruuner-Routledge, 2003.

Kharlamov, Vladimir. "Rhetorical Application of Theosis." In *Partakers of Divine Nature: The History and Development of Deification in the Christian Traditions*, edited by Michael J. Christensen and Jeffrey A. Wittung. Grand Rapids, Mich.: Baker Academic, 2007.

Klein, Melanie. *Envy and Gratitude and Other Works 1946–1963.* New York: The Free Press, 1975.

Klenck, Margaret. "The Psychological and Spiritual Efficacy of Confession." *Journal of Religion and Health* 43, no. 2 (June 2004).

Kohut, Heinz. *The Analysis of the Self: A Systematic Approach to the Psychoanalytic Treatment of Narcissistic Personality Disorders.* Chicago: University of Chicago Press, 1971.

————. *The Restoration of the Self.* Chicago: University of Chicago Press, 1977.

Kragiopoulos, Symeon. *Do You Know Yourself?* Translated by Monk Kosmas and Peter Xides. Manton, Calif.: Divine Ascent Press, 2010.

Larchet, Jean-Claude. *Mental Disorders and Spiritual Healing: Teachings from the Early Christian East.* Hillsdale, N.Y.: Sophia Perennis, 2005.

Larchet, Jean-Claude. *The Theology of Illness.* Crestwood, N.Y.: St. Vladimir's Seminary Press, 2002.

————. *Therapy of Spiritual Illness: An Introduction to the Ascetic Life of the Orthodox Church.* Montreal: Alexander Press, 2012.

Lossky, Vladimir. *The Mystical Theology of the Eastern Church.* London: James Clarke & Co., 1957.

Loudovikos, Nikolaos. *A Eucharistic Ontology: Maximus the Confessor's Eschatological Ontology of Being as Dialogical Reciprocity.* Translated by Elizabeth Theokritoff. Brookline, Mass.: Holy Cross Orthodox Press, 2010.

Louth, Andrew. *Maximus the Confessor.* London: Routledge, 1996.

————. "The Place of Theosis in Orthodox Theology." In *Partakers of the Divine Nature*, edited by Michael Christensen and Jeffery Wittung. Grand Rapids, Mich.: Baker Academic, 2007.

Luhrmann, T. M. "Redefining Mental Illness." *New York Times.* January 18, 2015. http://www.nytimes.com/2015/01/18/opinion/sunday/t-m-luhrmann-redefining-mental-illness.html.

Lysack, Maxym. "The Healed Leper Who Gave Thanks" (sermon). Christ the Saviour Orthodox Church. https://soundcloud.com/christthesaviouroc/2014-12-21-the-healed-leper-who-gave-thanks.

———. "On the Disintegration of Life Through Sin" (sermon). Christ the Saviour Orthodox Church. https://soundcloud.com/christthesaviouroc/2014-07-06-on-the-disintegration-of-life-through-sin.

———. "The Rich Young Ruler Who Knew Too Much" (sermon). Christ the Saviour Orthodox Church. https://soundcloud.com/christthesaviouroc/2014-12-14-the-rich-young-ruler-who-knew-too-much.

———. "Seeing Our Sins in Humility" (podcast). The Law of the Spirit. http://www.ancientfaith.com/video/lawofthespirit.

Matti-Karkainnen, Veli, *One With God: Salvation as Deification and Justification.* Liturgical Press, 2004.

Maximos the Confessor. *On Difficulties in the Church Fathers: The Ambigua.* Vol. 1. Edited and translated by Nicholas Constas. Cambridge, Mass.: Harvard University Press, 2014.

———. *On Difficulties in the Church Fathers: The Ambigua.* Vol. 2. Edited and translated by Nicholas Constas. Cambridge, Mass.: Harvard University Press, 2014.

Maximus the Confessor. *Ad Thalassium.* In *On the Cosmic Mystery of Jesus Christ: Selected Writings from St. Maximus the Confessor.* Translated by P. Blowers and R. L. Wilken. Crestwood, N.Y.: St. Vladimir's Seminary Press, 2003.

———. *Letter 2: On Love.* In Andrew Louth, *Maximus the Confessor.* London: Routledge, 1996.

———. *Maximus the Confessor: Selected Writings.* Translated by George C. Berthold. Mahwah, N.J.: Paulist Press, 1985.

———. *The Philokalia: The Complete Text.* Vol. 2. Compiled by St. Nikodimos of the Holy Mountain and St. Makarios of Corinth, translated and edited by G. E. H. Palmer, Philip Sherrard, and Kallistos Ware. London: Faber and Faber, 1981.

McDougall, Joyce. *Theaters of the Body: A Psychoanalytic Approach to Psychosomatic Illness.* New York: W.W. Norton & Co., 1989.

McGuckin, John A. "Classical and Byzantine Christian Notions of the Self, and Their Significance Today." Lecture given at the "Andrei Saguna" Faculty of Theology at the "Lucian Blaga" University of Sibiu, Romania. Nov. 13, 2014.

———. "The Eros of Divine Beauty in St. Maximus the Confessor." In *The Concept of Beauty in Patristic and Byzantine Theology,* edited by John A. McGuckin. New York: Scholars Press, 2015.

———. *The Orthodox Church: An Introduction to Its History, Doctrine, and Spiritual Culture.* West Sussex: Wiley-Blackwell, 2011.

———, trans. and ed. *Prayer Book of the Early Christians.* Brewster, Mass.: Paraclete Press, 2011.

———. *St. Gregory of Nazianzus: An Intellectual Biography.* Crestwood, N.Y.: St. Vladimir's Seminary Press, 2001.

———. "Symeon the New Theologian's Hymns of Divine Eros: A Neglected Masterpiece of the Christian Tradition." *Spiritus: A Journal of Christian Spirituality* 5, no. 2 (Fall 2005).

———, trans. and ed. *Two Akathists.* New York: Theotokos Press, 2011.

———, ed. *The Westminster Handbook to Origen.* Louisville, Ky.: Westminster John Knox Press, 2004.

———. *The Westminster Handbook to Patristic Theology.* Louisville, Ky.: Westminster John Knox Press, 2004.

McGuire, Anne. *Skin Disease: A Message from the Soul.* London: Free Association Books, 2004.

Muse, Stephen, ed. *Raising Lazarus: Integral Healing in Orthodox Christianity.* Brookline, Mass.: Holy Cross Orthodox Press, 2004.

New Oxford Annotated Bible: New Revised Standard Version with the Apocrypha. Edited by Michael D. Coogan. Oxford: Oxford University Press, 2007.

Ng, Nathan Kwok-kit. *The Spirituality of Athanasius: A Key for Proper Understanding of This Important Church Father.* Bern: Peter Lang, 2001.

O'Keefe, J. "Allegory" in *The Westminster Handbook to Origen*, edited by John McGuckin. Louisville, Ky.: Westminster John Knox Press, 2004.

O'Leary, J. "Grace" in *The Westminster Handbook to Origen*, edited by John McGuckin. Louisville, Ky.: Westminster John Knox Press, 2004.

Palamas, Gregory. *Mary the Mother of God: Sermons by Saint Gregory Palamas.* Edited by Christopher Veniamin. South Canaan, Pa.: Mount Thabor Publishing, 2005.

Palmer, G. E. H., P. Sherrard, and K. Ware, trans. and eds. *The Philokalia: The Complete Text.* Compiled by St. Nikodimos of the Holy Mountain and St. Makarios of Corinth. Vol. 2. London: Faber and Faber, 1981.

Papanikolaou, Aristotle. "Liberating Eros: Confession and Desire." *Journal of the Society of Christian Ethics* 26, no. 1 (Spring/Summer 2006).

Pseudo-Dionysius Areopagite. *Pseudo-Dionysius: The Complete Works.* Translated by Paul Rorem. Mahwah, N.J.: Paulist Press, 1988.

Pseudo-Macarius. *Fifty Spiritual Homilies and the Great Letter.* Translated and edited by George Maloney. Mahwah, N.J.: Paulist Press, 1992.

Rist, John M. "A Note on Eros and Agape in Pseudo-Dionysius." *Vigiliae Christianae* 20, no. 4 (December 1966).

Russell, Norman. *The Doctrine of Deification in the Greek Patristic Tradition*. New York: Oxford University Press, 2004.

Sandler, J., E. Person, and R. Fonagy, eds. *Freud's "On Narcissism: An Introduction."* London: Karnac, 2012.

Schmemann, Alexander. *Of Water and the Spirit: A Liturgical Study of Baptism*. Crestwood, N.Y.: St. Vladimir's Seminary Press, 1974.

Smith, J. Warren. *Passion and Paradise: Human and Divine Emotion in the Thought of Gregory of Nyssa*. New York: The Crossroad Publishing Company, 2004.

Steenberg, Matthew C. *Of God and Man: Theology as Anthropology from Irenaeus to Athanasius*. London: T&T Clark, 2009.

Studer, Basil. *Trinity and Incarnation: The Faith of the Early Church*. Translated by Matthias Westerhoff and edited by Andrew Louth. London: T&T Clark, 1993.

Symington, Neville. *Narcissism: A New Theory*. London: Karnac Books, 1993.

Theokritoff, Elizabeth. *Living in God's Creation: Orthodox Perspectives on Ecology*. Crestwood, N.Y.: St. Vladimir's Seminary Press, 2009.

Thermos, Vasileios. *In Search of the Person: "True" and "False Self" According to Donald Winnicott and St. Gregory Palamas*. Translated by Constantine Kokenes. Montreal: Alexander Press, 2002.

———. *Thirst for Love and Truth: Encounters of Orthodox Theology and Psychological Science*. Montreal: Alexander Press, 2010.

Thunberg, Lars. *Microcosm and Mediator: The Theological Anthropology of Maximus the Confessor*. Chicago: Open Court Publishing, 1995.

Tollefsen, Torstein T. *The Christocentric Cosmology of St. Maximus the Confessor*. Oxford: Oxford University Press, 2008.

Toronen, Melchisedic. *Union and Distinction in the Thought of St. Maximus the Confessor*. Oxford: Oxford University Press, 2007.

Torrance, T. F. "Karl Barth and the Latin Heresy." *Scottish Journal of Theology* 39 (1986).

Trader, Alexis. *Ancient Christian Wisdom and Aaron Beck's Cognitive Therapy: A Meeting of Minds*. New York: Peter Lang, 2011.

Turner, Frederick. *Rebirth of Value: Meditations on Beauty, Ecology, Religion and Education*. Albany: State University of New York Press, 1991.

Twomey, D. V., and D. Krausmuller, eds. *Salvation According to the Fathers of the Church: The Proceedings of the Sixth International Patristic Conference*. Maynooth/Belfast: Four Courts Press, 2010.

Tympas, G. C. *Carl Jung and Maximus the Confessor on Psychic Development: The Dynamics between the "Psychological" and the "Spiritual."* New York: Routledge, 2014.

Ulanov, Ann B. *Attacked By Poison Ivy: A Psychological Understanding*. Lake Worth, Fla.: Nicolas Hays Press, 2001.

———. *The Feminine in Jungian Psychology and in Christian Theology*. Evanston, Ill.: Northwestern Press, 1971.

———. *Finding Space: Winnicott, God and Psychic Reality*. Louisville, Ky.: Westminster John Knox Press, 2005.

———. *The Functioning Transcendent: A Study in Analytical Psychology*. Wilmette, Ill.: Chiron Publications, 1996.

———. *Knots and Their Untying: Essays on Psychological Dilemmas*. New Orleans: SpringJournal Inc., 2014.

———. *Picturing God*. Einsieldeln: Daimon Verlag, 2002.

———. *Receiving Woman: Studies in the Psychology and the Theology of the Feminine*. Philadelphia: The Westminster Press, 1981.

———. *Spiritual Aspects of Clinical Work*. Einsieldeln: Daimon Verlag, 2004.

———. "Two Sexes." In *Men and Women: Sexual Ethics in Turbulent Times*, edited by Philip Turner. Cambridge, Mass.: Cowley Publications, 1989.

———. *The Unshuttered Heart: Opening to Aliveness and Deadness in the Self*. Abingdon Press, 2007.

———. *The Wisdom of the Psyche*. Cambridge, Mass.: Cowley Publications, 1988.

———, and Alvin Dueck. *The Living God and Our Living Psyche: What Christians Can Learn from Carl Jung*. Grand Rapids, Mich.: W. B. Eerdmans Publishing Co., 2008.

———, and Barry Ulanov. *Cinderella and Her Sisters: The Envied and the Envying*. Philadelphia: The Westminster Press, 1983.

———, and Barry Ulanov. *Religion and the Unconscious*. Philadelphia: Westminster Press, 1975.

———, and Barry Ulanov. *Transforming Sexuality: The Archetypal World of Anima and Animus*. Boston: Shambhala Press, 1994.

Velimirovich, Nikolai. *The Universe as Symbols and Signs: An Essay on Mysticism in the Eastern Church*. South Canaan, Pa.: St. Tikhon's Seminary Press, 2010.

Vlachos, Hierotheos. *Orthodox Psychotherapy: The Science of the Fathers*. Translated by Esther Williams. Levadhia, Greece: Birth of the Theotokos Monastery, 1994.

Von Balthasar, Hans Urs. *The Glory of the Lord: A Theological Aesthetics*. Vol 2. San Francisco: Ignatius Press, 2004.

Ware, Kallistos. "'In the Image and Likeness': The Uniqueness of the Human Person." In *Personhood: Orthodox Christianity and the Connection between Body, Mind, and Soul*, edited by John Chirban. Westport, Conn.: Bergin & Garvey, 1996.

————. Foreword to *Of God and Man: Theology as Anthropology from Irenaeus to Athanasius*, by Matthew C. Steenberg (London: T&T Clark, 2009),

Winnicott, Donald W. *Deprivation and Delinquency*. Edited by C. Winnicott, R. Shepard, and M. Davis. London: Routledge, 1984.

————. *The Maturational Processes and the Facilitating Environment: Studies in the Theory of Emotional Development*. London: Karnac, 2007.

————. *Psycho-Analytic Explorations*. Edited by C. Winnicott, R. Shepherd, and M. Davis. Cambridge, Mass.: Harvard University Press, 1989.

Yannaras, Christos. *Relational Ontology*. Translated by Norman Russell. Brookline, Mass.: Holy Cross Orthodox Press, 2011.

Zizioulas, John D. *Communion and Otherness: Further Studies in Personhood and the Church*. Edited by Paul McPartlan. London: T&T Clark, 2006.

————, and Jean Zizioulas. *Being as Communion: Studies in Personhood and the Church*. London: Darton Longman & Todd, 2004.

INDEX

Pia Sophia Chaudhari holds a doctorate in theology from the Department of Psychiatry & Religion at Union Theological Seminary in New York. Her research interests include theological anthropology, depth psychology, processes of healing, and the engagement with aesthetics and beauty. She is a founding co-chair of the Analytical Psychology and Orthodox Christianity Consultation (APOCC).

ORTHODOX CHRISTIANITY AND CONTEMPORARY THOUGHT

SERIES EDITORS
Aristotle Papanikolaou and Ashley M. Purpura

Lucian N. Leustean (ed.), *Orthodox Christianity and Nationalism in Nineteenth-Century Southeastern Europe.*

John Chryssavgis (ed.), *Dialogue of Love: Breaking the Silence of Centuries.* Contributions by Brian E. Daley, S.J., and Georges Florovsky.

George E. Demacopoulos and Aristotle Papanikolaou (eds.), *Christianity, Democracy, and the Shadow of Constantine.*

Aristotle Papanikolaou and George E. Demacopoulos (eds.), *Fundamentalism or Tradition: Christianity after Secularism*

Georgia Frank, Susan R. Holman, and Andrew S. Jacobs (eds.), *The Garb of Being: Embodiment and the Pursuit of Holiness in Late Ancient Christianity*

Ecumenical Patriarch Bartholomew, *In the World, Yet Not of the World: Social and Global Initiatives of Ecumenical Patriarch Bartholomew.* Edited by John Chryssavgis. Foreword by Jose Manuel Barroso.

Ecumenical Patriarch Bartholomew, *Speaking the Truth in Love: Theological and Spiritual Exhortations of Ecumenical Patriarch Bartholomew.* Edited by John Chryssavgis. Foreword by Dr. Rowan Williams, Archbishop of Canterbury.

Ecumenical Patriarch Bartholomew, *On Earth as in Heaven: Ecological Vision and Initiatives of Ecumenical Patriarch Bartholomew.* Edited by John Chryssavgis. Foreword by His Royal Highness, the Duke of Edinburgh.